Hunting for the Pot, Fishing for the Pan

An Outdoor Life Book

Hunting for the Pot, Fishing for the Pan

Byron W. Dalrymple

Drawings by Ted Burwell

Outdoor Life Books

Stackpole Books

Harrisburg, Pennsylvania

Published by

Outdoor Life Books
Times Mirror Magazines, Inc.
380 Madison Avenue
New York, NY 10017

Distributed to the trade by

Stackpole Books
Harrisburg, Pennsylvania

Library of Congress Catalog Card Number: 80–5887
ISBN: 0-8117-0840-3

Manufactured in the United States of America
Second Printing, 1981

To Joshua

Contents

Introduction

On a recent evening we had goose for dinner. A wild goose. I have long been an avid goose hunter. There is something about sitting out in drizzle and fog in a rice stubble field when the geese are crying down the wind by hundreds, most of them unseen but now and then a brace or half dozen dropping out of the scud to examine decoys and listen attentively to the calling of a guide, that is a thrill like no other.

The sport, the enjoyment and drama of goose hunting console me for the suffering I experience, cold and wet, slogging and sitting in mud. Yet when I sit down at the table, in this instance with the dark, savory bird on a big platter before me, candlelight flickering over it as wisps of delicious vapors assail my senses, I am suddenly at a loss to evaluate the two experiences. Which is more thrilling, the hunt or the eating?

My wife is an excellent game and fish cook, chiefly because she allows the game or fish to assert its own personality and does not try to interfere too perversely with it, to block or overwhelm it, but seasons delicately only to enhance the natural flavors. The goose, a mature blue, was superb, its gleaming brown breast dappled with a gentle dusting of garlic powder, a hint of rosemary, and a dash of red pepper flakes. We sat long over the meal, discussing which was more important, the hunting or the eating, and decided that hunting (we might even call it hunting for the pot) and fishing (fishing for the pan) are not singular endeavors but activities that have several facets.

The sportsman who does not eat his fish and game, who in some cases even spurns it, in my view is only half a sportsman. Surprisingly there are quite a few of these. Their enjoyment is short-changed, inferior. Their philosophy of the outdoor sports is stunted. They never realize the full potential.

The Indians hunted to eat, and yet they hunted to *hunt*, too. The endeavor may not have been termed "sport" by them, but the hunters, during the chase, seethed with primitive excitement. And the drama afield was followed by a celebration with highly stylized ceremonies and a feast. Their very subsistence was based on hunting, but hunt itself was the dramatic forerunner, a veritable religious experience, a kind of celebration of life.

The Colonists, explorers, the earliest pioneers—all were hunters and fishermen. They hunted and fished for a livelihood. Then came the time of settlement, and the hunt continued for subsistence, but the tradition of a recreational festival of sorts was also carried on. The plainsman who took time off from the endless work of putting together his small primitive farm or ranch to go after a deer, an antelope, a mess of trout, a bushel of suckers speared in a nearby creek in spring, or a covey of young prairie chickens would have been hard put, if asked, to say whether the thrills and homely enjoyments of the hunt were as important—or more so—than the result on the family table. The fact is, hunting and fishing from earliest times to the present have always been double-barreled ventures: the drama of the chase coupled with the satisfaction of the eating and of providing a livelihood for the family. They were one, inseparable.

Only in modern times, dating chiefly from the beginning of this century, did the sport hunter and fisherman arrive on the scene claiming the recreational value dominant to the feast. There is a hazy time in between when there was a transition from subsistence and market hunting to sport hunting. But the interesting part is that even the market hunters, who killed waterfowl and deer, wild turkeys, prairie chickens, doves, and shorebirds by thousands, thought of their work as enjoyable, and their own tables were heavy with the results of their labors. Commercial fishing evolved somewhat differently because it was not quite on such a one-to-one basis.

Eventually, market hunters fell into disrepute, and both commercial hunters and fishermen came under severe regulations. Most popularly edible birds and animals were metamorphosed in human opinion into creatures available, and so regulated, only for recreational hunting, and many fish species fell under the same types of regulations. There were not enough for both market and sport. Sport fishing and hunting reigned supreme for several decades, and the idea of admitting that you enjoyed the eating as much as the sport sometimes came to be looked at by "purists" as proof that you were no sport at all. You were a meat fisherman, a meat hunter. Curiously, there was a growing stigma attached to the admission of enjoying fish and game as food—which is what it had been since history's dawning.

This reminds me of an amusing incident a friend related to me. He is a successful outdoor writer. Obviously, since that is his business, when he prepares his income tax statements he deducts various expenses incurred while fishing, hunting, shooting pictures, and gaining whatever experience necessary to complete assignments. An IRS agent questioned him once, and he explained why he had made certain deductions.

His interrogator said, "But come on now, admit it, you had *fun*, didn't you?"

He readily admitted he had enjoyed every minute of it. Was that a criterion for whether or not an expense could be deducted? Was one supposed to hate every moment of making a living? The comparison is apt. During past years there was a time when if you admitted that you just dearly loved to eat trout, or venison, you were relegated by some to the meat fisherman/hunter category. If you had fun eating, you couldn't very well be a "sport."

In the past few years, so-called conservationists, often misguided, and "environmentalists," whatever they are, have often harangued for the release of fish and the stockpiling of game, which in many instances is like trying to put 2 pounds in a 1-pound bag. These people are neither all wrong nor all right, just poorly informed. To be sure, on certain trout streams pressure is too severe. To keep taking trout out depletes natural stocks, and hatchery-raised fish for replenishment in many instances have become too expensive and don't amount to much anyway, for either sport or eating. Here, catch-and-release—fishing for fun only—certainly is logical. But there are numerous fish (and game) species that are overpopulous and short-lived that should be utilized. In fact, proper management most often requires utilization.

A classic example, about which more will appear later, concerns the brook trout. Over most of its native range in the eastern half of the continent, it has drastically declined. In the West, where brook trout were long ago introduced, it never did well in the large trout streams, but erupted in populations in the small, frigid creeks and beaver ponds of the high country. In hundreds of these, brook trout are stunted. Few people fish here. Some states encourage cropping by offering bonus limits, hoping for better use of the resource. Here, it is good management—and a marvelous experience in ample eating—to keep the trout rather than release them.

Curiously, just within the past several years opinions have begun to change again. The back-to-the-good-earth concept among many young people had something to do with it. Although, nowadays there is some stigma against hunting among certain factions, the more thoughtful segments, though somewhat negative about trophy hunting, do not object to hunting *if* the sportsmen eat what they kill. A recent long-term national survey, supported by the federal government and done by one of the eastern universities, shows that so-called subsistence hunting and fishing are perfectly acceptable to the majority of people.

Admittedly, fishing and hunting today are, and properly should be, fundamentally recreational pastimes. But the plain fact is, in our energy-pinched and inflation-riddled economy, *the kill and the catch are ever more valuable as food*. There is absolutely nothing wrong with looking at a stringer of fish, after the fun is over, as an entity of so much monetary value, or of a deer as a certain number of dollars in the freezer.

In the area where I live, and on our own ranch, the range is far overpopulated with whitetail deer. Limits are high, management encourages the harvest of antlerless deer. Die-offs regularly occur because population overwhelms food supply and living room. So, each fall we put several deer into our freezer. I have hunted deer for over forty years now. I love the hunting, but many times I enjoy far more the eating of an especially excellent venison roast than I do the actual bagging of the deer.

Furthermore, the meat *is* extremely valuable. One researcher has determined that at the current average price of ground beef, the annual deer harvest in the United States is actually worth at least $150,000,000! Why not then, while enjoying the recreation of hunting or fishing, revel also in the satisfaction of the economic aspects—the pot and the pan? There shouldn't be any guilt connected with it. As in primitive times, the eating should be a kind of celebration of abundance. Certainly the word "sport" should be prominently kept in the connotation of outdoorsmen's activities. But learning the value of the end result is also important. It is in fact more important than outdoorsmen have made it in the past.

What I am suggesting, then, is a new philosophy of hunting and fishing. There are rare species that should not be molested. There are some fishable and huntable species that are not prolific enough or populous enough to allow more than very modest attention from sportsmen. But there are also a number of super-prolific and abundant varieties of both fish and game that *should* be harvested heavily for proper management, and this in turn offers not only mere sport but more food. It is a matter of enlarging your present philosophy of the outdoor sports to include these facts.

When we speak here of hunting for the pot and fishing for the pan we aren't saying that outdoorsmen should switch their focus toward "making every trip pay for itself in meat." That would be ridiculous, as well as impossible, and it would also be an uneasy relationship with the outdoors for most sportsmen. What we are saying is that as we all know fishing and hunting are nowadays expensive pastimes. The recreation may well be worth the cost. But regardless of cost and recreation, while you're out there you should focus more closely on the importance of fish and game as food *as well as* recreation. It is almost a sacrilege not to do so.

Again, it's not a matter of "making it pay." It isn't necessary to plan a trip *only* to try to take home enough meat to offset expenses. But you can plan how to derive more enjoyment from the eating. And you can plan to make trips you haven't previously considered in order to gather good food, or more food, or both. That, too, can be a substantial part of the delight of the outdoors.

Byron W. Dalrymple

Part I

Hunting for the Pot

1

Abundant Species for the Pot

The hunter with his eye on the return in meat as related to his effort in the field should first realize that certain animals and birds will be more important in his planning than others. Which species on the game list, in his area or in areas to which he will be able to travel for hunting, should receive the focus of his attention? Bear in mind that as far as the sport, the recreation, is concerned, this he'll automatically obtain, but by putting special emphasis on certain species, or emphasis on a particular one during an especially high-crop year for it, he will glean more value for the table.

DEER

Among the big-game animals, deer are the classic example. There are places, to be sure, where deer are not abundant. There are far more where they are overpopulous. In order to keep ahead of the annual buildup of deer herds in many states, game managers have to establish antlerless quotas. Often these quotas are set much higher than the harvest the biol-

3

ogists desire, because for no good reason there is a traditional stigma connected with shooting does. Biologists must offer more doe permits in order to get a large enough, but smaller, harvest. Many years ago, when whitetail deer especially were heavily market hunted, and then went through a period of forced adaptation to burgeoning civilization, bucks-only laws were passed in numerous states. Does were left so there would be fawns to grow up for the future.

As the tradition grew stronger, many hunters simply would not shoot does. Now the situation has changed and improved somewhat, because in most states hunters have been educated to the facts of life about deer. The sex ratio of deer at birth is close to 50–50, with a slight tilt on the average toward a few more males than females. When bucks only are harvested, herds soon reach serious imbalance. On optimum range, deer are astonishingly prolific. During good years the birth rate may be as high as 160 or more fawns to every 100 does. Natural attrition of course accounts for some. On some ranges this is higher than on others. Nonetheless, if no antlerless deer are taken, the range is obviously soon overwhelmed by a preponderance of does and fawns, which multiply even faster. When a certain peak is reached, the range cannot sustain more, and a die-off occurs.

Game managers often practically have to beg hunters to help harvest antlerless deer. It is ridiculous that any doe-hunting stigma should exist. Where antlerless quotas are offered, the hunter who legally takes his share is actually the better sportsman than the person who refuses. He is helping keep the herd in proper balance. And, in addition, he is often able to make his hunt a two-, or even three-, deer hunt, thus adding both to the sport involved and far more to the amount of venison for the pot.

Deer, then, are one of the most important species that— not everywhere, but in many states or portions of states—fit the category of abundant animals for the pot. I think of an excellent example not far from my home in Texas that well illustrates how one can focus on the dual goals of recreation and a full freezer, and most wisely spend his money. A big ranch where I have hunted nowadays offers a special hunt for sportsmen after a trophy whitetail buck, with guide, transport and varied amenities furnished. Another big ranch not far from that one, where I also have hunted, has abundant trophy bucks but, as this is written, is far overpopulated with antlerless deer.

The management of the second ranch recognizes that unless some of them are taken off, the size of the trophies is going to slip because of overcrowding, and eventually there will be a debacle in the deer herd. This ranch also offers a trophy-buck hunt. However, it insists that, included in the fee, each hunter also take two does, or antlerless deer. (Three whitetail deer are legal in that area on the Texas license.) By making this stipulation the owners and manager assure themselves of proper doe cropping right along with their trophy-buck hunts.

The point of comparing the two hunts is that the cost is the same. Granted, a hunter isn't going to cover that cost by collecting the extra meat. That's not the point. What he can do, however, by choosing the second of two hunts of like costs, is extend and enhance his recreation, still have his trophy, plus three deer in the freezer, an actual money value of at least several hundred dollars. Further, he hasn't harmed the deer herd but rather has helped to keep it vigorous and properly tailored to its range.

RABBITS

The truly abundant animals and birds, or those short-lived varieties seasonally abundant and cyclic, with periodic highs and lows, are the ones to which the hunter for the pot should turn his main attention. Among small game, rabbits are excellent examples. Rabbits of all species are extremely prolific. Almost all states offer high daily limits, some have no limit, and a few no closed season. Where there are seasons, they're invariably long.

Rabbits are short-lived creatures. Because they are an important item in the food chain for all predators (mammals, birds, reptiles) they annually sustain awesome natural attrition. If the hunter doesn't harvest them, something else does, or they die from natural causes. Studies have repeatedly shown that an average of 85 percent of rabbits born one year don't live to see the next, regardless of hunting pressure. A rabbit in the wild that is two or three years old is a rarity. Therefore, there is no reason not to diligently harvest rabbits.

Rabbits are also astonishingly cyclic. They build up prodigious populations, then because of overcrowding and the ease under such conditions of transmission of diseases, plus the stress of reduced living room, they die off in great numbers. The rabbit population then may stay at a low for several years, and suddenly erupt once more. I remember winters in the northern Great Lakes region when a group of us hunted the big snowshoe hares practically every afternoon all winter long. During those years I've seen places in a cedar and balsam swamp when the snow was so deep and the hares so ganged up, you couldn't lay your hand on the snow without touching a track or two.

These big hares are delicious eating. My two boys, my wife, and I ate them many meals during several winters. The meat—each rabbit weighed up to four pounds—was a most welcome and valuable addition to our winter menu. Then suddenly there'd come a winter when hardly a track would be seen. During these low cycles, we gave up hunting as unrewarding for either sport or meat. This is part of the pot hunter's scheme: harvest the big crop; turn attention elsewhere during poor-crop years.

Wherever you live, though, there are almost certain to be rabbits—cottontails, swamp rabbits, snowshoe hares, pygmy rabbits—and regardless of how hard you hunt them, you cannot possibly keep ahead of them when they're on up cycles. Millions of them go to waste, recreationally and as table fare, surplus for both predators and man.

SQUIRRELS

Squirrels are in the same category. Fox squirrels and gray squirrels are locally or regionally abundant. They, too, follow high and low cycles. Gray squirrels seem particularly prone to severe ups and downs. Some of the tales from early pioneer days of the migrations of gray-squirrel hordes, millions of squirrels presumably moving from an area where they had consumed all the forage and trying to find new sources, are all but unbelievable. Some of these migrations, not as large, still occur. Tom May, a game warden in Van Buren, Missouri, told me that he had on several occasions floated the Current River in the Mark Twain National Forest, fishing, during a high cycle for gray squirrels, and in a short stretch he could have dipped up dozens of squirrels in his landing net. They were swimming all in the same direction across the river, apparently attempting to migrate to new foraging grounds.

I relate the incident to illustrate that squirrels, like rabbits, are "expendable" animals. To be sure, they are already popular among hunters. But thousands of hunters never go squirrel hunting. Here is a resource, a far from fully tapped reservoir of both sport and good eating. Squirrels, like rabbits, swiftly replenish harvested populations. Because they, too, are short-lived, many that the hunter does not take are simply wasted, lost to natural attrition. With both rabbits and squirrels, or any game that is cyclic, the low periods take care of themselves. When a hunter cannot locate enough of the animals to make a day of sport, he loses interest and turns to something else, then turns back to them again when they are plentiful.

POT-HUNTING PLUSES

One of the most interesting slants on the idea of pot hunting is that many a hunter who has switched to the meat-hunting ethic in combo with his recreation has switched also from his staid routine of always hunting the same species and worked up great enthusiasm for game varieties to which he has previously paid little attention. He discovers enjoyments he'd never known before: more varied hunting, longer seasons, and along with them much more table-fare value. I have a friend, a Texan, who used to make fun of me because I hunted cottontails down in the south-Texas brush country. The small rabbits that dwell in the cactus and thornbrush are sprightly, sporty, and utterly delicious. But nobody, just nobody, in Texas hunts rabbits. They're not even on the game-animal list. Upshot was that I talked him into a cottontail foray as an interim activity after we'd filled limits on quail. He's been an enthusiast ever since, but tries to keep his other nonrabbiting Texas friends from finding out, while I incessantly threaten to blackmail him.

On our own small ranch in the Texas hill country we have fairly abundant fox squirrels. There is no closed season on them in our county. I never paid much attention to them because I always considered that there were only a scattering. Then my older son, Mike, who has children of his own now, showed me that we actually had lots of squirrels—we just didn't look sharply enough for them. He started taking his son, Michael, squirrel hunting after deer season was over. No closed season allowed them to extend their fall hunting as well as take up late-spring squirrel hunting after the young were raised. Consequently, we all have turned to doing some pot hunting for squirrels during off seasons. We've added some fine meals, along with new and economical experiences on our own land and a long extension to the shooting season.

BIRDS

Among game birds, the mourning dove is one that is capable of sustaining far more hunting than it receives. To be sure, doves are exceedingly popular game birds in many states. But almost without fail surveys by game biologists show that 75 percent of the total dove kill, in a season that may last a couple of months, is made during the first week. It's not that doves are gone after that. It's simply that most hunters have a dove shoot or two when the season opens, a traditional get-together of a group of hunters, and from there on pay scant attention.

In my state, as in numerous others, we have had for some time a split season, a late segment falling in January. Practically nobody hunted doves during it. Yet that is a time of year when all birds are mature, fast flyers, the sportiest hunting of the year, and the finest eating. Because the mourning dove breeds in every state, is tremendously abundant and swiftly renewable, it is a perfect candidate for the abundant-species-for-the-pot list. Many hunters have never hunted doves. Here is a perfect focus for the new philosophy, invariably close to home.

Although waterfowl are of course limited as to how much hunting they can stand, they are also managed with meticulous care. Some are excellent examples of abundant birds that are candidates for more attention by the pot hunter—if selected by species. For example, not all hunters by any means are waterfowlers. But among those who are, on the average the Canada goose is doted on while the snow goose is not held in such esteem. There is no very good reason for this, and the hunter who pursues the idea to purist lengths short-changes himself. There are many places where several varieties of geese are available. As a rule the limit on Canadas is one, or occasionally two, birds. Conversely, in several goose-hunting regions the limit on snow geese (and blues, which nowadays are considered simply a color phase of the lesser snow) is five daily, or five in aggregate with perhaps one Canada or specklebelly. The hunter who gets his mind in gear, concentrates on snows and blues and lets the Canadas come as they may gets a triple-barrelled bonus: he carries home five geese on a good day—a great deal more value as far as the pot is concerned; he has several times more shooting sport; and, just for fun, if you want to consider energy consumption, he uses no more on five meals than on two of the other geese.

Much the same situation exists among duck hunters. The point system is in use in a number of states nowadays. Each duck counts so many points. When you reach or exceed 100, you must quit. The less abundant varieties are high-point ducks; the more abundant—and commonly less popular—are low-point birds. I shot one fall where an unusual variety of ducks was present, feeding in cut-over rice fields. As any waterfowl hunter knows, rice-fed ducks are delicious. But what many a purist-type duck hunter doesn't know, or refuses to learn, is that *all* species of rice-fed ducks are fine eating.

Hunters with whom I shot turned down gadwalls and widgeons. The gadwall is a big duck, the widgeon is fair sized. Some duck hunters claim the gadwall, and sometimes the widgeon, are trash ducks, not fit to eat. Amusingly, my wife and I have fed roast gadwalls to a couple of these hunters who expansively complimented the superb mallards! At any rate, during that hunt the mallard drake was a 20-point duck, while gadwalls and widgeons were only 10-point birds. My shooting companions were through at five birds each. I was only half-

way through. As far as the end result—birds on the table—
it was as if they threw away five excellent ducks each. I took
in ten, and thought of it each time we had a meal of wild
duck.

This should give you a basic idea of how to dovetail pot
hunting with recreational hunting by concentrating on the
perennially abundant species, or by concentrating during seasons of overabundance on specific varieties, or by paying
closer attention to the need for herd management among big
game and collecting extra fare for your table while enhancing
the sporting value as well. A hunter who begins to think in
these terms winds up with new experiences, changes in hunting endeavors that bring new enthusiasms. He often stretches
out his hunting seasons. And in dollar value, which shouldn't
be in the least distasteful to mention, he cuts costs while easily
tripling the booty the traditional hunter brings in.

2

Planning the Best Deer
Hunt for the Pot

Few hunters ever consider planning well ahead of time so they can get not only the greatest amount of enjoyment from a hunt but also the largest return for the pot. This can be especially important on deer hunts because so many people hunt deer, the meat is of such substantial amount, and the fare so excellent. A mule-deer hunt I made several seasons ago serves as a good illustration.

For a number of years I have made an annual trip to western Texas to the Trans-Pecos area where desert mule deer are plentiful. The deer from this region are the best venison imaginable, always fat and well flavored; these animals have long been favorite "eating deer" in our family. Texas game laws allow a total of four deer on a license. Only one may be a buck mule deer. Two may be whitetail bucks, and under special permit available from the landowner a bonus antlerless deer may be taken. This antlerless deer actually can be either a whitetail or a mule deer, but so few west-Texas ranchers allow shooting of does, even with state-issued permits available, collecting a doe mule deer is uncommon.

Competition for mule-deer hunts in Texas is always severe, because of limited mule-deer range. As I mentioned, I fortunately had a place to hunt where I had gone for some years. Early in the year I heard from a friend who hunted on another ranch and who wondered if I'd like to join his party. I was going to say no because of my annual commitment, but my friend mentioned that the owner of the ranch was starting a management program and firmly believed he needed to crop some does.

My ears perked up. I looked at hunt dates, figured I could make one hunt, then go directly to the other, about 50 miles away—a short hop in western Texas. I replied that I'd accept if the landowner would allow me a doe permit; I'd be a doe hunter. He was happy to have at least one taker. Most hunters, of course, wanted a buck, and the party I was going to join would never have considered shooting a doe.

My twofold plan, formulated months in advance, worked perfectly. I bagged a big, awesomely fat doe on the one ranch, then went to the other for my annual buck hunt. The desert mountains of that Big Bend country appeal to me greatly as hunting country, and I got an extra couple of days in them and a big bonus of prime venison.

This of course cut me out of one whitetail deer at home. However, thinking purely in terms of venison, the doe I would probably have shot at home to fill my bonus tag—or to fill one or more of my whitetail buck tags, also legal if permits are available—would have been small. Whitetail does where I live field-dress seldom more than 50 pounds. It takes a good buck indeed to scale 85 or 90 pounds field-dressed. But when my west-Texas hunt was finished, I had collected a stunning 10-point buck that weighed in, field-dressed, at 160, and a doe that was 110.

ADVANCE PLANNING

When you are organizing a deer hunt, it is smart to check the regulations in several states or areas of states within your time and travel limitations. Deer management today is a fine-honed affair. State after state has hunt units set aside annually, often differing year to year, where more than one deer may be taken in order to help tailor overpopulous deer herds to the available range. Often one must make application for these special hunts. But by a little digging and pre-hunt research well in advance you can often as not ferret out a chance to double your haul of venison. A great many such hunts require making application months in advance. Be sure you contact the game department in the state in question early in the year. Start your planning for fall way back in winter or early spring. That way, you'll be in under the wire. Maybe you won't "draw lucky," but it's worth trying, nonetheless.

There are also countless opportunities where an extra deer is allowed in certain counties, or on certain management units. Scan regulations end to end, carefully. Let's say you don't get a chance to hunt an extra-deer unit for a buck. But it is still legal for you to apply for an antlerless permit. If it is within reasonable distance of the place where you'll make your buck hunt, why not try for a two-deer hunt. Plan a couple of extra days of enjoyment in the outdoors, and perhaps bring home double the expected meat for the pot.

Look closely at regulations for each state to which you may be able to make a deer-hunting trip. You will discover that laws as to limits differ widely. You may discover that rich experiences await you—a state in which you've never hunted, a type of terrain entirely new to you—and that you are allowed more than one deer on your license. At various times there have been laws in states of the northern Rockies where two deer were legal, but one of them had to be a whitetail. The reason for this is that whitetails in these mule-deer states are more difficult to hunt than the mule deer. Most hunters, natives as well as visitors, shun the whitetails and go for mule deer only. In Montana this law was in force at one time—two deer, one a whitetail. Wyoming also has from time to time had incentives to crop more whitetails. The point is, whitetails in these states usurp mule-deer range, and have been spreading their own range. This is currently true, especially in Wyoming. Mule deer are too easily overbalanced by the more adaptable whitetail spreading into their territory. If you make yourself aware of these problems of deer management, and where they occur, you can rather easily find an opportunity to take more than one deer.

Even if your time on a deer hunt is limited, it still is advantageous to research state laws to locate places where you are at least allowed more than one animal. As I have mentioned, Texas has a four-deer limit, if you wangle the permits and carefully plot what species and sexes you intend to try for. You would have to also plan with care to make sure your trip dovetailed with seasons where you intended to hunt for both whitetails and mule deer. So, you see, this isn't a hit-and-miss idea that can be approached carelessly. It requires precise planning. But it results in some great hunts. A few years ago as a kind of trick deer-hunt story I made a west-Texas hunt on assignment for *Outdoor Life* magazine, during which I bagged three kinds of deer in three days—a desert mule deer, a Texas whitetail, and a Carmen Mountains whitetail, the latter a diminutive subspecies present in modest numbers in the Big Bend region. The fact that a license allowed multiple kills made the opportunity possible.

As I write this, the regulations in Louisiana, in certain specified areas, allow one deer per day, six per season. In Alabama the limit is one deer per day, period. In other words, you could collect, in theory at least, a truckload in an Alabama season. Obviously that is carrying things much too far. The game department in Alabama realized nobody could bag a deer a day all season. Or at least it would be rare. Probably nobody wants that many, or even six as in Louisiana. On the other hand, if you were plotting a deer-hunting trip, aiming at Louisiana or Alabama would put you in a situation where, even on a brief trip, you *could* legally take a second deer, maybe even two extra, if you had the chance. A hunt in

Louisiana or Alabama that costs the same as a hunt where only one animal is legal would certainly be provocative, both from the viewpoint of the sport and from the result tucked away in your locker or home freezer.

TWO-STATE HUNTS

Numerous possibilities for two-state hunts exist, as well. Admittedly, that can be expensive nowadays, considering the rising costs of nonresident licenses. Yet an extra license may be worthwhile in meat value alone. Scads of hunters hunt in their own state, then move across the line of a neighboring state, a short run, buy a license and hunt there. The advantages of the two-state hunt, however it's done, are several. From a standpoint of energy used and economy, if you drive, say, 400 miles from your home to the Black Hills in South Dakota to make a hunt, and the seasons there and in the pine-ridge country of Nebraska just south across the state line, fall properly, you could purchase a Nebraska license and also hunt there with only a moderate number of added driving miles, and perhaps fetch back two deer.

Because of my many years as a full-time professional outdoor writer, I have made a number of such two-state hunts, saving on time, expense, travel, gathering material for several assignments, and bringing home enough venison to keep us eating all winter. I vividly recall a classic trip of this nature to northern Arizona's Kaibab, with a short drive up to Kanab, Utah, for a second hunt.

LOCATING LARGE POPULATIONS

The hunter who is ever alert to better chances for the pot automatically raises his potential chances of success. An excellent example is the deer hunter who makes it a point to know where the *most* deer are, in his state or in other states where he hunts. The counties or management units where the deer population is highest may not furnish many trophy or record-book deer, but it stands to reason that if you are in an area where there are twenty deer to the square mile, your chances of getting a shot are going to be better than if you were in an area with three deer to the square mile.

Many hunters do not realize that estimated population figures of deer by county, hunt unit, or other designation can often be obtained from game-management officials of numerous states. If population figures aren't available, another immensely useful statistic is the kill per county, or unit, and in some instances even average per square mile during the previous or several previous seasons. Aiming your hunt at a high-kill or high-population area gives luck a boost.

For years New Hampshire has kept track of deer kill by counties. You can look at the records and instantly see where the most deer are taken. To be sure, this may simply mean in some instances that more hunters are present. But if the harvest is high and sustained over several years or longer, it is obvious that this is a county that *produces* a lot of deer. New Hampshire also has made computations of kills per square mile by towns (townships). Looking randomly at a report from several seasons back, I note that Dummer township in Coos County had a kill of 4.81 per square mile.

Although townships differ state to state in size, they are relatively small tracts. If an average of close to five deer per square mile is bagged in a small area, it is certain deer are plentiful. The state of Washington several years ago had an overabundance of blacktail deer in certain western counties. High antlerless quotas were offered, and the kills ran as high as three or four deer per square mile. Obviously, one's chances are excellent on such a hunt, even though there may be a lot of hunters. One caution, however: when you study available county and township and square-mile deer kills, be sure to look back several years. A steady high level will authenticate the tract as a populous deer area. A single high-harvest year may simply indicate a decisive cropping of overpopulation.

New Mexico offers an excellent example of a state in which one can easily get a fix on where to go for the best chances of bringing home venison. The lines are clearly drawn. In the north, the Carson National Forest and Rio Arriba County produce almost all the trophy bucks and record-book heads. But hunter success is not by any means as high as in the south. If you want to have the best chances of bagging a deer in New Mexico, the Lincoln National Forest and the Sacramento Mountains year after year show by harvest and success percentage per hunter that this is the place to go.

For all those who consider the meat almost as important as the recreation, another smart scheme is always to try to arrange for deer hunts in either-sex areas. These are numerous these days. Usually either-sex hunts, sometimes called "hunter's choice" hunts, occur where deer are too abundant. Their advantage over a buck's-only hunt, for the meat hunter, is that his chances are so much better. Maybe he'd like to collect a buck, but if he doesn't get the chance he can settle for a doe.

SPECIAL HUNTS

Always be on the lookout for special hunts. Some states allow an early bow hunt, then a gun hunt. Now many states also have special black-powder hunts. In some states a hunter must choose his weapon and stick to it, and gets only one hunt. In others, he can hunt during the archery season and again during gun season or seasons. Chances of success are enhanced simply because of a longer hunting period. In a few instances there are archery and gun licenses, and one may hold either or both, and take an extra deer by success with both.

In addition to the methods already mentioned for adding to your opportunities, thoroughly check state hunting regulations for special seasons. Here and there you'll find early-season deer hunts. Colorado has had one in August in the high country. Preseason antlerless hunts are becoming more common. There are also occasional postseason hunts. Some of these are to crop deer—mule deer as a rule—from remote country that have moved lower and within hunting reach on winter range. Now and then there are special crop-damage hunts. New Mexico had one of these just before spring several years ago; after many complaints in one of the southern areas, the game department surveyed the deer and decided how many could be taken, then turned them into a recreation (and food) resource by issuing permits.

These suggestions should help point any reader toward not only more deer hunting, therefore more enjoyment afield, but also toward adding substantially to the venison on the table. I chuckle to recall when my two boys were doing their first deer hunting, and how we cropped off as many does on our ranch as we could possibly use in accordance with the land-owner permits we received, given on an acreage basis. One season among the three of us we put six deer in the locker, and then on magazine assignment trips I made out of state I brought in two more. Eight deer is a lot of venison. We all like it, and we ate it until we just had to have a change. My wife prepared a delectable beef roast and when it came to the table both boys sniffed, made wry faces, then tentatively tasted it, putting on a deadpan act for their parents.

Mike winked at his brother and said, "Gamey tasting old stuff, isn't it, Terry?"

3

Hunt Planning for Other Game Animals and Birds

Planning to give yourself the best chances of collecting meat, of course, applies to other big game besides deer, and to some game birds. If among big game, for example, you have always wanted to go on a black-bear hunt, *how* you plan to hunt may make a big difference in your chances of success.

BEARS

A spring bear hunt over bait, in states or provinces where that is legal, is invariably more successful than simply wandering around the forest in the fall. Unlike antlered game, bears are not easily tied to specific places. Hunting black bear with dogs, where legal and where you can find a guide with trained dogs, also is much more successful than helter-skelter, aimless hunting.

Where you hunt also makes an immense difference, for bears are by no means plentiful in many states, yet abundant in a few. Here again, careful research beforehand is the most important part of the scheme. You will discover that in the

East, Maine and New York State's forest reserves invariably turn up the highest kills. Ontario, where spring hunting over bait has long been legal, shows extremely high success. Largest black bear populations are in the West, with Washington leading, followed by Oregon, Idaho, Montana. Alaska also rates very high.

MOOSE

When you make a point of total familiarity with your state game laws, you can often spot a special big-game hunt for a certain year, or several years running, that offers not only unusually heady experiences but a big bonus in meat for the pot. I think offhand of Minnesota, where for the past several years there has been an open season on moose, with rather high success. This so far has been a hunt for residents only.

I talked to one Minnesotan who told me, "So many people will apply there's no use me fooling with it. Chances of drawing a permit are too slim." That's a poor attitude. Why *not* put in an application? If you don't draw a permit, that's that. But if you do, you have the immense thrill of the hunt, and if you fill your tag you have collected perhaps as much as 450 pounds of cut-up meat, excellent meat at that. Translated to cold-turkey monetary value, comparing it to beef, that's $700 to $900! In today's world, it's like getting paid handsomely to go have a good time.

Be sure always when planning big game hunts to look for places, just as I suggested for deer, where either sex is legal. I made an Ontario moose hunt one year in the Wintering River region, where that year any moose—bull, cow, calf— was legal. We camped far back in the bush, going in by boat and towing a canoe to hunt with. I never did get a chance at a bull. But toward the end of the hunt a group of seven huge timber wolves jumped a big cow and ran her right out to me as we paddled down a lake. The thrills of that experience stay vivid in my memory, and instead of going home empty-handed I had the big cow, which was excellent meat. Had I hunted a bull's-only area, I probably would have had neither thrill nor meat.

Either-sex hunts are commonly offered in certain portions of elk range. I know guides in the West who wait until their hunters have filled on bulls, then they shoot a cow elk for winter meat. Cow elk, they all claim, and I heartily agree, is far better than a bull, invariably fatter, and during the rut (the breeding season) bulls may be strong, and then afterward thin. Of course, you can't always get a license in an either-sex elk area, and in some instances you have to apply for one sex or the other. Even if you want a bull, perhaps a trophy bull, it's still smart to apply, if possible, for an any-elk area. During the bugling season (the rut), for example, each mature bull will have a harem with him. That harem may consist of anywhere from a half dozen to thirty or forty cows. Obviously, if you don't get a whack at the trophy, you stand a high chance of settling late in the hunt for a cow. Because elk are western animals, and especially desirable, practically every eastern big-game hunter wants to make at least one elk trip. By trying for an either-sex hunt, after going so far, even if you don't get that trophy bull, your chances of a fine piece of meat are doubled.

ANTELOPE

Some big-game animals are simply so low in population, and range restricted, that hunting is too severely regulated to make them candidates for hunt planning toward extra sport and meat. The wild sheep fall into this category. So does the mountain goat. The pronghorn, or antelope, however, occasionally fits the better-meat-hunt planning group. Prong-

horns, once awesomely abundant on the plains, were brought
to the brink of extinction early in this century and were re-
established in substantial numbers by the influence—and
money—of sport hunters. Today pronghorns inhabit virtually
all country of the West suitable for them. Because their range
is precisely limited, exceedingly careful management is necessary. They are prolific, and their range cannot be expanded.
Only so many can exist on a given range, so they are annually
cropped meticulously after careful population surveys.

Very occasionally this means issuance of some antelope doe
permits. It also occasionally means issuance of bonus buck
permits. To get in on one of those hunts, which are not especially common and usually occur only in the high-population
pronghorn states, one must keep careful tabs on the situation
annually, checking with game departments to discover
opportunities.

A few years ago I was planning a hunt in Wyoming, and
discovered that several hunt units were going to offer extra
antelope permits. In other words, if you had a hunt set for
one unit, which I did, you might be able, if any permits
remained, to acquire a second one in the same or another
two-antelope area. I was going to hunt in the Kaycee area,
south of Buffalo. I had my first antelope permit there. I also
had a mule-deer permit and on it could hunt anywhere in the
region. We were living in Michigan at the time, and with a
friend who also had his licenses I drove out to Wyoming.
There were some extra-buck antelope permits left in the Gillette region. We would pass right through Gillette. Upshot
was that we bought permits for that area also.

I bagged a fine buck there the first day out. So did my
partner. We skinned and cooled out the carcasses overnight,
cut them up and got them into a locker, and went on to
Buffalo. Two days later I brought in my second buck antelope,
and the next day bagged a tremendous buck mule deer. It
was one of the most dramatic big-game hunts I've ever had.

By carefully planning to dovetail open seasons, and keeping my ear bent for special opportunities that resulted in the second antelope, I laid in our winter's meat before my hunting at home even started. Later on, in November, I added a Michigan whitetail buck taken within 5 miles of my house.

WILD HOGS, BOARS

A meat animal in the big-game category almost entirely overlooked by the average hunter is the feral hog. Feral swine are simply domestic hogs that have reverted to the wild. In the South as far back in history as early settlement days hogs were commonly allowed to free-roam the woods, and then rounded up for butchering. Many never were found, and became wild.

A number of states have feral hogs. In Texas, where I live, there are lightly inhabited areas of the southern brush country, and also locations in the "piney woods" of eastern Texas where feral swine are abundant. Florida has them in the big swamps. There are many in Arkansas and in the Carolinas, Tennessee, and elsewhere.

Make no mistake, domestic hogs that have lived for generations in the wild are tough, wary critters, as difficult to hunt as whitetail deer. Most of them get so they forage chiefly at night and lie up in dense thickets by day. Thus, the sport is exciting, and in places where hogs are well fed they are excellent eating. They are never as larded with fat as domestic swine, but have just enough to make quality pork. On many of the preserves in the South that advertise "wild boar" hunting, the hogs are simply feral stock. The Russian or European boar is a quite different animal. In a few areas these have crossed with feral swine.

Several years ago I made a hunt in the cactus and thorn-brush of southern Texas on a ranch where wild hogs are abundant. I hid by a water hole late in the afternoon and watched two huge animals move warily toward it at dusk. I was able to down one of them, a boar weighing 300 pounds. You have probably heard that a boar hog is inedible. Don't believe it. Some old boars, if not most carefully handled in dressing, are too strong to eat. But I shot this big fellow, which had short tusks and was young, in the head, and we dressed and skinned it with extreme care. It was excellent eating. On the same ranch one year a friend and I shot several shoats. They were gourmet fare.

On our own ranch we have an occasional European boar wandering in and have killed several. We also have crosses between those and feral hogs. We hunt annually for them, whenever we see signs, and if the opportunity presents itself, we try to collect animals up to a hundred pounds. We've never had better pork.

Hunters who want to try hunts for feral hogs must check state regulations carefully. In certain states wild hogs are presumed to belong to somebody, so you can't indiscriminately kill them. It's best to hunt by permission on private lands. However, I know of one hunt, on a Wildlife Management Area owned by the state in eastern Texas, where for the past few years permits have been offered by application and drawing. The wild hogs had become so plentiful they were destroying the habitat. The game department decided the animals might as well be used for sport and meat, and the hunt has become popular. A few National Wildlife Refuges have also offered controlled wild-hog hunts occasionally, to pare down an over-population. Feral hogs make a top-notch subject for a meat hunt as well as an unusual hunting experience.

Although the javelina of the Southwest is not a true swine, it is a piglike distant relative, and should be considered here. Curiously, on its home grounds the javelina has never had as much respect as it deserves as either a game or a meat animal.

For some years now it has been fairly popular as an off-trail trophy among hunters visiting its range, but even among those hunters there seems to be some stigma attached to eating the meat.

That is patently ridiculous. Indians, Mexicans, and early pioneers in the Southwest regularly ate the little desert pigs. I have hunted them often over the past twenty-five years or so, and we have always eaten the meat. The javelina is never fat like a hog. Nor does it grow as large as many sportsmen unacquainted with it believe. The average is around 35 pounds, with large ones weighing 50 or 60.

Javelina are hunted in Texas, New Mexico, and Arizona. Texas has the largest population, Arizona is second, and New Mexico third. Hunters should note that it is often possible to combine deer and javelina or quail and javelina hunting. In Texas, for example, the animals are found in the southern whitetail range and also in western Texas in mule-deer range. The Texas license includes all game, so a deer hunter within javelina range can easily plan to add both trophy and meat. Further, a close look at game laws will show that in this state in most counties the bag limit is two javelina, but in the other states it is only one. Also, certain Texas counties have no closed season and no bag limit. Thus a multiple kill is legal. Because the animals run in droves of anywhere from several to a couple of dozen, when a group is spotted and stalked it's often easy to collect more than one.

QUAIL

One great stride game management has made during recent years is convincing legislatures to give it leeway to swiftly change limits when game populations drastically change—up in numbers, or down. This is an especially important consideration where short-lived game is concerned, and has been applied lately with excellent results especially to quail. The populations of quail, and several other ground nesting birds such as wild turkeys, are far more severely controlled by weather than by predation. During a perfect "hatching" year, with a follow-up of suitable weather for raising chicks, quail populations skyrocket. Conversely, there are many years when the hatch is poor and only a few of the baby birds that hatch survive. Time was when a bag limit was set and there was no way to change it at the last minute. The state legislature had to do it, and the process was so unwieldy that it had to wait until the next year. By that time, perhaps just the opposite—a higher, or lower—bag limit would have been better.

Nowadays many, although not all, states have given their game-management people more leeway. In my state a year ago there was a tremendous quail crop, both of bobwhites and blue quail. I'm not sure readers would believe how many quail "a tremendous crop" means in desert country. I've seen blues and bobs both, where the two range together, so plentiful you could walk out without a dog, put up a dozen coveys in an hour and, if you could shoot even halfway efficiently, kill a ten-bird limit in half that time.

At least 80 percent of the quail hatched one spring are gone by the next, with or without hunting. Thus, game managers reason, when crops are especially high, they should be harvested. Fortunately, in my state we have a system where the game department can make last-minute population surveys of quail populations and raise or lower the limit. So, during last season's quail explosion, the limit was raised to twenty birds a day, sixty in possession. Scores of hunters had no trouble whatever filling limits. All across the Southwest the same situation, with the limits differing slightly, occurred.

Therefore, the astute meat-hunt planner keeps tabs on such ups and downs, and plans to put in a lot of quail hunting during the high-population, high-limit years. On occasion turkey limits are upped to more than one bird, pheasant limits are raised, grouse limits ditto, in state after state. Hunters who make sure to stay up with the regulations and plan to take advantage of the high side not only have much more enjoyment, but much more meat for the pot.

Similar situations of expanded bag limits commonly occur with squirrels and rabbits. There is one other consideration, especially with squirrels. Several states with high squirrel populations traditionally offer spring hunting. The season usually opens in May or June, depending on latitude, after young squirrels are about grown. Some of these states allow squirrel hunting all summer. Or they have a spring and a fall season. Or the season opens in the spring and runs clear through until end of the year, when it closes during gestation, birth, and raising of young. I've hunted in both Oklahoma and Missouri, for example, when such an arrangement was in force. Obviously, having such a long squirrel season, and being able to hunt in spring when the animals are at their population peak of the year as well as later, gives the meat-for-the-pot sportsman an edge. If you live in or near a state with similar regulations, it pays to familiarize yourself with the laws and any annual changes in them.

Not only should you stay informed about the seasons and limits, you should also keep yourself informed about the game populations each season. As I write this I have just returned from a sage-grouse hunt in northwestern Colorado, combined with a trout-fishing trip. The reason I planned the recent hunt is that a check with the Colorado game department informed me that there was an excellent hatch and survival of sage grouse this year. The season opened in early September. I also made a point of fishing high-country small waters for brook trout, on which a bonus daily limit is allowed. The two endeavors dovetailed perfectly, and, to add to enjoyment and meat, I also worked in an antelope hunt.

Several years ago I had planned a sage-grouse hunt, then

cancelled it when I learned the population was drastically down. Keeping up with game-population cycles, especially for small game and birds, allows you to plan ahead and to some extent bring about your own success, in both sport and meat. Stay flexible. If quail are down this year and rabbits up, concentrate on rabbits.

EARLY-SEASON ADVANTAGES

For the sportsman with one eye on the pot, the *timing* of concentrated hunting during the season is also extremely important. When the season opens there will be far more game, especially among small game and birds, than week by week as the season progresses. It's not so much the hunting that severely pares a population of short-lived creatures, but natural attrition. Certainly hunting has some effect, particularly if coverts are crowded with sportsmen and pressure severe. However, suppose you are after quail, and the season lasts from November 1 until February 15, as it does in some states. Say you have a place to hunt where nobody else hunts, perhaps a quail-hunt lease or an agreement with a land owner. If you were to hunt opening day, and not go again until early February, it is absolutely certain there won't be half as many birds on the February hunt. Natural attrition will have removed them.

Thus, early-season concentration for cyclic or short-lived game is always advantageous, for both sport and meat. Further, keep in mind nature's rule that the higher the population, the more certainty of a severe die-off. I remember vividly a quail hunt I made a few years ago near the Mexican border. A friend of mine had a big hunting lease of several thousand acres on a cattle ranch, and maintained a permanent camphouse on it. Blue (scaled) quail peaked that year in fantastic numbers. My friend staked out a rough circle in the cactus and brush of 200 yards around the camphouse, and just to tantalize guest hunters allowed no shooting within the circle.

We made several tours of this "refuge" and roughly estimated the quail population within it. As the hunters ate meals the camphouse yard was always swarming with quail, talking and calling as blues are wont to do. We figured that within the 200-yard circle there surely were upwards of 300 quail! They were just as abundant everywhere. That year the daily limit was twelve, possession thirty-six. Five of us hunted the opening three days and killed limits within an hour each morning. We just drove the ranch trails until we saw a covey run, then got out to chase them. That year quite literally hundreds of thousands of blue quail were in that region.

I went back for deer hunting the last week of December. The quail season was still open, and the lease owner decided we'd make one hunt for quail within the refuge circle. Four of us combed it hard and managed to kill ten birds among us in three forays during the day. It was the same everywhere over the several thousand acres of the lease. The birds were gone. Extreme population highs, which crowd small game and birds, produce stresses that invariably mean drastic die-offs. The early-season hunter for these species is the one who fills the pot.

4

How to Be a "Meat Hunter" for Deer and Other Big Game

The term "meat hunter" has long been an epithet of sorts used often as a synonym for "poor sport," or for the hunter who is more "killer" at heart than sportsman. That is unfortunate, for the hunter who has as much regard for the meat as for the recreation of the hunt is in reality the true sportsman. And if high respect for the meat is a part of his creed, he will be extremely careful not to waste any of it after he shoots it. Just as important, he'll so place his shots that he will ruin as little as possible in the taking of the quarry, and sometimes none.

Let me point out that the hunter who is an all-out recreationist much too often slams a shot at a deer or other big-game animal any old way—as it runs, as it stands with its rear quartering or full on toward him. He is eager to get the animal on the ground. That is his first concern, whereas the so-called meat hunter—the person who has utmost consideration for the eating qualities of the animal after the shot—will elicit far more restraint. In the last analysis, restraint *is* sportsmanship. Placing shots on deer and big game to avoid wasting meat is the highest order of authentic concern for sportsmanship, and for the quick, clean kill.

Paradoxically perhaps, the purist type of sport hunter is in many ways synonymous with the concept of the old-time meat hunter. Go back in history to that time when our country was being explored and opened up, and certain rugged individuals were hired specifically to furnish meat, say for a wagon train moving across the plains, or perhaps for a frontier army encampment or fort. Who got such jobs? Not the wild-eyed, whoop-it-up roustabout who liked to hear his gun fire, but the quiet, stealthy dead-eye, the thoroughbred woodsman who knew game and how to collect it cleanly and efficiently.

Weapons were not of the quality of modern times. The hunter had to get within rather close range to be sure of success. He could not afford many misses. Ammunition might be at a premium. In addition, the less shooting the better, to keep from disturbing game or attracting the Indians. Although the frontiersman hired to hunt meat for a group might enjoy his work, ever honing his prowess, it was a dead-serious business. Each day he *had* to produce a certain amount of food.

SHOT PLACEMENT

The hunter's scheme, always, was to get close, never if it could possibly be helped shoot at a running deer or antelope or elk. Craftily he waited for the animal to stand just so. The hunter was astute at contriving some sort of rest, and his stalks invariably were timed and coordinated to come out so that he had, at the end, a support for his rifle. He didn't aim "at the deer." He aimed with exceeding care at a small *vital* area, so that the deer, or other big game, went down instantly or would move only a short distance from the spot. Chasing animals that were wounded was a waste of time, and the meat

was never as good. It might even be lost, so that he'd have
to start over, or go in empty-handed and perhaps be fired.

Of course, he could place a shot to "break down" a deer,
aiming, say, for the shoulder. That would anchor the animal
and if it required another shot, that could be administered.
However, no meat hunter worth his pay ever operated that
way. Breaking a shoulder (or if the animal were broadside,
perhaps both shoulders) ruined a substantial amount of meat.
A second shot, if needed, only added to the damage. That
meant the hunter had to make excuses for a partially shattered
animal and catch hell from the cook and the boss. He might
also have to keep hunting to make yet another kill, to help
replace the ruined venison.

Thus, what the meat hunter of the frontier did—and what
the modern sport-meat hunter does or should do—was think
in terms of shot placement that was quickly lethal while doing
as little harm as possible to edible flesh. Therefore, absolutely
no difference exists between the meat-hunter concept of how
big-game should be killed and that of the modern recreational
hunter with the highest motives of sportsmanship. The reasons for hunting may differ somewhat, but the desired result
is the same.

The modern hunter who proceeds with an eye cocked toward the pot is actually to be lauded. Invariably he will be
the best hunter, showing the most restraint and sporting judgment, with as much respect for the animal after its demise as
before, wasting as little of it as possible as he squeezes the
trigger. This is the hunter, mind you, who does not let the
deer dictate to *him* when, where, and how to make the shot.
He the hunter is in control and foregoes shots rather than
accept one he doesn't like, one that wastes the venison.

This, then, is the basic philosophy of the modern-day meat
hunter who is combining the desire for fine table fare with
recreation. I have read, and been astonished by, accounts by
gun writers and others that claim the best way to make certain

of deer is to take a shoulder shot and "break the animal down."
I will agree that broadside shoulder shots will invariably put
deer and other big game on the ground and keep it from
moving away. I will also note that it is a surefire way to collect
only part of a deer. It is a disgraceful practice and a deliberate
waste of as much as a third of the meat.

The plain fact is, a shot placed *behind* the shoulder is no
more difficult. In fact, it's easier. It is instantly or very swiftly
lethal. It damages virtually no edible meat except a small
amount of ribs. It also avoids bloodying much edible meat
because the bullet shock is chiefly to a small portion of the
ribs and not carried into the more substantial portions of the
skeleton. Proper shot placement is the key to becoming a
conservation-minded (and pot minded) big-game hunter, and
odd as it may seem, the old-time commercial-hunter placements are best.

Only a few shot-placement areas are acceptable for the very
best results, but, as the early meat hunters who hunted to
sell venison knew, those few are the only clean, instant, or
quick-kill aiming spots. So the idea is, if you are truly a hunter
in control of yourself, you refuse to accept any shots but these.
You learn to make them deftly, and you'll experience pride
in clean kills and meat with barely a blemish.

There is a surprising amount of confusion among hunters
as to precisely where those lethal spots or areas are. One of
the most useful pieces of advice about this was set down in
a deer-hunting piece written by Bob Brister, shooting editor
of *Field & Stream*. He said an old border-country rancher
once told him to forget about all of the deer except the *front
end*. That end, the man said, is where you can kill him; the
other half is where you just wound him.

Deer and other large animals, it might be said, "live" up
front. The lungs, heart, brain, spinal column—these are the
four areas where a bullet of sufficient power for the job results

in an instant or very quick kill. However, when considering meat, one must take into account how to reach any one of those areas with minimum flesh damage. The spinal column from above the shoulders on back is not only a tricky shot, often resulting in a miss or wounding, but results in undue damage to venison as well. Trying this shot is likely to wind up ruining the most desirable meat of all, the loins or backstraps. My advice is to forget about this shot. It's seldom if ever necessary, anyway.

The shoulder shot I've already talked about. Sure, putting a bullet through a shoulder gets into the lungs and also anchors an animal by breaking bones. But it is invariably avoidable and cannot do the job without unacceptable meat damage. Much has been made in hunting literature about heart shots for instant kills on big game. The heart shot certainly is lethal. Nonetheless, I never purposely try this placement. It is bad practice, can result in all sorts of unplanned problems.

The heart of all big-game animals is located very low in the body cavity, between the two sections of the brisket, and is well protected because it also lies near (and between) the front legs. I once hit a walking buck antelope so low the bullet sliced into the lower portion of the sternum and clipped the very lower tip of the heart. Indeed, the buck did not move more than 30 paces after the shot, but a half inch lower would have meant no serious wound at all. Only the fact that the animal was broadside and the front leg on my side happened to be stretched out ahead as it walked saved me from breaking its leg. In that case, it is possible the animal would have run off, the leg bone having kept the bullet from doing any serious immediate damage. Conceivably the wounded animal might have gotten away, only to die later, a total waste.

On dangerous animals, the heart placement, especially low through the shoulder, may be reasonable. It may be on authentic trophies, as well. For the sportsman who prizes the meat, too, it is in my view not only unacceptable, but also one of the poorest bets for clean kills imaginable, because of the difficulty of exact placement.

This would seem to leave very few opportunities. By number, that's true. But what I have always wondered, in reading millions of words about hunting, and writing several million myself, is why a big-game hunter *needs* more than two or three options. After all, a deer or other big-game creature either faces you, faces unacceptably away from you, stands quartering front-end or rear-end on (in the latter instance often with head turned back to look), or appears broadside or nearly so. Remember that if you pursue my tactics, splitting your interest between sport and meat, you don't shoot at running animals, and you wait for unaware standing or walking animals to present the stance you desire. So why do you need any wide variety of bullet-placement possibilities?

There is a crucial area just behind the shoulder of a deer or comparable game that spans from there to the paunch and reaches from the brisket (what is seen of it as the animal stands well braced) up to just below the spine. The only physical structures over this rather large area—so large in moose and elk it should not be missed by any controlled hunter—are hide, thin flesh coating, and ribs. This area—make a firm mental note of it—is the most vulnerable part of any big-game creature. It might even be considered an error in nature's design, yet if the animal is to move with agility, it must exist.

Behind this relatively thin exterior coating of ribs and skin with very meager flesh is the most vulnerable and vital part of the animal: the lungs. An animal hit here—anywhere from top to bottom, but preferably spang in the middle vertically— either drops instantly or runs very briefly and is easy to find. At long ranges, this is the *only* placement I recommend. It offers the largest lethal area on which to lay a sight. The ribs and their coating are of minor importance as meat. Yet a big-game animal hit there is downed cleanly. When possible, this placement, aimed a bit high to strike a short distance below the spine, does very little backstrap damage yet sends shock overwhelmingly along the nerve and bone system and is almost without fail instantly lethal.

I feel strongly that I must repeat: every hunter should be concerned about instant, clean kills. I repeat also, you don't *need* to consider all those shots the books and magazines tell you about. I have bagged well over a hundred deer in some fifty years of deer hunting. For the last half of that period at least I have accepted only a very limited number of shots at deer. The rib shot already described can be slightly varied, from a deer facing you at a broad angle to one looking away. But let me warn against angles too shallow. It's easy to put a bullet into the paunch or into a shoulder. Better wait for a broadside or almost broadside stance.

Meat hunters of the old commercial school, and poachers with their jacklights, did and do shoot deer and other big game animals in the head. Obviously this is an instant-kill placement. Some years ago when I was teaching my boys to hunt deer, I restricted each in turn to a head or neck shot for his first deer. I was able to get them into close range. Mike, the older and thus first to start, placed his first shot perfectly between the eyes of a buck facing him. My thinking was that a hit was certain to drop the animal, and a miss, though easy on small deer especially, would do no damage. From broadside the placement should be in the ear. Although I have shot a few deer with head shots, admittedly the target is small, the placement is not logical for any but short ranges, and for bucks remotely of trophy proportions skull shots should be passed up.

This leaves only neck shots. For some twenty-five years I have stuck with only neck and ribs. Some hunters complain that neck shots are too difficult. I would reply that you should simply train yourself thoroughly enough so they *aren't*. There is some meat in a big-game animal's neck. It is by no means choice, and often also a bullet does the required job without harming much of it. Further, trying a neck shot, you get either a kill or a clean miss.

The neck shot can be administered from the front, point of aim at the throat area well below the chin. It can be done easily from the side. A deer standing, quartering away and looking back, presents an easy neck shot. One broadside and looking at you also offers easy placement. A careful rifleman with a good rest can even make the neck shot from behind on a deer or other big-game animal standing rear end on, with its head up. My rule is: short shots, try the neck; long shots, try the ribs. The neck shot administers such shock that the

Three most lethal spots on a deer or other big-game animal: (1) lungs; (2) neck; (3) heart. Of the three, the lung shot is the best choice at long range; the neck shot up close.

kill is instantaneous. A rib-shot deer may run, but only a short distance.

Think again about forgetting all of the animal except the front half—actually somewhat less than a whole front half, only from the diaphragm forward. Beginning hunters, and some old hands who never get fully under control through experience, too often see the whole animal. A deer looks like a lot of target. A moose or elk looks like far more. It *is* difficult to look at an animal broadside and not be tempted just to haul off and shoot. So train yourself to ignore all but that front portion, and of that all but the couple of areas I have suggested. One immense advantage for success is that by doing this you are never confused about where to aim.

Countless hunters I've talked with about my theories of

The three spots seen on a deer partly facing the hunter. Again, the neck or lung shot would be the best bet.

A deer quartering away from the hunter could be killed with a spine or neck shot, but it would be better to wait for another chance.

Perfect setup for a neck shot: deer at close range, partially facing hunter, with tree blocking part of body.

lethal, meat-saving shots insist on going through endless "But what if. . ." illustrations. What if the deer moves and turns its backside to you and starts to walk into the brush? What if you spook it, or something does, and it runs? What if it never presents anything but a shallow going-away angle, and you can't get into the ribs without hitting the paunch? So on and on. My reply is always the same: what if you simply forget that animal and go look for another?

During some forty years of making my living writing about outdoor matters, I have been around scores of deer camps, have seen hundreds of deer hung from meat poles, many of them mangled unmercifully, shot six or seven times. A wounded animal that gains time to get adrenalin flowing has astonishing tenacity. It also becomes, after several tries at collecting it, practically worthless as meat. Deer especially are not scarce in this country. You don't have to lay down a barrage wildly at the first one you see. Restraint is the one quality that separates the true sportsman and meat hunter alike from the slam-bang shooters.

RESTS AND SIGHTS

Early in this chapter I noted that the old-time commercial hunters invariably took a solid rest when aiming. The buffalo hunters on the plains, where natural rests were scarce, carried their crossed sticks so they had a solid rest and could place bullets accurately. The modern pot hunter after big game should get the rest habit so instilled that he is never at a loss. In timber, a rest is usually accessible. If you can't get the gun barrel across a limb that's steady, seize a sapling with your nontrigger hand and lay the gun across your wrist.

Always pad the rifle somehow if you must rest on a hard surface such as a rock. Put your sling and hand, or a jacket, under the forepiece. I have often contrived rests with my hat.

In timber country the basic rest is a downed log. If possible, pad the log with a folded coat.

Here author uses sling to pad rifle on rock rest (left), but an even better way would be to use your hand (right).

Crotch of dead tree provides a rest, with cap as padding.

A rest improvised of two crossed sticks, picked up
at random.

One year while hunting antelope on the bald plains I wore a fairly stiff crowned and brimmed western felt hat. I laid my hat on the ground, gingerly placed the rifle fore end lengthwise in the hollow formed by the crease, and dropped an excellent buck with a rib shot at long range. On another occasion I took my hunting knife and its sheath from my belt, steadied the sheath point into soft turf, laid the rifle across my hand where I gripped the knife handle. It worked just fine.

A good rest is an integral part of meat hunting; it makes correct bullet placement easier and eliminates wobble. I formed a habit long ago of always thinking positively about a rest. Don't say to yourself, "I'll never be able to get a rest

A long stick leaned against vehicle served as rest for a high-bluff shot.

Using sling in kneeling position, author steadies himself
against small tree.

here," but instead "What are the rest possibilities here?"
There's always a way, and even the most makeshift rest can
be the difference between filling and not filling a tag, or between much ruined venison and very little that is spoiled.

A word needs to be said about sights, too. It is astonishing
that in this age of highly refined telescope sights, and after
many decades of their use, there are some holdouts who still
claim open sights are better. That is pure nonsense. All the
arguments about how scopes won't allow you to shoot in brush
or at jumped (running) deer are ridiculous. My view, as I've

Two ways to use a standing tree for a rest

stated, is that nobody should be shooting at a running deer anyway, and the fact is, a scope sight lets you discover and aim through tiny openings in brush that the naked eye behind open sights would never find.

The telescope sight is, in fact, one of the mandatory tools of the meat hunter. In effect, it is the mechanism that allows you to forget about that big "other half" of the animal that isn't "where it lives," and to place a bullet with pinpoint finesse where it will do the most good and waste the least meat.

5

Deer and Big Game—Be Selective for the Best Meat

A meat hunter should train himself to be something of a trophy hunter. The average deer hunter going into the woods begins by looking for the largest antlered animal he can find. In many instances he really does pass up chances for shots, hoping to get a more striking set of antlers. It is all relative, however, for the fact is, only a very small percentage of big-game animals bagged annually are even remotely true trophies. Maybe a hunter collects a whitetail deer that has a rack 2 inches wider than last year's. But at that it is only a so-so specimen, judged by the antlers.

Everyone has heard the old resigned statement, "Oh, well, you can't eat the antlers anyway." How true! So, given the fact that undoubtedly 99 percent of the deer and other game brought in is far from trophy class judged by antlers or horns, it would make more sense perhaps to hunt primarily for a "trophy meat animal," that is, a specimen that is fat, large, and in prime shape. Obviously, if one has a chance at a stunning set of antlers, the word is bound to be "go." But if you are seeing so-so bucks and a lot of big, fat does, why not consider learning to judge the quality of animals on the hoof, and balancing your trophy hunting at least 50–50 between skull adornment and meat for the pot?

Of course, you can't walk up to a deer and pinch it, run your hand over its flank, and otherwise check it out as you might a beef critter you are about to buy for butchering. And you can't look at the carcass hung for aging to make sure of the general quality. There are, however, a number of ways to judge game animals on the hoof, according to what has been happening during the year with their food supply and the weather. I have been told by some hunters that it's ridiculous to pass up opportunities for shots. After all, you might not get another chance to fill your tag. On a very short hunt, granted, you might be wise not to linger. But in most deer woods and on many other big game hunts today, there are enough animals available so that with several days of hunting you can do at least a modest amount of picking and choosing.

When my sons and I hunt our small ranch in the Texas Hill Country, admittedly we do some antler hunting. But because we have multiple tags in Texas, with three whitetails the legal bag in most counties, we routinely pass up certain deer and collect others strictly because some are in better physical shape. Two seasons ago my son Mike, sitting on a stand on one of our oak-covered hills, saw each afternoon for three days straight the same group of does. He wanted a good buck, and so he left them alone. Two of these does, he had told me, were awesomely fat. They waddled when they walked. They were also mature and large.

On the last afternoon of that hunt, about an hour before dusk he had seen no suitable buck. The does came trailing along right on schedule. I had signed two doe permits for him, which he was carrying. He collected both. By the time I picked him up in my vehicle he had them gutted. We hung them from a limb, and, as we usually do, skinned and rough-cut them up then and there. Both were simply larded in fat. They made some of the finest venison we have ever taken off

the ranch. It was a matter of looking over and picking the best meat specimens available.

In this instance, he had done his trophy-antler hunting, but had kept an eye out for the best "eating" deer, as well. Of course, hunters are bound to be eager to fill tags and dubious about passing up chances. Yet if you want to revel in the eating along with the sport, you may want to do some "meat scouting," control your eagerness, and be willing to go home with an unfilled tag rather than with some scrawny, mediocre-antlered buck hardly fit for table fare. At least when hunting on any range where the quarry is known to be reasonably abundant, selecting a particular animal that will furnish the best meat makes sense.

In order to do this, you must know how to judge animals on the hoof, and you must make a point of looking them over in detail. This calls for a quality binocular. I firmly believe that no big-game hunter can hunt at his best without a binocular. One good reason is that a glass allows you to study deer and big game from a distance while the animals are unaware, and to judge by sizing up each specimen not only which is the trophy rack but which is prime locker material.

It shouldn't be difficult for anyone to distinguish a fat animal from a skinny one. It can, however, be confusing, under excitement, or at a distance, or in dim light. If an animal is in shadow but about to step into better light, don't be hasty. Give it a chance. Your shot placement is easier in good light, and more light may show you it's an animal you don't want. Deer and all antlered and horned animals are, bear in mind, never as fat as domestic animals. They are not line bred to allow fat buildup, but actually by nature just the opposite. Game animals never have meat marbled with fat like beef, either. They are active and hard muscled, and fat is always an overlayer, put on fast and often lost just as swiftly.

But before you even try to judge how fat and prime an animal is in flesh, look at its coat. The coat of a game animal tells you a lot about its general health and vigor. In fall, for example, all big game puts on a new coat. Deer, which have worn thin, reddish coats all summer, change to thick, gray coats. In late fall, when most hunting seasons are open, a deer that is still reddish in color might as well be wearing a printed sign saying: "Don't shoot; I'm in mighty poor shape."

That reddish coat will not be thin and sleek as it perhaps was in summer. Usually it is rough looking and scraggly. Animals with such coats are invariably in poor health. Don't go entirely by the reddish color, either. Any deer, or any other big-game specimen, with a poor, scraggly coat should be passed up. You can't tell by looking what causes its problem, but a lusterless, rough coat indicates some kind of health disability.

In trying to spot a choice animal, always look for rounded lines. If the ribs of a buck show, or the hip bones of a big doe are prominent, look for another target. "Sleek" aptly describes how a vigorous game animal in prime condition should look. The coat should be glossy and thick.

Especially when judging deer, look at the neck. If it looks too long or scrawny, the animal isn't much. Also, run your eye along the backbone. Not a vertebra should show on the best, high-prime animals. The sides should be smooth and rounded. A deer puts fat first around its entrails, and then across its back and hams. If the ribs also are larded, it is in top condition, so those rounded sides that all but ripple when it walks tell you much about the shape it is in.

A lot of pure hokum surfaces annually among deer hunters regarding age of deer and its relation to physical condition. For example, many an old hand allows that, by gum, when he goes after a fat doe, he always picks a barren one—that is, one that does not have a fawn or fawns, or has ceased having them. It may be that some trained biologists can make fair guesses as to which are the barren does. I've seen those "old hands" shoot several, and watched twin fawns of the year,

Don't be fooled by large antlers. Both bucks are thin, ribs show, and coats lack gloss.

This buck's coat is sleek and dark; he looks "round"—evidence of ample butterfat.

Buck is in extremely poor condition: meager antlers; pale, dull coat; protruding ribs; skinny neck.

grown and no longer dependent but still hanging around the mother, run off. Forget about barren does. Just pick one that shows all the attributes of being healthy and in good physical condition.

Next are the matters of the "tough old buck" and the "tender young fawn." Some of the best venison I've ever eaten has come from ancient bucks that were gray in the face. Find a buck that is about over the hill in his breeding life, yet in vigorous health otherwise, and when he is fattened up in fall he'll be superb eating. Any stockman will tell you that age is no criterion for good meat. The criterion is whether an animal

A buck in beautiful physical condition—round, shiny, fat, with excellent antlers.

is "putting on" or "losing." A deer that is losing weight will invariably be tough, even though it may look in fair shape. One that is gaining weight in fall, will turn out to be tender, delicious venison. I've seen old gray-faced mule-deer bucks with antlers beginning to run out to misshapen spikes that were hog fat and tender.

The up-or-down business applies to fawns, too. Many a hunter with an antlerless deer permit thinks a chance at a fawn—a deer of the year, one born the previous spring—is a sure way to venison in modest quantity that is certain to be tender as veal. The facts of fawn life are quite different. A

Group of whitetails in varying degrees of condition. Buck in left foreground is smaller but fatter than bigger buck at rear, although the latter is in acceptable condition. Modest sized doe in center, head down, is quality venison on the hoof. Larger doe at right and slightly above looks old, poor.

fawn that has persisted in following its mother and trying to nurse into late fall will, in all probability, be without an ounce of fat and so tough you can't inhale the cooking odor without choking. An early fawn that soon learned to feed itself and went into its first fall gorging on acorns will be fat, tender, and a delectable piece of meat. My advice, though, is if a big, fat doe is available, take it in preference to a fawn any time.

TIMING OF THE RUT

A certain amount of hunt planning for proper time is needed to assure that chances of bagging the best meat animal or animals are high. Part of this concerns the timing of the rut in your area. Males of all horned and antlered animals, if in basically good health, are at their most vigorous just prior to the beginning of the rut. This is nature's way of helping guarantee that the race will continue. The rut is a severe physical ordeal for big-game males. Buck deer may endlessly chase after does, breed many of them, meanwhile eating very little. A bull elk may gather a harem of as many as forty cows, incessantly patrol his charges to fend off interloper bucks, fight a great deal, service the cows constantly, and spend vast amounts of energy—and fat—in the process.

If you are going to be hunting big-game males, the rut is naturally one of the best times as far as ease of success is concerned. Males are less wary and watchful of danger. They are addled with the mating urge. However, if you're thinking of meat, a buck deer taken during peak of the rut, or an elk or moose taken toward the end of it, is a poor table specimen. Fat has disappeared, the meat may look stringy and blue, and it will be tough and strong. Many a bull elk at the end of rut is hardly fit to eat. He is totally done in.

Thus, one needs to know when the rut begins, in a normal year, in the area where he'll hunt. Getting right in at the start finds males in good shape. After that, meat hunting is hardly worthwhile—for buck or bull. However, it should be noted that females of the big-game animals do not suffer any serious physical strain during breeding season. They are in heat only for brief periods. A deer is in breeding condition for barely twenty-four hours. If she is not bred at that time, she does not come in heat again for twenty-eight days. She hardly misses a meal all through the breeding season and her physical condition stays on a high level.

Therefore, a hunter who intends to try for an antlerless animal (deer, elk, moose) has no reason to avoid the rut period. It may, in fact, be a help. Does lead bucks on magnetized chases, elk gather large groups of cows, which can be located because the bulls are bugling. As I noted early in this book, many a guide I know lets his hunters get all excited over the big, noisy bull elk, then he puts his own tag on a fat cow, for winter meat.

It's a good idea to look at seasons, or season openings, when many hunters like to go, in relation to the rut. Some states have a bull-elk season set during the "bugling season." In some places the deer season spans the peak of the rut. This can be an advantage or a disadvantage for the meat hunter, as I have shown. Some seasons fall before or after the rut. If a season opens immediately after the rut or the peak period of it concludes, yet stretches along for some weeks, it's often best to wait a few weeks, giving males a chance to recoup lost weight.

I think especially of antelope season. Pronghorn bucks are great harem gatherers and chasers, wearing themselves frazzled. A hunting season during the rut often sees the bucks in poor shape, and strong tasting. Conversely, a few antelope seasons are set early, in late summer, when the bucks are in beautiful shape, their horns glossy black and lots of fat on their bodies. I hunted antelope in New Mexico this past August, and the bucks were among the primest of the prime.

Not long after the rut, antelope lose the outer sheath of their horns, which grows new each year. I have hunted in late antelope seasons—in late October and early November, for example—when horn sheaths were loose. Once a friend of mine shot a buck and when it hit the ground the horn sheaths fell off—not a very heart-gladdening experience. So always watch for early antelope seasons, when both the trophy and the meat are best.

KNOW THE RANGE

In virtually every state, game management personnel have plotted ranges. They know, for example, which areas are the best deer range, and how many animals to the square mile (or whatever unit they use) fill the carrying capacity of that particular range. An overpopulation means less forage for each animal. So it is not always an advantage to hunt deer, for example, where they are "simply swarming." A most interesting, rather recently discovered tool of deer management is a parasite count in one of the stomachs. All wild animals carry a number of parasites. Certain ones found in various states in deer stomachs are common, and the more deer are crowded together, the more easily the parasites are distributed and thrive. By the parasite count in deer stomachs, from deer taken as samples from areas suspected of overpopulation, biologists can tell with amazing precision how much cropping of that herd is needed to tailor it to the carrying capacity of the range. Needless to say, general vigor of each animal is in direct proportion to the lessening number of stomach parasites.

If you discover, for example, that an area has only a mild overabundance of deer, this would be a good place to plan a hunt. But if you learn that a certain hunt unit is heavily overpopulated, it is quite possible that the animals are not in very good physical condition. In this case, you might better hunt where deer are not so abundant. You'll take better animals, both antlers and meat.

Food of course is the key, both long-term and short-term. In my part of Texas there are ranches that have abused their acres for many years by grazing too many mohair goats, which directly compete with deer for forage. These overbrowsed lands often have plentiful, but pitifully runty, deer, the result of poor forage for countless generations. Conversely, in southern Texas, in the brush-country cattle ranges, whitetails are big, not strikingly abundant, but usually in fine shape.

The hunter, particularly the deer hunter, who makes a point of knowing the history of the range where he hunts, whether it is public or private land, can key his hunting to the best deer-range conditions, judged against long-term use of the land. If he does this astutely, he'll always bring home tasty venison. The same hunter must also consider the short-term availability of food. What happened during the previous late winter and early spring may well have an emphatic bearing on the physical condition of deer this hunting season.

For example, a year ago on my area we had a tremendous acorn crop, along with ample rain and a good growing season following a moderate winter. Deer (whitetails, in this instance) came out of winter in excellent condition. Antler growth was exceptional. For them, everything about weather and the growing season simply jelled. By fall all animals were in top shape, and with winter—and deer season—coming on there was lots of nutritious browse; in addition, there was a bonanza acorn crop.

We have in this area a half dozen different kinds of oak, and all of them were loaded. I observed deer on our ranch gorging beneath huge chestnut oaks. They could fill up in a few minutes because these acorns are as big as your thumb. They are also sweet acorns, loaded with quality nutrition. The deer started into fall fat, and became fatter and fatter.

Unfortunately, 1980 started dry and continued until by spring and summer we were in a severe drought. On our home place, separate from our ranch, we have a good many deer, which we can observe around the yard off and on all summer. In early August we saw deer with ribs and hips showing, feeding in the middle of the hot days—trying to find food, at least. By fall it was authenticated that the best hope in our area for recovery, the acorn crop, was a failure. Acorns had started to form but withered or failed to develop. There simply were none. A deer die-off had begun long before the season opened.

Under such conditions it is obvious that deer hunting can be predicted as poor, and that most of the deer killed will be thin, hardly fit for sausage. The lesson to be learned from such observations, for the pot hunter, is to keep tabs on the season and plan a hunt where conditions are better, away from the food-scarce area. Or, if that can't be done, perhaps it is as well to turn attention to other game and wait for next season to take up deer hunting again.

Of course, seasons are seldom that drastic in bringing big game to desperate straits. Sometimes a year starts out hard on the animals, but, remember, wild creatures rebound quickly. All deer hunters have seen times when as buck antlers hardened they were unimpressive, thin, and with a whitish cast, not the mahogany hue of trophy bucks. It is easy to misjudge meat quality by a year that sees thin, whitish antlers form. Usually this phenomenon occurs because at the time the antlers are forming, in early spring, a high-protein diet was not available; around 16 percent protein helps grow the best antlers. Forage in total perhaps was meager.

Antler formation thus was not up to par. A scouting trip that found deer in this condition during late summer, or as velvet came off in early fall well before season, might cause a hunter to suspect a lack of trophy racks and quality venison that year. Yet summer rains, a substantial acorn or other mast crop, or availability of grain perhaps still could result in fine, fat deer at opening of the season.

To be sure, following all these rather intricate leads to assure the best meat on the table is not simple. It does, however, add immensely to the interest of the big-game hunting art. And when you eat the result of a successful pot-and-sport hunting scheme put together by a gathering of sound facts, there's a pride in the savoring that adds a new dimension to the recreational endeavor.

6

Calibers and Loads for Meat Hunting

Much of the quality of any game meat is directly related to the choice of gun caliber and load, or shotgun shot size and load, that are used in collecting it. Meat that is "shot up" loses appeal in looks and is difficult to clean properly. It is also by no means as tasty, and is more difficult for a cook to handle. Further, some is invariably wasted. Choices of calibers and loads must depend to a great extent upon the judgment of the hunter, but there are some basic rules that can serve as guidelines to achieving clean kills without decimating the targets.

Consider first the choices facing the big-game hunter. The main problem is that there are so many rifle calibers and bullet weights, and so many fads coming and going incessantly among gun writers and gun and ammo manufacturers. Over past years, for example, numerous magnums have been highly touted for big game. A certain number of hunters fall for the idea of "big" for no very sound reasons. There are many hunting jobs that a heavy magnum caliber will do better than a lighter caliber-bullet combo. Trouble is, some hunters get the idea that the loud report, the heavy recoil that slams the shoulder, and the massive energy of a projectile that instantly flattens the animal are somehow better.

Loud is not necessarily better. Big isn't either. The hunter with the moderately conservative view will ask himself one question: what calibers and loads will efficiently do the job (a specific job—collecting deer, bear, moose, antelope, etc.), yet, with proper bullet placement, do the least *unnecessary* tissue (meat) damage?

Granted, there are no precise measurements for the answer. It would be ridiculous to claim that the .243 caliber with a 100-grain bullet is an adequate combination for all big game, and even more so to claim it as a perfect moose killer. It will down a moose. But only under perfect situations and with expert handling. By the same token, it is just as ridiculous to carry around a .300 Winchester Magnum with a 180-grain bullet if you intend to shoot a whitetail deer.

I well realize that talking down a fellow's pet firearm is like kicking his dog. The point is, however, that many hunters go far overgunned. Though I don't believe in being undergunned, I am convinced that the caliber and load are not half as important as the judgment of the man pulling the trigger. If you follow the advice on bullet placement in Chapter 4, and select a caliber and load combo simply logical for the taking of the animal in question, you will have no wounding problems, nor much meat loss.

Overgunned hunters, even when they use the "meat hunter" shot placements I have suggested, still cannot avoid being meat wasters. I have a deer-hunting friend who is a big-magnum addict. I've been with him on mule-deer hunts when I nearly cringed to watch him shoot. His claim was that it didn't make much difference *where* he hit a deer, because the power of his big bullet was certain to zap it, regardless. This may be handy material for bragging, but it's a sorry attitude for a hunter to carry into the woods with him, and a good way to wind up with a freezer full of field-pulverized meat.

I have not missed a year in the past twenty-five making at least one mule-deer hunt each season. Most of the time I have used the .243 with a 100-grain load, sometimes with 85-grain handloads. Remember now, mule deer may be burly, but I pick my shots, select the particular deer I want, and wait for the proper stance so I can be sure of putting the bullet where I want it. Every kill has been quick and clean.

Lots of other calibers with comparable loads would have done just as well, some of them, to be sure, a little bit heavier. The .270, 30/06, .308, 25/06 are good examples. My point is, however, that I decided long ago how I wanted to hunt, and in my scheme the meat is extremely important. The fairly light .243 is perfectly adequate for deer hunting, and if properly used it is kind to the part that goes into the pot. Calibers heavier than needed for the game under consideration are meat wasters to some extent even when bullet placement is done expertly and carefully. One year I helped skin and quarter an antelope shot through the ribs with a .300 Magnum. Tissue damage was so great over such a large area that even the loins were barely edible. Big-game hunters need to think about what the meat is going to look like after they've got the hide off. A sensible friend points out, "There's no reason for going overgunned for any big-game animal; you only have to kill it once!"

BIRD HUNTING

Interestingly, there are not the fads nor the bristling opinions among bird and small-game hunters about the choice of shot sizes and loads. There is much more logic and practically no emotion involved. Yet this, too, is far less than an exact science. You certainly should select a shot size (talking now of shotguns), and a powder charge backing it, that is logical for the game you are after. There are extremes, in the case of each species, that are not logical. It would be silly, for example, to carry No. 9 shot shells with low powder charge into a goose blind, and just as much so to go after doves on opening day with high-base No. 2's. The aim of every bird hunter should be to match shot and powder to the species he's after so that *under the particular shooting circumstances* the birds will be put down cleanly but will not be mangled.

The emphasis on shooting circumstances is important. For example, I shot mourning doves at a waterhole last year on opening day when birds drifted in over a tree under which I stood, circled within 20 yards, lazing along. Easy targets. Shooting a shotgun with improved cylinder barrel, I used field loads in No. 8 and cleanly killed a limit with no crippled birds, and with no shot-mangled birds in my bag. Two days later all was changed. I shot a high flight of doves, pass-shooting, the sky overcast and the wind a small gale. The ranges were long, the birds going all out. I switched to a full-choked barrel, and stuffed the gun with express loads of No. 6 shot. I missed a lot. When I did manage a hit, the heavier shot with more punch behind it tumbled them; yet at the extended range the close choke of the gun still did not result in any shot-riddled birds.

You will be surprised, if you pay close attention to selecting bird loads not by species alone but by field circumstances on a given day, how much better your bag will look when the collected birds are readied for the pot, their meat much less bloodied and punctured. Sometimes it pays to be prepared to change combinations in the field to match a switch in conditions.

I think offhand of a sage-grouse hunt I made in western Colorado during the early fall of 1980. The sage grouse is a large bird. Mature cocks weigh as much as 4 or 5 pounds. Hens are a bit smaller. However, a sage grouse is not an especially tenacious species, and not difficult to put down.

My host on this hunt was much more experienced than I with this bird. He also knew the country and the type of cover the birds would use most, short sage. Further, this was opening day, and he knew that most game birds are not as wary on opening day as they will be after the shooting has gone on for several days. This gentleman equipped himself with a moderately open barrel and loads of No. 7½ shot. I carried a full-choked 12-gauge loaded with high-base sixes.

It did not take long to discover that the birds were going to sit close, and flush from under foot. Shots were at 15 or 20 yards, and sage grouse have a habit of often flushing straight away, not across. It had been perhaps twenty-five years since I had hunted sage grouse, and I was overeager. My first bird, centered rear-end-on with my heavy load and choked barrel at short range, was badly shattered.

Fortunately, I was able after that first distasteful experience to change gun and loads. In addition, we began waiting out birds that flushed close. This is often difficult for a hunter. The impulse is to hurry up the shot before a bird gets out of range. Sometimes a wait-out of a couple of seconds, with any species, can compensate for too heavy a load or too close-choked a gun. It's better by far, however, to match the load and choke to field conditions. Late that afternoon, for example, after birds had been pushed about some, the scene changed, and so did we. Birds flushed wild. Some were much too far out. Others, however, were efficiently taken care of by the full-choke barrel and the heavy load I'd started with in the morning. To illustrate how drastically individual situations can differ, I've talked to hunters who shot sage grouse in Montana late in season when they flushed wild. They used express loads in No. 4, just as for big ducks or, on occasion, geese.

Day to day experience under varying conditions teaches a bird hunter much about how to drop his targets in the best shape for the kitchen. A classic illustration concerns hunting pheasants early on a frosty morning when they have roosted overnight in dense weed cover. Dozens of times I have practically stepped on cocks before they'd flush. Or a pointing dog would have one right at its nose. When they lie snug in heavy cover, reluctant to fly on a crisp dawn, an experienced shooter knows they'll go straight up, standing on their tails in air so to speak, wings beating to gain some altitude. When the bird reaches 10 or 15 feet, it heels over to begin level flight.

At that instant of changing direction, a rooster is almost standing still. I learned as a young fellow shooting pheasants on our small Michigan farm that if I'd wait for that second, I could aim point blank and kill every bird. I also learned that I'd better have an open gun and medium shot, or I'd decimate them. My brother and I actually tried to shoot slightly above a rooster as it rose, commonly putting only a few shot into the head and neck, leaving the edible meat hardly blemished. When need be, we also waited them out, allowing them to get out to 30 yards or so before firing. My suggestion: if you shoot on the top of the rise, use No. 7½ in a field load and hold slightly over; if you wait them out, better be loaded with No. 6 shot.

Quite an opposite situation occurs when you hunt pheasants in grain stubble where they may run and flush wild, or at least at substantial range. Now they don't beat up standing on their tails. They take off from running and are going like blazes the moment they're airborne. Last season I hunted pheasants in the Texas Panhandle in a cut-over milo field. I used a Remington 12-gauge automatic, with No. 6 express loads. The problem here was that you *had* to compromise. Better to have a bird with a few extra shot in it than to bring one down wounded. In milo (or corn) pheasants run, and even with a dog are often never retrieved.

It strikes me as not asking too much of any bird hunter to consider his choice of loads and chokes at least partly in relation to the quality of the resultant table-ready birds. Actually this consideration, too commonly overlooked, is couched in plain good bird-hunting sense. You want to drop the targets but not mangle them. The time of season will have bearing on your choice of shot sizes; so will overhead cover, or lack of it.

When bird seasons open, the largest number of birds of the year are present. Among most upland birds, which are short-lived, 70 to 80 percent each fall are birds of the year. These individuals are more naive than older birds that have gone through one or more hunting seasons; they are also smaller, invariably more lightly feathered, and weaker flyers. Sometimes when there have been late hatches I have seen half-grown quail, numerous short-tailed young doves, and occasionally grouse only half the size they should be. On that sage-grouse hunt I mentioned, we flushed two birds from practically under our boots that were barely one-pounders. Apparently they were from a late-hatched covey. A solid hit at short range on these tender youngsters would have ground them to a pulp.

Thus, when the season opens a compromise for lighter shot and more open barrel is a sensible pot-hunter idea. As the season progresses, birds fill out and wise up. Ranges are longer, birds more fully feathered and tougher. So, you raise the punch a bit. Toward the end of a long bird season (some quail seasons last over four months) mature birds are wary and much harder to put down. Now you should think about a closer choke, possibly one size larger in shot, and with a bit more powder behind it. These switches add to success, and to enjoyment of the eating.

My mention of overhead cover or lack of it concerns the differences, for example, between hunting woodcock and jacksnipe. The woodcock is, except in most unusual instances, in spots of fairly open ground cover but with timber overhead. It is small, lies close, and is not difficult to bring down. So, you need small shot to keep from unduly pocking it at short range, but an open barrel, if you hope to pop them among the crisscross of cover. The open barrel and the small-shot, low-based shells get the job done but leave the birds in good shape for the pot.

Conversely, the jacksnipe is also a small bird, of open wetlands. It hides well enough, but when it flushes there is seldom any interference from brush or timber. It gets away fast and low to the ground, presenting a difficult target, then often circles high, flying a straight course. (I recall vividly how the picture on the Peter's ammo box of No. 9-size shells years ago was of a jacksnipe.) Because of its small size, you need small shot, just as for woodcock. You can also get by with a low powder charge. But you need a less open barrel if you hope to center these exasperating birds. They're small enough and fast enough so you're not likely to shoot them up badly, even so.

In general, then, the shot sizes and the loads most efficient for bagging birds cleanly are the ones that do the least unacceptable damage to them as table fare. Never use shot sizes or powder charges that might be considered "overkill loads." A basic guide follows. (Compromises are dictated of course by field conditions—cover, weather, hunting pressure, time of season, etc. Choke should be tightened as range lengthens.)

Species	Load, average	Long range	Extreme
Woodcock, doves, jacksnipe, bob-white quail	Low-base, No. 8	No. 7½	No. 6 (doves)
Western quail: scaled, Cal., Gambels, mountain, Mearns	Low-base, No. 7½	High-base, No. 7½	Low-base, No. 6
Hungarian partridge	Low-base, No. 7½	High-base, No. 7½	Low-base, No. 6
Chukar	Low-base, No. 7½	High-base, Nos. 7½,6	High-base, No. 6
Ruffed, spruce grouse	Low-base, No. 7½	High-base, Nos. 7½,6	High-base, No. 6

Sharptail grouse, prairie chickens, pheasants, sage grouse, blue grouse	High-base, No. 7½	High-base, No. 6	High-base, Nos. 6,4
Ducks	High-base, No. 6	High-base, No. 4	High-base, No. 4
Geese	High-base, No. 4	High-base, No. 2	High-base, No. 2

These are very general listings. Chokes properly matched to ranges—and avoiding too-quick, close-in shots, thus giving shot a chance to spread—will put lightly marked birds into your bag, seldom with any shot-up specimens.

Turkeys, so far not mentioned, are a rather special proposition. The majority of turkey hunters use shotguns and accept head shots only. Seldom is there opportunity to shoot a turkey on the wing. Those called up, or waylaid, should never be body shot. It is wasteful of the meat, and not always successful. A wounded turkey is generally a lost one. The average turkey is downed within 40 yards. Target the head only, using a full-choked shotgun, preferably 12 gauge, and either express No. 4 or No. 6 load. This procedure results in a "clean" bird, not a shot marring the big, meaty body.

SMALL-GAME HUNTING

Selection of shotgun loads, and light rifle calibers and loads for small game (rabbits and squirrels) also deserves attention. Cottontail rabbits can be bagged with a variety of loads, but No. 7½ or No. 6 shot in field loads are standard for modest ranges, express loads when cottontails are run with a dog and ranges are longer. Extremely short shots should be avoided whenever possible to save meat quality. Big snowshoe hares need 6's at least, when before a dog. But if you still-hunt them, which means short shots as a rule, finer shot is adequate, and the head should be the target.

Squirrels are a small problem for the shotgun hunter. Their hides are tough. And, often as not, one must shoot through leaves or twigs. Some squirrel hunters use No. 7½ or No. 6 shot sizes, but many go for No. 4, the large shot giving better penetration.

My own slant on squirrel hunting is somewhat different, and it applies also to prowl-hunting after rabbits, too. In my view, a .22 rifle is by far the best weapon for small-game hunting for both recreation and the pot. It is sporty as can be. It forces a fellow to have to meticulously learn his craft and become an expert shot. Also, when properly used, it wastes no edible meat. The .22 should be equipped with a scope. On several .22's of mine, I have mounted full-fledged big-game scopes, not the so-called .22 scopes, cheap, small-diameter models. These—one is even a 3x–9x variable—pick out the smallest shooting holes through leaves and limbs, or on rabbits through dense brush and weeds. In woodlands where light is dim, the scope is a marvelous light-gathering device.

The whole idea of using the scoped .22, as far as meat hunting is concerned, is that you again pick the most lethal bullet placement that does the least edible meat damage. The target is always the head. Granted, you have to learn to shoot. Meanwhile, it's a clean-kill or clean-miss proposition. Every squirrel or cottontail is dispatched instantly, and the meat is wholly unblemished.

There are advantages in big-timber squirrel hunting. I recall hunting in Arizona for tassel-eared squirrels—the Abert squirrel which dwells in a few areas of the Southwest, in yellow-pine country. Trees 100 feet tall towered over us, and trying with a shotgun to kill one of the big squirrels that had run up to the top of a tree was virtually impossible. A scoped .22, however, reached up and picked them off neatly.

There is always a way to get a rest when .22 hunting for

For small-game hunting, .22s mounted with big-game scopes are the best rifles for accurate, meat-saving shots. At left, Remington pump with Redfield scope; at right, Browning auto with Weaver scope. At center is Winchester pump with Weaver .22 scope.

squirrels. The animals are always peeking around a limb to see what's going on, the head or part of it usually showing. The little rifle is the perfect tool, not only from the sport hunting standpoint, but in relation to the pot as well. Once you begin hunting rabbits and squirrels this way, I can almost promise you'll never carry a shotgun on such hunts again— and every animal will be in perfect shape in the kitchen.

In some states there are even opportunities for hunting certain game birds with a .22. For an expert shot this can be a great meat saver, as well as a sporty hunt. Be certain to check regulations carefully as to the legality of the .22, however. In some states it may not be used for any game birds. In several others, it is legal for hunting such birds as the big blue grouse of the western mountains, the spruce grouse, and even for some other grouse and quail. Some western-quail species can be stalked to fairly close range, close enough for head shots with a .22, although the shooter must have a steady hold and a keen eye. The western blue grouse is often a rather naive bird, easy to approach within a few yards. Ptarmigan are also sometimes hunted in their northern ranges with a .22. A careful shooter can enjoy a unique kind of sport this way, and bring to the kitchen birds with bodies unmarked by shot.

HUNTING TURKEYS

A word needs to be added about rifles for turkeys. A few hunters use them. The .22 is not enough gun. It wounds and loses too many, and is not legal for this work in most states. Few rifle hunters after turkeys are able to get close enough to make good a head shot. Even if they could, the birds don't hold still long enough, and the target is awfully small. Many hunters, though, have learned to their sorrow about shooting turkeys through the body with standard centerfire-caliber rifle ammunition. Most "deer" loads utterly ruin a turkey.

There are ways to avoid this. A few hunters use the .22 Magnum, with hollow-point bullet. I have used it often. This bullet does some meat damage, but if you place your shot in the crop area, the back, or under a wing—not through the wing butts where big bones lie—it will drop a turkey, and the modest amount of damage is perfectly acceptable. Gun buffs

also down-load many a deer caliber. I have tried loads in my
.243 that are full-jacketed bullets with enough powder to send
them only at around 2000-to-2400-foot-per-second velocity at
the muzzle. These kill turkeys with virtually no meat damage,
unless you strike a large leg or wing bone.

Getting a proper turkey load fixed up for heavy rifles is
tricky, and a matter for hand loaders who are long experienced
and can make tests for velocity. Bullets must be hard jacketed
so they don't upset, or they'll ruin large quantities of meat.
The .222, a fine caliber for accuracy, can be down-loaded to
become a good short-range turkey rifle. Don't be misled into
thinking the jacketed regular .222 will collect a turkey without
damage. The bullet goes too fast and will often result in vast
damage. The best approach is to think of rifles for turkeys
only as a means to stretch range *modestly*, perhaps to 75 or
100 yards. Then use either the .22 Mag or work up a big-rifle
load using a full-jacketed bullet and a powder charge to keep
velocity somewhere around 2000 to 2200 feet per second.
Rifle hunting for turkeys is an intriguing undertaking, but
using ammunition that results in gross tissue damage should
always be taboo.

7

Offtrail Wild Meats

There are a number of animals, and some birds, that are legal to take, furnish good eating, but that have never been called "game." Some are classed as furbearers, others are simply pests. Quite a few of these have been used regionally, or very locally, for meat since early settlement of this country. The average outdoorsman, however, seldom if ever hunts them, and indeed in some cases wouldn't think of trying them on the table.

As everyone knows, the various meats we eat—many fruits and vegetables, too—are considered "good" simply because we were brought up eating them. And "good" is related to nations or regions: not many Yankees eat okra, but old-line southerners couldn't do without it. Mexicans eat goat as a staple meat; *cabrito*, young goat, is in fact a delicacy. A number of Anglos in southern Texas eat it regularly because of the bicultural mixture along the border. But goat meat as a market staple would be impossible to find over most of the United States.

It is not quite true, as the old saying goes, that there is no accounting for tastes. Tastes are based on what is readily available and thus long ago became traditional—blubber for Eskimos, shark fins for the Chinese, plantains as a starch staple in some tropical locations, dog meat many years ago for some Indian tribes. So it is really ridiculous to shudder at the thought of eating something someone else calls "good" just because we've never tried it or because it is not traditional in our country, state, or region.

I think offhand of two rather striking illustrations. Some years ago I was in southern Florida, and a hunter down in the 'Glades killed a cougar, or mountain lion. The big cats there ranged in fair abundance at one time, although they are endangered today. Florida in those days wasn't much like it is now. Some of the villages down in the big swamps were thoroughly isolated, truly another world. This hunter brought the big cat into the village where he lived, hung it up, and began skinning it. Before he was finished a number of his neighbors had gathered, asking if they might have a piece of the meat. Cougar had long been considered a delicacy in that area, as it was in a number of places throughout its vast domain years ago.

The second illustration is an amusing one. When we lived in northern Michigan some years ago, we had an old gamewarden friend who was renowned as a bobcat hunter. I went with him on many long, exhausting chases on snowshoes in winter as he cast his burly hounds on fresh bobcat tracks in the forest. One evening we attended an annual game dinner held by an organization of outdoorsmen in our area. The fare was always highly varied and at times a bit exotic. This one year some pranksters took all the meat off the bones of a fresh-killed bobcat and made a simply superb stew. It was served at the dinner without fanfare or identification.

Several of those who'd concocted it plugged it especially hard to my old warden friend, the cat hunter. He was a hearty sort, and with a drink or two warming him, dug into it grandly. He pronounced it the best dish served that evening. They then dropped the bomb on him. When he learned what he'd eaten, the numerous bobcats he'd brought in passed through his mind, and he went outside and was ill. His stomach and brain simply couldn't hurdle tradition regardless of how delicious bobcat stew might be.

MUSKRATS

When I was a youngster we lived in the country and I ran a trap line. My main catch was muskrats, the hides of which at that time were quite valuable. The muskrat, which lives in clean creeks and ponds, is chiefly vegetarian, feeding on various aquatic roots and leaves, from cattail tubers and stalks (which are perfectly edible and excellent fare for humans, as well) to watercress, various grasses and reeds. It also some-

times eats crayfish and fresh-water mussels. The meat is dark, and as I can enthusiastically attest, delicious.

I asked my mother, as I skinned a fresh-caught and -killed muskrat, why we didn't try it. My mother was practical about such things, and she saw no reason not to. She cut up a couple of muskrats, parboiled them gently until the meat was tender, then browned and roasted the meat in a covered earthen dish. Muskrat, we learned, has a most delicate and individual flavor.

Many a person to whom I've mentioned muskrat has been aghast. The word "rat" and the "rat tail" are usually given as reasons. The fact is, muskrats are far cleaner in habits than pigs in a pen, or chickens running free about a barnyard! Historically, coastal Louisiana was a center of muskrat abundance. That has changed some over past decades, but years ago tens of thousands of muskrats were trapped annually in the Louisiana marshes, chiefly for the hides. However, routinely the carcasses were put up about 300 to a barrel and shipped refrigerated to New York City and other northeastern cities, where the meat was used as a filler in expensive terrapin soup. Somehow it amuses me to think of the artistocratic diners most likely to be reveling in a pre-entrée bowl of gourmet terrapin soup, munching cubes of meat and murmuring over it, never knowing that a short time before it was swimming around in its coat of fur down in a Louisiana bayou. If you forget prejudice, and think of a turtle and a muskrat, neither one *looks* any more, or less, appetizing than the other.

So you see, the eating of muskrat meat is not as far-out a suggestion as many sportsmen might consider it. Up until the 1930s and for a short time after, marshes along the southern Lake Erie shore were heavily trapped for muskrats, for fur. But I vividly recall the highway between Toledo and Cleveland, then a two-lane road with the lake often in view, with numerous small roadside restaurants bearings signs that advertised muskrat lunches and dinners. The meat was heavily used. As late as World War II there was a roadhouse outside

Saginaw, Michigan, where I ate occasionally that did a capacity business serving muskrat dinners, the meat supply coming from the trapping operation on a privately owned nearby marsh.

Muskrat *hunting* is hardly feasible. But trapping for this common wide-ranging animal is possible for numerous outdoorsmen, even within the fringes of suburban areas. It is profitable, an enjoyable outdoor experience, and making use of the meat doubles both attributes. All one has to do is put aside prejudice, if any exists. There's no logical reason for it, anyway.

BEAVERS

In fact, a number of animals considered furbearers for the most part make unusual and delicious table fare. The beaver,

once trapped by millions for its fur and, indeed, responsible for much of the early exploring of this continent, was relished as meat both by Indians and frontiersmen. Today it has adapted itself to numerous areas, and causes problems with its dams and digging. Beavers are legally trapped during specified seasons in numerous states. They are large, and the meat, especially of younger animals, has a most agreeable flavor. The big, flat tail—roasted in its skin, which loosened and could be peeled off—was considered by pioneer Americans and native Indians one of the finest of wild meats.

COOKING TIPS

Perhaps I should pause here to offer a suggestion or two about cooking these offtrail and other wild meats. It has long surprised me that hunters and their wives, who so often do the kitchen honors, seem to think that because a bird or animal is termed "game" there must be some secret mandatory method of turning it into an edible dish. "How do you cook a pheasant?" is, if you stop to think about it, a rather silly question. How do you cook a chicken?

There are, to be sure, countless ways to make *exotic* game dishes, just as there are many ways to make exotic chicken or beef dishes. Condiments and varied ingredients make most of the differences. If you ponder kitchen lore sensibly, there are only a very few *basic* ways to cook *anything*. You fry it, simmer it, boil it, bake or roast it, braise it, broil it. These are the standard approaches. Even among them there are overlaps, small nuances of difference. These methods are used on the off-trail as well as the traditional meats. Since this is not a recipe book, but a book about hunting and fishing for pot and pan that takes you only up to the point of the cooking, I won't get into formal recipes. Fundamentals, however, are simple. If you think a piece of meat may be tough or a bit

strong—a cut-up beaver, for example—either marinate it or
soak it in salted water. You can also parboil (partly boil, or
tenderize) it first in tumbling salted water. Then start over,
broiling, baking, pan frying, however you wish, adding seasonings of your choice. That's really all there is to it.

When I was a small boy, nobody in our area ate "fryer"
chickens. We'd never heard of them, and probably would
have thought them pallid, a waste of grown-up meat. I've
always remembered how my mother, who cooked on a wood
stove most of her life, handled any old barnyard rooster so
tough, as one relative said, you had to keep clubbing it back
into the kettle. She turned it into the most full-flavored,
tender meat you ever tasted. She was a great hand to parboil
all sorts of meat, from the tough rooster to an old cock pheasant, from muskrat to raccoon. After it was thus tenderized,
it could be put away to cool and the next day slowly fried or
baked, or it could be prepared immediately.

There were for years (probably still are) in Michigan several
German restaurants renowned for their huge, multicourse
chicken dinners. The chickens were invariably not cut-up,
bland-tasting fryers, but adult hens. The meat had been tenderized first by the old-fashioned parboil approach, then was
flour-coated and gently fried in butter, or baked. I suggest
this simple, general approach, with your own variations, for
all sorts of game and off-trail meats, especially if you have
doubts about how to proceed or misgivings about toughness
or strong taste.

NUTRIA

Another marsh animal, in addition to the muskrat and the
beaver, should receive attention as a meat source. It is not
a native, but was introduced to this country years ago as a fur
animal. This is the South American nutria, or coypu. In appearance it might be described as a giant muskrat. Average

adults weigh 6 to 10 pounds but some may weigh double that. The nutria, long raised on fur farms in South America, was introduced in the U.S. for the same purpose. Its fur, though used, has never been as popular and valuable as the native muskrat. It soon established itself in the wild as a competitor with the muskrat, particularly in southern marshes. In Louisiana, the competition decimated muskrat populations.

In Texas, the state game and fish department tried nutria as weed eaters, hoping they'd solve weed problems in ponds, lakes, and streams. Instead, the nutria became utter nuisances, digging holes in cattle tank dams, and in some places even ruining vegetable crops. They are strictly vegetarians, living on cattails, sedges, and tough grasses along lakes and streams. They are adaptable to both fresh and salt water.

In some southern waters the nutria is considered a pest, with no laws protecting it. In others, it receives seasonal protection as a fur animal. But nowhere has it been much used as food, truly a great and unfortunate waste because the nutria is delicious. That is not hearsay. On our small Texas ranch we have a stream on which we built a couple of lakes; when we bought the place twenty years ago nutria were already there. We heard all sorts of predictions about what pests they'd be. Actually, in our rocky, canyon-cut country there was nothing they could harm. They didn't bother the one dirt dam we built; the other was concrete.

My older son, Mike, early teen-age, wanted to collect a nutria hide. I had brought my boys up not to shoot indiscriminately. There was a rule: if you shoot it, you eat it. Mike shot an adult nutria in our stream with a .22. He hung it to a limb and began skinning. As he peeled the hide off, he was at first dubious, then decided the meat really looked good. He cut up the carcass, his mother cooked it, and it was unbelievably excellent.

Anyone within the range of this introduced animal can scout out where colonies live. Many a landowner who has them welcomes having them controlled. Where it is legal, they can be hunted at night, from a small boat, with a .22. Otherwise, they can be trapped. During the fur season, the hides now bring a good price, and many pounds of quality meat can be put up.

RACCOONS

The raccoon is also a prime candidate for the pot. Raccoon has been eaten locally and regionally since the country was young. Some southerners thought they had a corner on it, but when I was a very small lad in Michigan old-fashioned country neighbors of ours introduced us to raccoon, and we ate it often. Mrs. Kyle, a widow whose grown sons were trappers and hound hunters along the Flint River, brought over a dressed raccoon ready for the oven. She suggested that my

mother roast it. The Kyles were very poor people; so were we. Nothing was wasted, including Mrs. Kyle's gift of raccoon. To this day I can remember the delicious taste of it.

With the exception of the high Rockies, raccoons range throughout the contiguous United States and southern Canada. They are abundant, common on the fringes of cities and in farm country and woodlots, and available to any outdoorsman who goes after them. Most years, the hides are valuable. In most states the raccoon is considered a furbearer. It is trapped, and also a favorite of hound men, who enjoy the excitement of night chases after it. Most states have protective laws, open season for fur trapping, and regulations about hunting. Invariably the raccoon, either trapped or when hunted with dogs, is shot with a .22, the head the target, for a clean kill and no pelt damage.

In most parts of its range, during the hunting and trapping seasons raccoons are often exceedingly fat. The fur season falls when hides are prime, in early to mid-fall and on into winter. By then the animals have fattened up to tide them through cold weather. I have seen adult raccoons taken in winter in the Great Lakes region that weighed almost 40 pounds, at least a third of it fat. The fat is not strong, and the oil from it extremely soft. However, many a winter-larded raccoon is far too fat to make a good roast; the pan would overflow.

Earlier I mentioned that my mother, from whom I learned as a young fellow much about cooking offtrail meats, often parboiled various kinds. She used this method with super-fat raccoons to remove much of the fat. She'd boil the meat briefly and pour off the water, which then had accumulated a certain amount of oil. Then she'd peel off as much fat as possible, which had been firmed, and repeat the process. After the desired amount of fat was removed, she prepared the animal for roasting. My brother and I took very seriously the business of "trying out" raccoon fat and using the resultant oil on our leather boots, to soften and help waterproof them. We also took very seriously the business of eating mother's roast raccoon!

OPOSSUMS

In the South particularly, the opossum is invariably mentioned as a sport and eating animal right along with the raccoon. The opossum, which has enlarged its range in our time, is found from Maine to Florida, to Texas, to the southern Great Lakes, and is also present along the western slope on the Pacific coast. Across the southern half of its range especially, it is often extremely abundant. It is trapped for fur, and the down-home sport of night hunting with dogs for 'possums is as traditionally southern as grits and gravy—or "possum and sweet taters." Long ago the blacks in the South were the main consumers of 'possum meat, because it was a creature easy to catch and abundant around settlements, as well as in the woods. But the acceptance of this dish by poor whites, and many not so poor, eventually became just as widespread. In some sectors it still is.

The opossum is, like the raccoon, often unduly fat. It can be treated the same way in the kitchen. Roast opossum and sweet potatoes as a combination dish did not make its way down through southern history as any joke. It is delicious. Incidentally, some pot hunters try to take 'possums alive, not a difficult endeavor when one "plays dead," and pen them up for a few days before butchering. The ordinary diet of the opossum is rather indiscriminate, and "sweetening them up," as it's called, on a table scrap diet washed down with milk enhances the flavor of the meat.

Roasted opossum, many enthusiasts of the dish say, is much like suckling pig. I know one cook who parboils 'possum with onion, sage, and chili peppers, and meanwhile boils several sweet potatoes with the skins on until they are almost tender.

After draining, the 'possum and the potatoes are put into a Dutch oven, a dollop of southern cane syrup poured over them, and the combo baked until done. The pot hunter who'd let prejudice keep him away from the result simply doesn't know what "good" means.

WOODCHUCKS

Throughout the Northeast, the Great Lakes region, and the middle South the woodchuck is a common farm animal that has over the years come to game status. In Pennsylvania, for example, the animals are carefully protected, and chuck hunters avidly pursue their sport. The western counterpart of the woodchuck is the marmot, or rock chuck, found over a wide range in the mountain states, and the hoary marmot, which ranges to the north, up through British Columbia and much of Alaska.

The woodchuck is another of those animals, often considered pest, that has served as food since Colonial times. The younger animals make the best eating. Although western rock chucks are seldom eaten, they are just as edible as eastern woodchucks. Both animals are vegetarians. I fished for trout several weeks in the Colorado high country during the summer of 1980, and camped in a mountain meadow where abundant rock chucks were in sight, or else whistling in alarm at my buddies and me from every direction. I kept thinking that there were many pounds of good meat going to waste all around us. However, in most states one needs a small-game license to shoot any animals, even pests and nongame, and in eastern states there are seasons as a rule on woodchucks.

Where members of either of the chuck tribes are available, pot hunters should not overlook them. They can be handled in the kitchen like muskrat or beaver or any of the "fur" animals. Our family has even tried a long-tailed relative of the

chucks, the southwestern rock squirrel. Although I was not especially enthused over the flavor, it was certainly not unpleasant.

There are other possibilities in the West for pot hunters who are brave enough to stray far from traditional standards. Many plains Indians thought fat prairie dogs, also vegetarians, were excellent fare. In the high country of several western states there is a good-sized, handsome rodent, the Columbian ground squirrel. Peter Barrett, executive editor of *Field & Stream* magazine, told me that each year when he and Ted Trueblood make a trout-fishing camp trip near Ted's home they collect several of these fat little animals, and Ted, a veteran camp cook, turns them into a superb meal. No accounting for tastes? Good is good, regardless of its packaging!

There is one cleaning instruction that should be observed

meticulously in relation to all of the fur animals, plus the chucks, and, for that matter, even the small-game tree squirrels. All of these animals have kernels or glands in the small of the back that should be removed. They also have similar kernels, often larger, under each foreleg, between the ribs and the forelegs. These, too, should go. There is nothing harmful about them, but if left in they are likely to create a strong, unpleasant flavor. The muskrat and the beaver have, in addition to these, twin musk glands at the rear of the abdomen. Removal of these without rupturing them is an important step in the cleaning process.

Once you begin trying various off-trail wild meats, interest in seeing how far you can extend the possibilities grows. Adding to your off-trail meat list becomes a hobby in itself, as well as an addition to the larder. I recall that when we first moved to Texas, we occasionally heard someone mention eating armadillo. They are plentiful in our area, and barbecued armadillo is fairly common. So are armadillo tamales. Armadillo has some of the qualities and flavor of pork. Soaking the meat overnight in lightly salted water helps dispel a slightly earthy taste. When chili "cookoff" contests were becoming popular and getting some national publicity armadillo chili was one of the highly touted varieties that won a few prizes.

In parts of Texas armadillos for years—ever since the "big depression"—have been called "Hoover pigs." Many a native back in those days blamed the sorry state of the economy on Hoover, and claimed country families were reduced to eating armadillo because of the depression. The armadillo has now spread its range from its original domain of south-central Texas and portions of Mexico clear across the South into Florida. In general, it is unprotected, fairly common, easily stalked, and collected with a .22 rifle.

Some small birds in the pest class also make excellent eating for pot hunters not averse to tidbits. When I was young, Italian families used to come out into the Michigan countryside from Detroit, equipped with fine-mesh large nets which they threw over haystacks at night and in which they collected hundreds of English sparrows. The tradition in Europe years ago was that ordinary song birds of many kinds were useful as food. The Italians patiently cleaned the sparrows and used them in various dishes.

The "Four and twenty blackbirds . . . " nursery rhyme was not made up without solid founding in early traditions. Blackbirds were commonly used in "pies." Years ago I hunted doves and quail in southern Georgia several falls with an old gentleman who had had poverty-status beginnings and who said he had practically been brought up on blackbirds. Again, the tradition had been brought to America from the Old World. It is curious that certain birds have so well adapted to present-day civilization that they are more numerous than ever. The handsome redwing blackbird has recently been proclaimed the most abundant bird on this continent. Several of its relatives—other blackbirds, grackles, starlings—are not far behind. There are millions of them, and they have become utter nuisances in many areas. In portions of the South, redwings are called rice birds, are exceedingly destructive, and are destroyed (legally) whenever possible.

The fact is, blackbirds, especially those that have been feeding on grain, are authentic delicacies. One fall in south Texas the late Paul Young and I fed quail in the vicinity of his hunting camphouse, just to have many of them around to observe. Scores of redwings began gathering and stealing our quail food before the quail could get it. We decided to eliminate as many as possible.

After a few shotgun barrages we had gathered several dozen. We decided to see what sort of fare they'd be and took the breasts out, washed, and dried them. Then the idea of a prank hit us. Some northern hunters, visitors to Texas, were coming down, so we decided to broil the tiny breasts *en brochette*, daubed with bacon drippings, and tell the newcomers we were serving breasts of jacksnipe. Having never hunted snipe, they'd never know that snipe breasts should be larger. If the birds didn't taste very good, they'd be stuck to laud them anyway, and we'd avoid being the testers. Trouble was, our guests, tasting very gingerly at first, soon fell on the birds like gluttons. Before Young and I got a chance, the blackbirds, which were superb, were almost gone.

The legality of collecting pest birds must be checked beforehand, obviously, but it offers some possibilites for gourmet eating that have virtually remained untried. I've eaten feral (barn) pigeons and found them excellent. A few hardy pothunter souls even now and then cook up a batch of grain-fed crows. The meat is dark and dry, but not bad. Coastal fish crows, of course, aren't edible.

Even a few try-anything types draw the line when it comes to rattlesnake, but in the Southwest it is rather common at game dinners and at various festivals. Rattlesnake can even be bought, canned, in some stores. Some of the big rattlesnake roundups in the Southwest serve hundreds of pounds of fried rattlesnake during their "doin's." Last year I attended one of the most famous of these out of curiosity. It was in Sweetwater, Texas, and what an eye-opener. I saw car licenses from New York and California, hundreds of people gathered on the grounds, and quite a few visitors from foreign countries. Concessions sold all sorts of rattlesnake-rattle jewelry and even fancy plastic toilet seats with whole baby rattlers embedded. Hundreds of snakes were in evidence. Scores of them, after being milked of venom, were butchered and the meat sold fresh or fried by one of the concessions. It's actually very tasty.

Prospective snake hunters should be cautioned, however, that within recent years numerous states have enacted laws pertaining to the taking of reptiles. There are also federal laws involved concerning endangered reptile species. Check first. Also, rattlesnake hunting for the common, abundant varieties, traditionally done with a snake hook and bag, is a dangerous undertaking unless you have ample know-how.

JACKRABBITS

One other group of animals deserves attention: the wild hares known as jackrabbits. Over most of the vast area west of the Mississippi River jackrabbits are abundant. The two chief varieties are the blacktailed jack of the southern two-thirds of the range, and the white tailed jack of roughly the northern third. For some curious reason, these big hares that

during peak population cycles are a scourge upon grazing lands have never been favored as good for eating. Literally millions of pounds of jackrabbits have gone to waste over the years, when great drives were made to control the animals, or by pest shooters who have tried to keep them under control.

Yet, curiously, cookbooks and recipes from frontier times on the plains and elsewhere in the West show that jacks were definitely not shunned. They had a surprising amount of attention, in fact, with many detailed recipes. True, hares have a stronger flavor than rabbits. Old jacks are inclined to be tough. Nonetheless, jackrabbit, especially the younger animals taken in winter, are surprisingly good. In Mexico they are as prized as the cottontail. The outsize white tailed jack of the north, which turns white or partially so in winter, furnishes fur of some value, and is perhaps a bit tastier than the blacktail.

Jack meat needs to be soaked in salted water, then marinated or parboiled before the final cooking. Most of the old recipes I've run onto call for baking, or making a stout stew with chili peppers, braising, or barbecueing. A few even suggest grinding the meat for patties. Hunting jacks for the pot, using a .22 rifle or pistol, calls for some expert stalks in order to get close enough, and is a sporty proposition. It is hardly proper not to mine this source of wild meat when some experimenting in the kitchen can make it as common and edible a dish as cottontail.

8

Hunting You Didn't Know Was There

In addition to the offtrail pot-hunting possibilities discussed in the previous chapter, there are a surprising number of opportunities to gather standard game species that a major percentage of hunters aren't aware of. Hunters, like everyone else, are inclined to form habits from which they seldom deviate. The routine may be, let's say, pheasant hunting in October, deer in November, rabbits in midwinter, with few changes over many years.

Some lesser known game varieties may be readily available and virtually unknown, in terrain you've hunted for years, and they could just as well be added to the pot. Or, there may be one or two rather obscure species in your territory, or in an area to which you travel—game with open season that is bypassed unwittingly for lack of knowledge or careful perusal of the game laws. In addition, some of the top game species may range much more widely than you realize, be present in at least moderate numbers yet hardly touched, simply because of lack of awareness by the average hunter of their presence over a certain range.

Early in my hunting career I learned about these "unknowns," and formed a habit, which has lasted all my life, of making certain I knew what was available with open season both in my home bailiwick and in areas where I made distant hunting trips. Many new and enjoyable experiences and many with well-known species but in out-of-the-way places have come to me because of this habit. We have eaten and put up in our freezer each season numerous game varieties we'd never have known about otherwise.

I can recall as plainly as yesterday where and when this habit began. I was nineteen and had a beagle hound that was a real rabbit-running whizz. We had abundant rabbits, also pheasants, in the Thumb area of Michigan where I lived. The dog quickly sensed that pheasants were game, too, and she'd put them up but never chased one if we missed. It was easy to tell when she was on a pheasant trail. She didn't bark, as when she hit a cottontail track, and she moved very slowly, sniffing and meandering with intense eagerness until she flushed the bird.

A friend and I, hunting one blustery fall morning, had picked off a couple of rabbits after exciting chases, and one rooster pheasant. Presently in an expanse of moist swale the dog began acting "birdy" again. The area had ground cover of scattered marsh grass in clumps with damp spots of meadow in between. There were intermittent bunches of low willows and a few scrub poplars.

"Get ready," my companion said tensely. "We're going to get us another pheasant."

At that instant a bird burst from under the dog's nose. It was small, mottled gray and brown, with long legs and a long bill. *Screek, screek, screek,* it called, as if cussing our presence. It flew low to the grass at first, in an amazing corkscrew pattern, appearing to tilt first on one wing and then on the other. By the time we recovered our senses it shot higher into the air. Even though it was small there was a dramatic game-bird quality about it.

"Shoot!" I yelled, and we both shot. The bird flew right on, swiftly, now rising high in perfectly level flight, its scimitar wings really scooping the air. We had just missed our first jacksnipe. We quickly realized what it was, from pictures we'd seen, but didn't have any idea jacksnipe were in our country. We also were now worried about whether there was an open season.

There was—and that five acres or so of swale was teeming with birds—a flight that, we deduced from a quick check at home in a bird book, had tumbled in during migration. That afternoon we quit the rabbits, forgot the pheasants, and dedicated ourselves to missing snipe. We finally collected half a dozen, which turned out to be strictly gourmet fare. I had instantly become a dedicated snipe hunter, and began to wonder what else I might be overlooking.

Since that time I've shot snipe from upper New York state to Minnesota, Louisiana, Texas, and even southern Arizona. They are marvelous sport, and sinfully good eating. Jacksnipe are not scarce. At least forty states usually have open season with, as a rule, an eight-bird daily bag limit. In at least half of the open-season states, the birds during migration or on their wintering grounds are supremely abundant—along creeks, around ponds, on wet meadows, moist southern or midwest prairies, and marsh edges. Louisiana, where the heaviest winter concentration gathers, is estimated at times to hold as many as five million.

Almost any U.S. hunter, therefore, could add jacksnipe to his bag each fall. Because the birds are water and wetland oriented, they can be dovetailed perfectly with waterfowl shooting. Here is a wonderful bonus for the pot, as well as a unique hunting experience. Yet the joys of jacksnipe hunting and eating are known only to a few specialists. Thousands of hunters do not even know what a jacksnipe is.

Just as with the waterfowl-jacksnipe combo, most of these "unknowns" can be worked in as extras on hunts for the more popular or better known species. They add new zip to any hunt and often become the high point. The extra meat is like being handed a valuable gift. And, in most instances, because some of these species are lightly hunted the hunting terrain is uncrowded.

An example that illustrates all those points crosses my mind. I was hunting pheasants in South Dakota some years ago under rather crowded conditions. Nonetheless, we bagged limits almost too quickly every day, until we had a possession limit. I knew that briefly west across the Missouri River, a short drive from our location, were prairie grouse, mainly sharp-tails, and that year the season was open at the same time as pheasants.

Most bird hunters have never seen, or bagged, a sharptail grouse. Several states and provinces have seasons each fall, and good shooting. These compact birds weigh as much as 2½ pounds and are delicious eating. They are strong-flying, exceedingly dramatic targets before the gun. I talked our party into extending the trip to take in a sharptail hunt. Hunting was uncrowded, the experience exciting, and we packed home a number of these fine bonus birds along with our pheasants.

Although most of these lesser known pot specialties are birds, some small-game animals are also involved, and in a couple of instances big game, as well. As an example of the latter, a most intriguing hunt with an exotic variety of venison has occurred some seasons for a limited number of people on Chincoteague National Wildlife Refuge in Virginia. It is the sort of hunt you have to be aware of well in advance if you hope to apply for a chance as a participant the years it is held.

SIKA DEER

Somewhat more than half a century ago a few sika were released on Assateague Island. The sika is a dark-colored deer with indistinct lighter spots, native to Japan and Malaysia. In due time, the animals became so abundant on what is now Chincoteague Refuge that a hunt to control their numbers was begun. Generally, this has been by permit during the regular archery season, and also during a trophy primitive-weapons hunt, by drawing, with details available from the refuge manager.

These same handsome, exotic deer are also available in modest numbers in Dorchester County, Maryland. Originally released on an island in the Chesapeake Bay years back, they became so numerous that some apparently swam to another island and eventually to the mainland. They have been legal at times during the regular deer season, and for an interested hunter quite a trophy, as well as excellent and unusual meat. I have taken several sika in Texas, where numerous ranches have them running wild. They are handsome, shy, as difficult as whitetails to bag, quite a conversation piece, and delicious venison.

In Kentucky hunters have occasionally had chances during deer season at another exotic big-game animal, the fallow deer. There is a herd established in the Land Between the Lakes region. This is a broad swath southeast from Paducah between Lake Barkley and Lake Kentucky. Although it also extends into Tennessee, practically all the fallow deer are in the Kentucky portion. These deer, originally native to southern Europe and Asia Minor, have palmated antlers, and color varies among them. Most are tan with light spots. They're striking trophies and also quality venison. In the past, regulations have lumped fallows and whitetails together, but that could change.

Certainly such unusual big game offers a bounteous supply of both thrills and meat, but obscure small-game opportunities should also be ferreted out. As I've suggested, they can be worked in with other hunts and can add their bit to both sport and pot. Earlier, I told of a two-state mule-deer hunt I made one fall to Utah and Arizona to take advantage of a chance to collect two deer with very little extra travel, thus making the long trip from my home much more worthwhile in resultant venison. What I did not mention earlier was that I had a couple of days to fill between the two hunts, and I stumbled upon a plan by which I could fill the time to excellent advantage.

ABERT SQUIRRELS

I stopped to visit an old friend in Williams, Arizona, Levi Packard, who worked for the state game department. He mentioned that the squirrel season was open. That sounded interesting, and it suddenly came to me that the squirrels he was talking about must be Abert, or tassel-eared squirrels. Most squirrel hunters are unaware that these animals exist, and only a few have ever hunted them.

The Abert squirrel ranges only over portions of Arizona, New Mexico, Colorado, and Utah. It is a large, handsome animal with tufted ears, stunning rufous and gray colors along its back, and a huge partially frosted tail. It's a rather specialized animal, adapted to and locked in by feeding habits to the yellow-pine forests. The area around Williams, Arizona, is perfect habitat for it, and the animals were abundant that year. (A relative, the Kaibab squirrel, differing a bit in color patterns, is present only on the Kaibab plateau, on the north side of the canyon. It is fully protected.)

With .22s we prowled the forests of huge pines. Not another hunter was in sight. A squirrel, startled while feeding on the ground, would streak through the forest, bound onto a great pine trunk, and race clear to the top in seconds. Talk about sporty hunting! This hunt was a perfect and most interesting way to wait out the beginning of the second deer hunt. The bonus for the pot also was very much worthwhile. Daily limit was five, with two days possession. These squirrels, full grown, weigh on the average 2 pounds each, a substantial total in extra meat. I took home the legal limit with my venison. They were the most delicious squirrels we've ever eaten.

RABBITS

Another small-game experience I stumbled into and dovetailed with a standard hunt also illustrates how provocative and important as bonuses the unknowns can be. This one occurred in the Yazoo Delta country in Mississippi. I had been invited duck hunting in flooded pinoak flats. We used boats. The duck hunting turned out to be so fast that morning that we were through in a rush. Here and there in the flooded timber there were shallow places with tussocks of grass or small mounds of earth thrusting above water. A good many of these had a big swamp rabbit hunched atop it, taking the morning sunshine after a crisp night. We eagerly went after them.

These rabbits are much larger than cottontails. Some weigh as much as 5 or 6 pounds. They think nothing of swimming. Although they are hunted by locals, most U.S. hunters don't even know they exist. They're found in proper lowland habitat from the Carolinas south, across the Deep South, and on into the Ozark bottoms and bottom lands in Oklahoma. It was a rather comic and intriguing experience to hunt rabbits from a skiff. We'd take turns paddling and popping rabbits, even as they fled by swimming. Ordinarily, of course, swamp rabbits are hunted with dogs, or walked up in lowland tangles and cane brakes. In this instance, they filled out a too-good duck shoot and sent me home with a dozen or more pounds of excellent bonus meat to boot.

There is another type of rabbit hunting, little known to American hunters, just waiting in the West to be mined by smart pot hunters. This is for the tiny pygmy rabbits of the dry sagebrush and grass in portions of Oregon, California, Nevada, and Idaho. These diminutive animals get virtually no attention, yet are abundant and exceedingly sporty.

COOTS

Another virtually wasted opportunity concerns an abundant, well-known bird found in waterfowl habitats all over the nation. It's a bird known to every duck hunter, yet one almost entirely passed up because it has somehow always received derogatory publicity: the common coot. Granted, coots are not very wary, and sometimes it's difficult to get them to fly. They are vastly underharvested because the more discriminating waterfowlers have long scorned them and also tacked a poor table reputation on them. With the limit often as high as fifteen a day and thirty in possession, gunners could have a lot of sport and a tremendous amount of good food that is seldom sampled. Occasionally on certain waters there are special coot shoots with even higher limits to try to control overpopulations.

Somehow the idea spread years ago that coots are not fit to eat. Yet in Louisiana's Cajan country *Poule D'Eau* ("chicken of the water") stew is a famed dish. So, I can attest, is coot gumbo.

Because so many cooks may approach coots with trepidation, I'll outline briefly how we've prepared them: Simmer the breasts and legs until tender, with celery and a pinch of salt. Then drain, flour, fry them brown, and set them aside while you sautée chopped onion and green pepper in the drippings. To these, add some of the water in which the meat was boiled, plus tomatoes, okra, and as much red pepper as you dare. Then put the meat in again and simmer for an hour; finally thicken with flour and serve over boiled rice. I pass along this simple recipe because so much hearty, delicious eating and scads of days of good shooting are passed up because the coot usually is.

GALLINULES AND RAILS

Relatives of the coot—gallinules and rails—get the same scanty treatment. Freshwater marshes, lowlands, and canals of Florida are the hot spots for several varieties of gallinules— common, Florida, and purple. Granted, these birds, quite similar to the coot, are not especially sporty shooting. Nonetheless, they are interesting, plentiful, fine eating, and almost entirely overlooked. There are open seasons in other Gulf and south-Atlantic states, and a few elsewhere, but the birds may be scattered.

Rails of several varieties always have high limits, and low hunter interest. These are the big king rail of the rice country and other freshwater marshes chiefly across the southern United States, the middle-size clapper rail of tidal marshes, and the Virginia and sora rails, smaller and found in brackish and freshwater marshes. They are superb table fare, and at least thirty states offer open seasons. Unfortunately, few hunters even know the birds.

Rail hunting is rather specialized. These narrow-breasted birds run through marsh grass and reeds and are tough to flush. On high tides along the east coast that push them out of hiding, they're flushed and shot from a skiff, one man poling, the other shooting. Along the Gulf where tides are lower, you just have to slog after them and try to get them airborne. Dogs sometimes help.

Curiously, the diminutive but delicious sora rail, which ranges over much of the interior United States, gets almost no hunting. One time in Michigan a friend and I chased the little devils in a marsh, splashing and plodding as fast as we could. They'd zip like tiny swamp rats through the vegetation.

But we managed to flush a few and put them in the bag. It was certainly a different sort of hunt, and awesome exercise, but the unique hunting and eating experiences were well worth the exhaustion.

In a few places in the rice-growing southern states the large (18-inch-tall) king rail is successfully hunted by shooters who follow a rice combine as a field is cut. The birds keep running into the diminishing, still-standing rice. During the last few passes of the machine, they keep popping up in front of the walking gunners. This has long been a successful technique used in the east-Texas rice-growing region. You have to admit that's a different kind of hunt, indeed.

Any fall, in any state, there's a chance that intriguing experiemental hunts for introduced birds may be set. Numerous states have long experimented with exotics such as red jungle fowl, tinamou, bamboo partridge, francolin, and particularly with several unusual pheasants. Among these have been the big Reeves pheasant and the green pheasant, both of which at one period were legal game in portions of Washington, and the green in Idaho. I attended the first hunt in the nation for the handsome and exceedingly wild Afghan white-winged pheasant, in New Mexico. We hunted with a mountain backdrop and on the edges of cactus- and catclaw-covered foothills—a unique pheasant experience indeed. It's not possible to predict when and where such unusual hunts may be held. Best bet is to check with your local game officer or a regional office.

WOODCOCK

Although many of the species that furnish "hidden" hunting are not well known, some very well publicized and popular game birds range in states where they are hardly known at all. A striking example is the woodcock. It is renowned and revered in New England and much of the northeastern United

States, in Pennsylvania, and the Great Lakes states. It is also little-known legal game, yet in some places amply abundant, in at least eighteen other states, from the Carolinas and the Central States, to the Deep South and Texas. But tell the average hunter from those areas that he could be putting the delectable woodcock on his table and he'd likely laugh. There's even fair woodcock hunting in places like the wild-plum thickets of eastern Oklahoma, the Arkansas river bottoms, and the moist woodlands of Mississippi. All this hunting lacks is hunters.

Further, the very best woodcock shooting on the continent is not where most hunters have long believed, in New England and northern Michigan, but in Louisiana. It is estimated that as much as 80 percent of the total continental flock spends the winter there! To be sure, local Louisiana hunters do partake of this sport, but the potential isn't even touched. I made my first hunt there recently, near Baton Rouge and Henderson, and was astonished at the abundance of birds.

BAND-TAILED PIGEONS, SANDHILL CRANES

Two marvelous and quite different game birds that need to catch the interest and attention of more hunters are the band-tailed pigeon and the sandhill crane. Band-tailed pigeons, as large as barn pigeons, inhabitants of the mountain passes and slopes of the West Coast and portions of the Rockies, furnish one of shotgunning's greatest thrills, and true gourmet eating. In the Pacific coastal states a fair number of hunters follow the sport, but in Arizona, New Mexico, Colorado, and Utah, where there have been open seasons lately, only a handful of shooters pay any attention. I've hunted bandtails in both Oregon and Arizona, and would rate them in a "super" category for both sport and the pot. Five-bird-per-day-or-more limits are not unusual.

The sandhill crane is a classic among underutilized game species. For more than a decade portions of the Dakotas, Montana, Wyoming, Colorado, western Oklahoma, much of Texas, and eastern New Mexico have had open seasons. I've seen these great birds, adults measuring 4 feet from toes to bill tip, and with a 6-foot wingspread, rise at dawn from roosting lakes (they roost standing in shallow water) literally by thousands. They then fan out over the grain fields to feed. Sportsmen often confuse cranes, which fly with neck and legs outstretched and are entirely grain feeders, with the various herons, which fly with neck crooked and live on fish and other aquatic food. Sandhill cranes are wary as geese, weigh 7 to 10 pounds average, and are delicious table birds. Often they can be combined in a hunt for geese and ducks.

I recall lying on a bluff high above Coyote Lake in western Texas, listening in predawn chill to the guttural chatter of several thousand cranes down below, as they prepared to make the morning flight. Presently I heard the rush of wings, the splashing. Groups lifted and circled the water to form up. Some flew away from my stand and some rose and climbed, spiralling, to clear the bluff. There was snow on the ground. My hands were numb from gripping my gun. My heart hammered. Then they were there, huge dark silhouettes right above me. Their great wings seemed to move in slow motion— but how deceptive. I swung, missed with my first shot, and then was overwhelmed with excitement as the following two shots caused two birds to fold and plummet.

Inconceivable as it seems, game managers have a hard time getting resident hunters interested in crane shooting. They hunt ducks and geese in the same areas and let the cranes "go to waste." Hunters outside the open states seldom even know this hunting exists. With limits usually three a day, six in possession, and oven-ready cranes averaging 5 to 6 pounds, hunters pass up a whopping value in both eating and recreation.

GROUSE AND QUAIL

These provide the most candidates for the hunting you may not know exists. All of these are not obscure species either. For instance, the famed ruffed grouse is pictured by most hunters as a bird of the forests of New England and the Great Lakes region. It certainly is abundant there. However, a little scouting around will also show you good ruffed-grouse shooting in locations as diverse as the Carolinas, Georgia, Ohio, North Dakota, the Rockies, and the Northwest.

Although the once awesomely abundant prairie chicken is, by comparison, now only a remnant, happily it is still huntable. A hunter who desires a nostalgic taste of yesterday might plan a pilgrimage during the brief seasons to one of the several states where there is usually an open season—South Dakota, Nebraska, Kansas, Oklahoma, Texas, New Mexico. Or, for a bird hunt like none other on the continent, go for the big sage grouse of the sagebrush expanses in Nevada, Colorado, Wyoming, Idaho, and Montana. There are occasional brief seasons for it in several other states, as well.

Sometimes the old cocks among these birds grow to be unbelievably big. In Wyoming one fall I glassed an alfalfa patch on a ranch where I was hunting and discovered a group of heads sticking up. The birds had flown in from the surrounding sage to feed in the green, fenced field. I eased over the fence. Without a dog, I simply stalked the birds. They were alerted and still kept their necks stretched. I presume they felt partially concealed in the clover.

With my attention on the flock, I stumbled slam into a single. It was an old cock. It flushed ponderously and with a great racket. The medium-size birds—up to 3 pounds—are the best eating, but I was so startled I whammed off a shot and connected with a jolt. The huge bird tumbled. It was the biggest grouse I've ever seen—an incredible 6 pounds.

Then there are the big blue grouse of the Rocky Mountain

and Pacific Coast ranges, birds of the forested high country that weigh 2 to 3 pounds or more, and the smaller spruce, or Franklin's, grouse, presently legal as a rule in Montana, Idaho, and Washington. I've had experience with both these birds, and admittedly they are naïve. It comes to eating them, though, their naïveté never bothers me. Besides, a big blue that suddenly goes hurtling down a mountain can present a most exciting and tricky proposition, and both birds, in the remote forest sanctuaries, offer a wilderness-hunt atmosphere and experience totally unique. When open season falls properly, sometimes big-game hunters can collect bonus blue grouse for the pot.

Another grouse that relatively few American hunters know about is the whitetail ptarmigan, legal quarry in Colorado. It is also found, along with relatives, in Canada and Alaska. It receives little pressure.

Then there are two imported partridges. The Hun, or Hungarian partridge, with fair populations in such places as New York, Wisconsin, Minnesota, and several of the central states, as well as in portions of the Rocky Mountain states and in the Northwest. In some of these places Huns are hardly hunted at all. The chukar partridge is the other. Most hunters residing east of the Rockies have never seen or hunted this grand and delectable bird. At least ten states now offer hunting.

Several species of western quail—the blue or scaled quail, the desert Gambel, the Mearns, the valley quail, and the big mountain quail—are locally hunted, but most hunters over more than half the United States know nothing of them. Often they are astonishingly abundant, with high daily limits and long seasons. For visitors as well as locals they make great bonus pot hunts, as well as heady recreation, and can be dovetailed, for example, as important extras by nonresidents with big-game trips to their bailiwicks in the West. Most of these species are larger than bobwhites, and each has its distinctive table qualities. For example, the flesh of the handsome Mearns, possibly because of its habit of incessantly digging and feeding on tubers of sedges, has a pearly, translucent hue and a most delicate and different flavor.

9

Where to Find the "Unknowns"

The following charts should help you find hunting you perhaps didn't know was available. They cover game birds and small game mentioned in the previous chapter, pinpointing portions of ranges of some well-known species, over which most hunters may not be aware of them. They also list species which receive only modest attention—in certain areas virtually none—and, in addition, species well known locally perhaps but hardly heard of outside their rather restricted ranges.

Hunters should be cautioned that the listing of a species for a given state does not necessarily indicate an open season. Populations of these often cyclic varieties may change drastically over a period of a few years, or even year to year. Habitat destruction also may influence or change "best areas" in just a few seasons. For example, widespread spraying of sagebrush in the West over past years and currently to kill it and allow grasses to replace it on cattle ranges has been totally destroying vast expanses of prime sage-grouse habitat and eliminating the birds from it. When planning a trip, and before hunting any of the species, check with the game department in question regarding open season, current population status, and any shift in prime range.

Jacksnipe

Snipe are migratory and therefore present in the cold states only up to and during migration. Flights may pour in, then move on in a few days. Seasons are federally controlled. Some states listed may not be allowed seasons during a given year.

State	Population	Best Areas
Maine	Fair	Duck-marsh fringes, bogs
New Hampshire	Fair	Duck-marsh fringes, bogs, beaver ponds, creeks
Vermont	Fair	Lowlands; Champlain Valley
Mass.	Some	Waterfowl-area fringes
Rhode Island	Some	Seapowet Marsh Preserve; wet fields
Conn.	Some	Marsh fringes
New York	Fair	Lakes Erie and Ontario marsh edges
New Jersey	Fair	Freshwater marshes
Delaware	Fair	Prime Hook and Bombay Hook refuges
Maryland	Good	Waterfowl-area fringes
Virginia	Fair	Waterfowl-area fringes
N. Carolina	Excellent	Currituck County marshes; coastal rivers
S. Carolina	Some	Lowland-marsh fringes
Georgia	Some	Most waterfowl areas
Pennsylvania	Some	Creeks, beaver ponds, moist meadows
W. Virginia	Some	Canaan Valley when wet
Kentucky	Very few	
Tennessee	Ditto above	

Michigan	Good	Marsh edges, creeks
Wisconsin	Good	Marshes, bogs, ponds, creeks, wet meadows
Minnesota	Excellent	Scores of wet places, potholes, etc.
Ohio	Fair	Great Lakes marshes; Little Portage, WA
Indiana	Fair	Any wet or moist open area
Illinois	Good	Bottoms, creeks, edges of wet fields
Iowa	Good	Marshes, river bottoms, creeks
Missouri	Modest	Wet pastures, marshes
Arkansas	Good	Lowlands; along Mississippi River
No. Dakota	Excellent	All wetlands
So. Dakota	Excellent	All wetlands
Nebraska	Excellent	Rainwater Basin, all other wetlands
Oklahoma	Some	Around lakes
Florida	Excellent	All suitable habitats
Alabama	Some	Rivers, marshes
Mississippi	Good	All lowlands
Louisiana	Best in U.S.	Marshes, wet prairies, all lowlands
Texas	Good	Eastern rice country; southern ranch tanks
New Mexico	Some	Waterfowl-area fringes
California	Good	Mud flats, marshes; Gray Lodge and Grizzly Island WMAs
Oregon	Good	Most wetlands and waterfowl grounds
Washington	Good	Northwest, South Puget Sound regions, salt marshes, wet fields

Rails

Seasons on rails and gallinules are federally controlled. Certain states may or may not be allowed seasons in any given year.

State	Population	Best Areas
Maine	Some	Duck marshes, bogs
New Hampshire	Low	Marshes
Vermont	Some	Marshes
Mass.	Some	Salt marshes
Rhode Island	Few	Tidal marshes
Conn.	Fair	Tidal marshes
New York	Fair	Hempstead, Oyster Bay
New Jersey	Good	Tuckertown to Cape May Point and up Delaware River
Delaware	Good	Tidal marshes, Woodland Beach WA
Maryland	Good	Tidewater areas
Mississippi	Some	Coastal
Louisiana	Excellent	Freshwater marshes and rice country, king rail; tidal marshes, clapper; brackish and freshwater marshes, sora and Virginia rails
Texas	Fair	Rice country of southeast
New Mexico	Few	Waterfowl areas
Virginia	Excellent	Mockhorn Island WA best public area
No. Carolina	Excellent	Currituck Sound; marine marshes
So. Carolina	Excellent	Tidal marshes and islands

Georgia	Excellent	Tidal marshes and islands
Pennsylvania	Low	Marshes
W. Virginia	Low	Marshes
Kentucky	Few	Marshy lake edges
Tennessee	Few	Marshy lake edges
Michigan	Fair	Marshes (sora rail— very difficult to flush; this applies to most inland states)
Wisconsin	Fair	Marshes
Minnesota	Fair	Marshes
Ohio,	Fair	
Indiana,	Fair	
Illinois	Fair	
Missouri	Fair	Fountain Grove and Schell-Osage WAs
Arkansas	Good	Rice lands, fish-farm areas
N. Dakota;) S. Dakota;) Nebraska;) Oklahoma)	Few	Pond and marsh edges
Florida	Excellent	Tidal marshes in Nassau, Duval, and St. Johns counties, and on Gulf in Bay, Franklin, and Gulf counties
Alabama	Fair	Coastal lowlands and rivers

Gallinules

Florida	Good	All freshwater marshes, lowlands, canals.
Other Gulf and south-Atlantic states	Fair	

Woodcock

The woodcock is well known and popular in New England, Pennsylvania, the Great Lakes region, and a few states of the northeast U.S. States listed here are those where woodcock are available but receive little attention. In all northern and middle-south localities they are erratically present during migration only. Seasons are federally controlled; check to make sure of open season.

State	Population	Best Areas
Maryland	Good	Eastern shore; north-south valleys in west
Virginia	Fair	Any damp areas with overhead cover
No. Carolina	Some	Piedmont and western damp valleys
So. Carolina	A few	Scattered flights in any suitable cover
Georgia	Some	Northeast; coastal plain; spring branch courses
W. Virginia	Good	Northern panhandle; Canaan Valley; Ohio River bottom
Ohio	Fair	Lake Erie shore east of Toledo; Pymatuning S.P. area
Indiana	Fair	Suitable habitat in northern counties; stream courses
Illinois	Some	Moist coverts in south
Missouri	A few	Stream courses
Arkansas	Quite good	Southwest; Miss. River bottoms; fringes of waterfowl areas
Kansas	A few	Along eastern stream courses

Oklahoma	Some	Northeast and east; stream courses; wild plum thickets
Florida	Some	Fields and thickets bordering northern woodlands
Alabama	Some	Most in western portion, fringes of waterfowl areas, stream bottoms
Mississippi	Substantial	Any moist woodland; southwestern counties; lower bottoms of Pearl and Pascagoula rivers
Louisiana	Best in nation	Probably winters 80% of total continental flocks Northeastern parishes (counties); Florida parishes; Atchafalaya River bottom
Texas	Fair	Along Louisiana border

Grouse

Listing of a state does not necessarily indicate annual open season on any of the grouse species. Obviously, regulations change with bird populations. Check legality before hunting. The important ruffed-grouse states of New England and the Great Lakes region are well known. Those listed below are others not so well known, where fair to good populations occur.

	Ruffed Grouse	
State	*Population*	*Best Areas*
Maryland	Modest	Western counties
Virginia	Good	National forests

No. Carolina	Excellent	Western border counties
So. Carolina	Modest	Oconee, Pickens, and Greenville counties
Georgia	Good	Counties along and just below northern border
W. Virginia	Good	Southeastern counties
Kentucky	Good	Eastern quarter of state
Tennessee	Fair	Along eastern border
Ohio	Good	Northeastern counties
Indiana	Some	Hoosier National Forest
Iowa	Some	Allamakee County
No. Dakota	Some	Turtle Mts., Pembina Hills
Utah	Some	Cache, Wasatch, and Ashley national forests
Wyoming	Some	Lincoln and Teton counties
Idaho	Some	Most forest lands
Montana	Some	Western forests, along stream courses
Oregon	Fair	Willow and alder thickets, burns, logged areas in most forest areas; along stream courses
Washington	Fair	Willow and alder thickets, burns logged areas in most forest areas; along stream courses

Prairie Chicken

So. Dakota	Fair	South-central counties west of Missouri River

Nebraska	Fair	Cherry, Rock, Holt, Garfield, and Thomas counties
Kansas	Good	Greenwood and surrounding counties, southwest counties
Oklahoma	Good	Osage and nearby counties; counties along Texas border in west
Texas	Fair	Northeastern Panhandle counties
New Mexico	Fair	Roosevelt and nearby counties

Sharptail Grouse

Michigan	Some	Seney area, Upper Peninsula
Wisconsin	Some	Parts of northwest
Minnesota	Fair	Northwestern counties
No. Dakota	Excellent	Western half of state
So. Dakota	Good	Eastern two-thirds of the region west of the Missouri River
Nebraska	Fair	Sand Hills area
Colorado	Low	Northwest: Moffat, Routt counties
Wyoming	Low	Sheridan, Johnson counties
Montana	Excellent	Judith Basin foothills; southern dry-farm areas; Missouri River breaks

Sage Grouse

No. Dakota	Low	Extreme southwestern area

So. Dakota	Low	Harding County and nearby
Nevada	Fair	Humboldt, Elko, northern Washoe counties
Colorado	Fair	Sagebrush plains of north and west
Wyoming	Good	Sweetwater, Carbon counties; also Fremont, Sublette, Lincoln, Natrona, Albany, Park
Idaho	Good	Owyhee, Washington, Camas, Gooding, Jefferson, Fremont counties
Montana	Good	Liberty, Choteau, Fergus, Wheatland, Sweetgrass, Carbon counties

Blue Grouse

New Mexico	Fair	Mogollon, San Mateo, Sangre de Cristo, Jemez, San Juan Mts.
Arizona	Low	Springerville-Alpine area in east
Utah	Modest	Northern Wasatch range
Nevada	Modest	Most high conifer-aspen habitats
Colorado	Good	All big-timber regions above 6500 feet
Wyoming	Fair	Lincoln, Teton counties, and in all Nat. Forests

Idaho	Good	High country of Panhandle counties, and in all high forests
Montana	Good	Western high-country forests
California	Good	National forests of northwest and north-central areas
Oregon	Good	Blue and Wallowa mts., coast ranges, western Cascade slope
Washington	Good	Coast ranges, Cascades, Blue Mts.

Spruce (or Franklin's) Grouse

Montana	Modest	Northwestern mountains (damp evergreen forests)
Idaho	Modest	Panhandle forests and others
Washington	Modest	Cascades and extreme northeast

White-tailed Ptarmigan

Colorado	Good	Above-timberline areas, scattered. Best to check any season with game department to locate known concentrations.

Hungarian Partridge

Huns are quite cyclic. During low-population periods seasons in some states could be closed. Also, Huns are quite dependent upon agriculture; invariably, they are found near or in grain fields with surrounding brushy cover.

State	Population	Best Areas
New York	Modest	Jefferson, St. Lawrence, Franklin, Clinton counties
Wisconsin	Substantial	South and east of Wisconsin River, best along border south of Green Bay
Minnesota	Fair	Western border counties (Polk, Norman, Clay, Wilkin)
Indiana	Some	Grant, Blackford, Gray, Tipton, Delaware counties
Illinois	Fair	Lee and northern border counties
Iowa	Good	Northwest quarter of state; check season boundaries
No. Dakota	Excellent	Northwest and interior counties
So. Dakota	Fair	Two tiers of northern counties east of Missouri River
Utah	Fair	Box Elder, Cache, Rich, Tooele, Juab, Wasatch counties
Wyoming	Some	Park, Bighorn, Sheridan, Washakie, Hot Springs counties

Idaho	Good	Western and Magic Valley regions
Montana	Good	Triangle formed by Harlowton, Lewiston, Great Falls
Oregon	Fair	Northeastern counties
Washington	Fair	Eastern counties

Chukar

So. Dakota	Check with game department	
Nebraska	Check with game department	
Arizona	Modest	Along Utah border or in Prescott region
Utah	Good	Box Elder, Uinta, Tooele, Carbon, Grand, San Juan counties
Nevada	Excellent	Western, northwestern and Elko counties, but fair over much of state
Colorado	Fair	Escalante and Gunnison River canyons; western counties
Wyoming	Good	Northwestern and north-central counties
Idaho	Excellent	Lower Clearwater and Salmon Rivers; Hells Canyon of Snake. Fair in many counties
Montana	Modest	Check with game department

California	Good	Southern third of state; eastern border counties except north; Shasta County south to Kern County
Oregon	Good	Deserts and stream drainages of eastern counties
Washington	Excellent	Snake River and Columbia River breaks; widely established over most of state in suitable habitats

Bandtailed Pigeons

Seasons federally controlled. Check with State Game Dept.

State	Population	Best Areas
New Mexico	Modest	Catron, Grant, Hidalgo counties
Arizona	Good	White Mts.; Payson-Long Valley area
Utah	Some	Monticello region
Colorado	Some	Del Norte, South Fork, Salida, Uncompahgre Plateau, Grand Mesa, Wolf Creek Pass
California	Excellent	Monterey, San Louis Obispo, Shasta, Santa Cruz, Santa Barbara, Humboldt, Trinity counties, roughly in that order

Oregon	Excellent	Cascades and Coast Ranges clear to saltwater
Washington	Excellent	Olympic peninsula; north and south Puget Sound areas; northwestern counties

Quail

Gambel Quail

New Mexico	Good	Desert and watercourses of southwest
Arizona	Excellent	Desert and foothills most of state, except northeast
Utah	Good	Washington county; lesser numbers across south in desert bottomlands
Nevada	Good	Clark County
California	Good	San Bernardino, Riverside, Imperial counties

Mearns Quail

Arizona	Excellent	Oak and grass zone of foothills: Pinal, Cochise, Graham, Santa Cruz counties

Mountain Quail

Nevada	Good	Foothills, medium altitudes— northwest

		Humboldt, southern Washoe counties; Sierra foothills of western border
Idaho	Good	Canyon, Payette, Washington, Ada, Adams, Valley, Twin Falls, Lincoln, Gooding counties
California	Good	Western Sierra slope from Kern to Shasta county
Oregon	Good	Most foothills; favored: Tillamook, Lane, Coos, Douglas, Wallowa counties
Washington	Fair	Coastal mountain foothills

Small Game

State	Best Areas

Swamp Rabbits

No. Carolina	Swampy areas of tidewater region
So. Carolina	Swampy areas of tidewater regions
Georgia	Northwest, and (marsh rabbit) swamps, marshes of south
Florida	Most marshes and swamps (both swamp and marsh varieties, close relatives)
Kentucky	Only a few, along Mississippi and Ohio bottomlands and a few other stream courses
Missouri	Modest numbers along stream bottoms of southern counties

Arkansas   Along Arkansas River and tributaries;
                      Sulphur River bottoms
Oklahoma   Stream courses and bottoms of southeast
Alabama   Moist to wet bottoms and swamps
Mississippi   Most lowlands
Louisiana   Southern counties along stream bottoms
                      and cane-belt areas

Pygmy Rabbits

Nevada   Most brushy, dry areas
Idaho   Sagebrush and grass areas
California   Sagebrush of northeast
Oregon   Southeastern counties

Tassel-Eared (Abert) Squirrels

Arizona   North, yellow pine forests
New Mexico   Southwest, yellow pine forests

10

Field Care of Deer and Big Game

Once a deer or other big-game animal has been downed and your license tag immediately attached, the most important period of the hunt begins, so far as the quality of meat eventually to reach the table. Tens of thousands of pounds of wild big-game meat is ruined annually during the hours from kill to destination (home or locker plant). Field situations differ widely, of course, from the often hot weather when a pronghorn is collected, or the warm climates where deer are taken, to cold and snow in the North during deer or moose season. A deer taken in the Deep South may be exposed to humid weather, and an elk killed in the Rockies, to air so dry a crust quickly forms on the exterior of the skinned carcass.

Good sense should guide you as to how best to handle an animal under most circumstances. The basics, however, remain the same everywhere. The prime and immediate concern is getting body heat out of the animal as quickly as possible. The size of the quarry will certainly have bearing on how difficult the various steps will be. Make no mistake, though any hunter can field-dress and care for deer or antelope, when an adult bull elk or moose hits the ground, the fun is over. The handling chore is prodigious. Most hunters usually need help, and all should plan beforehand what to do and what tools they will need.

There is an old rule among big-game hunters that if you find yourself in a situation where you need help to physically handle an animal, an elk, for example, or an extra-large deer, at least immediately open the body cavity, roll out the entrails, and prop the cavity open as best you can while you go for or wait for assistance. This allows much body heat to escape. Any animal left untouched for an hour, even in cold weather, will bloat severely. To be sure, for that short a period this won't spoil meat, but it certainly won't add to the quality.

Field dressing of deer and big game has been covered in detail in literally hundreds of magazine articles and books. I don't intend to more than skim the process here. I will observe, however, that any hunter after big game who goes into the field ignorant of how to get the entrails out properly, and how to get the hide off when the time comes, shouldn't be hunting in the first place. This is as much a part of big-game hunting as learning to shoot the gun. Sure, you have to experience that first time, but you should at least have the know-how in your head.

Most deer, and antelope, are usually field-dressed, then transported to camp, home, or locker plant, where they are skinned and finally butchered. But I must point out that in some situations it is just as easy, and far better for the meat, to field-dress, skin, and rough-butcher an animal on the spot. On our ranch, for instance, where the whitetail deer are small, we commonly field-dress a kill, hang it from a nearby limb, skin it right then because when an animal is still warm the hide peels off easily. Then we rough-cut it while it is hanging, sling the meat over a shoulder in a big, heavy plastic bag to carry it to our vehicle or camp. Instant skinning and rough-cutting allow body heat to dissipate swiftly, save loading and unloading the whole animal, or dragging a deer through the woods. In addition, they assure the best meat possible. As soon as the plastic carrying bag is at, the vehicle or camp, we immediately open it—never should warm meat be left closed up—so it will air, and at camp the individual pieces are laid out or hung to cool out throughly.

If you intend only to field-dress an animal where it falls, and then transport it whole, all you really need for tools is an adequate, sharp knife. If you intend to swing a deer from a limb and do as I've just described, then you also require a length of small-diameter, light but strong nylon rope, easily carried in a jacket pocket, and one or more bags for the meat. Regular garbage bags won't do; they're too flimsy and fragile. I buy sturdier bags at a locker plant for fifteen to twenty-five cents each. Sizes may differ place to place. The ones I use measure roughly 30 inches deep and 20 inches wide. They are extra-heavy and made to hold substantial weight. The meat from a whole small deer can be carried in just one.

Along with rope, knife, and plastic bag carried on me, I carry in my vehicle a good-size sharpening stone for my knife, and also a meat and bone saw. Sometimes we hang field-dressed deer, spread the body cavity open with a stick, then—if we can drive near it—go after the vehicle and skin and rough-butcher the hanging deer. The saw is mighty handy then. One other very useful piece of equipment is a large, heavy-plastic sheet folded and carried in a pocket. It is all but weightless, takes up little room, and is invaluable if you have to skin and cut up an animal on the ground, in places where there are no limbs from which to hang it.

The pronghorn, or antelope, usually with season open when the western weather on the plains is warm, commonly receives abominable treatment. Antelope are frequently left too long in the sun, tossed into the bed of a pickup for transport, and so on. Antelope is marvelous meat, but it spoils or taints easily. You can't successfully drag an antelope far. The hair is loosely attached and comes off easily. The hide is thin and wears through. It's no trick, however, to skin out and rough-butcher an antelope on the spot.

This is a good scheme especially for hunters who stalk antelope and often get a long way from base, with no vehicle to immediately pick up the kill. There aren't likely to be any limbs around to hang the animal from. So, after field-dressing you turn the animal onto its back, skin down the legs and sides and spread the hide flat as you go, thus keeping the meat areas only in contact with the fresh interior of the hide. As soon as the hide is down far enough, the shoulders can be taken off and laid on a plastic ground sheet. Hams come next, and then the rib cage is split. You can vary this routine by skinning completely, then laying the carcass on the sheet for rough-cutting. If you work methodically and patiently, you can get the hide off without one speck of dirt on the meat.

Wearing a pack frame with an old, clean pull-top laundry bag secured to it makes the rest of the chore fairly easy. Put the meat into the bag and pack it out, then make another trip for head and hide. (See instructions later in chapter for using pepper to ward off flies.) It's inadvisable, if you're a newcomer to pronghorn hunting, to plan on gutting your kill and backpacking the whole animal in. A mature buck pronghorn, field-dressed, weighs from 85 to 110 pounds, and is hard to handle. Not many average hunters can pack one.

If you intend to drag a deer or other animal, go for help to get it out, or ride horse or vehicle to it later, of course you don't need to carry rope, plastic sheet, and the big plastic bag. You do need a modest-size plastic bag, however, in which to put the liver, heart, and, if you use them, kidneys, in order to keep the meat clean, and any flies or other insects off it. For large animals (moose, elk), what you carry or take later to the scene of the kill depends entirely on where and how you are hunting. Tools to do the big skinning and quartering jobs most easily are, believe me, worth the bother.

For example, one fall while moose hunting in Canada I shot a big specimen which fell in 2 feet of water in the edge of a lake. We were hunting from a canoe. We had with us an axe, several large butchering knives, a sharpening tool for them, plastic sheets, several hundred feet of stout rope, and two pulleys. Just getting the animal onto the edge of the shore was a tremendous job, and without ample rope and the pulleys it couldn't have been done. The rope was then used to get the animal onto its back, and the legs spread and tied to nearby trees.

After field-dressing it and clearing the entrails out of the way, we skinned it, still on its back, peeling the skin down so that the carcass was on the inside of the green hide as we worked. This, of course, kept the meat perfectly clean. With saw and axe we then quartered front and rear, split the rib-cage barrel, and loaded safe amounts into the canoe, making several trips to camp. Currently there are several brands of light, small pulley-and-winch gadgets, complete with small-diameter nylon rope; they are cheap and compact, and can move or lift 1000 to 2000 pounds. Every big-game hunter should have one.

On another occasion while elk hunting I put a big bull down late in the day and we had to leave it in the mountain meadow overnight. Because of the thick hide and hair on the neck of a bull elk or moose, the meat up front will sometimes sour quickly if it lies on the ground that long before complete cooling. We dragged poles of fallen aspen and, after field-dressing the bull, rolled the front end onto several of them, and finally with much effort the rear. When you leave a big-game animal overnight, it's best to roll the entrails well away, to toll predators, if any, away from the carcass. They'll usually take offal and leave the meat alone. We propped the body cavity open. The weather was crisp and dry, and we found the bull in good shape next morning—no predator problems—

and discovered to our great relief that we could bring a 4WD right to the animal. We had big knives, a saw, axe, and sharpening tool, equipment which simplified the cutting-up chore.

Some outfitters and hunters quarter large big-game animals, leaving the hide on, if they don't intend to have the animal mounted or the hide tanned. This protects the meat from leaves and dirt. It does present problems, however, with hair, and with skinning later. With plastic sheets for wrapping, or large plastic bags so readily available, skinning is best. Often clean squares of canvas are used for wrapping to take meat out on horseback or in a vehicle. A neat trick, seldom used but beautifully efficient for transporting rough-cut meat or quarters of large animals, is to carry army-surplus laundry bags that have been laundered often and thus breathe well. They beat plastic.

Incidentally, if you must leave a field-dressed deer overnight or while going after transport or help, and it happens to be where no limbs are available for hanging, it is always possible to find stiff bushes, or down timber or dead brush, and to make a pile or a crisscross platform on which to lay it to get it off the ground. Turning a deer belly down on such a platform, the body opening spread wide, drains and cools it. The back, if exposed to any sun, is insulated by the hide and hair.

BASIC FIELD-DRESSING STEPS

In case you haven't properly done your homework, go back momentarily for a quick refresher on the rudiments of field-dressing. The procedure is the same, regardless of the species, even though the large animals are more difficult to handle. Assume you have killed a deer. Get it onto its back, if possible with head higher than rear. If you have help, keeping the animal on its back is no problem, or at least to start you want the rear end with legs up. Without help, prop the sides with rocks or deadwood. I commonly spread the rear legs of modest-size deer without any props. Just let the one at your left as you kneel at the rear fall as it may, and put the one at your right around behind your right shoulder and lean against it.

Just remember as I pursue these instructions, you can't be squeamish and dainty field-dressing big game. You do have to wade right in and get after it. If it's a buck, grab the testicles and cut them off. If a doe, remove the milk bag with a circle of skin. Firmly grasp a buck's penis and make a neat cut ahead of it. Keep cutting and peeling it back clear to the point near the rectum where it enters the pelvis area between the hams. With knife point snip the cartilage here. The penis and tubes are now freed of outer attachment.

Slit the hide over the lower abdomen. Raise a pinch of tissue covering the abdomen, inside the hide, and make a neat, careful cut of an inch. This is just a "starter" opening. Great care must be taken not to puncture the entrails, or, as you work upward, the paunch. Indeed, use *extreme* care, otherwise you have an utter mess. Work two fingers of the left hand (we're doing this right-handed) into the slit, palm up. Spread the fingers and press down against the gut while entering the knife point, cutting edge up, between your spread fingers.

Now cut upward and forward, inch by inch, following with fingers inside as a guide, opening the entire abdomen. If you wish, you can first cut the hide only, up across the abdomen, then cut the tissue inside. This often helps to avoid paunch or gut punctures. Now carefully cut from where you made that first small opening back toward the rear, so it is all open right to the round opening of bone that encases, between the hams, the bowel and bladder.

Holding the knife blade straight and flat with the bone, insert it from the rear just above the rectum. Cut around the rectum, freeing it from the tail. Ease the blade into edge of cavity and cut the tissue free all around the opening. Be careful. Obviously the caution here is to do this without puncturing the bladder. Some hunters prefer to split the pelvic circle with a heavy knife. It can be done if you cut just off center, but it is difficult for the inexperienced, without hammering the back of the knife blade with a rock. I therefore suggest the "reaming method," at least for the first few animals.

If you've properly freed all tissue inside the pelvic circle, you can now reach inside the extreme lower-body cavity, grasp the lower gut, and—with a gentle but steady pull—the bladder, rectum, penis, and remainder of the gut will all come through. Drop them outside the cavity. *Don't* cut off the bowel, or the contents will spill inside. Now you can tilt the animal to one side and roll out the entrails and the paunch to get them out of the way.

The opening of the cavity should have been made up to the bottom of the sternum, which will show as a white cartilage. With the fore end of the deer now on its back for sure, straddle the animal, place the knife, cutting edge up, just to the right side of the sternum. You'll probably need to grasp the knife handle, if it's large enough, in both hands. Rip upward. Watch this cut! Keep yourself—and a partner who may be holding the forelegs—out of the way of the knife. This operation cuts the ribs away from the sternum on that side, thus opening the lung and heart area above the diaphragm.

If the animal is to be mounted, with a cape mount, don't make this sternum cut along the ribs. If not, cut clear up to the neck. Either way, the diaphragm is now carefully slit on each side. If no mount is intended, a neat trick is to make a slit in the hide and flesh of the upper neck just back under the chin, and cut the windpipe. Now by reaching inside the chest area and seizing the windpipe, you can easily pull it out, along with the lungs and heart. If the head is to be mounted, reach up inside the lung area and slit the windpipe from below as high up as possible and follow through. A portion of the diaphragm will probably still have to be snipped. That's all there is to it. The necessity of removing all of the windpipe clear to the base should not be overlooked. If left in, it can sour the upper meat.

Cut the heart and liver free and put them into the plastic carrying bag. Be sure to leave them closed up no longer than necessary—they have to be cooled out. If the deer is small, one man can lift it by the head or antlers and allow blood inside the cavity to spill out through the pelvic opening. If it's large, two men are required. Or, the animal can be turned over by two hunters, perhaps draped atop a low bush to keep dirt from getting inside the body cavity, and allowed to drain. Needless to say, if you're going to hang a deer and skin it on the spot, it will drain when hung *if* you hang it head up. There are preferences about this. Some hunters insist on hanging by the gambrels (hind legs). If you do that, the deer must drain well first.

When a fresh-killed deer or other big-game animal is hung, hide on, afield or in camp, to be skinned later or transported out whole, the body cavity should be propped wide open with a stick or two. If hung by the gambrels, the legs should be secured wide apart; if by the antlers or head, they should be propped wide apart with a long stick in the gambrel (hock) area of each hind leg.

At that hock point, incidentally, on the inside of each of the deer's hind legs, is where the tarsal gland is located. Especially during the breeding season, this gland, easily identified by the long hair covering it, is wet and smelly. The musky smell, in fact, is all but impossible to get off if you get it on your hands or on the meat. Opinions differ about whether or not the tarsal gland should be removed. If it appears dark and wet, I always gingerly take it and a husky expanse of hide around it out as the first step in field-dressing. It's not difficult and avoids any chance of fouling meat.

Saving the heart and liver of big-game animals should be emphasized. Thousands of hunters discard them; in fact, over the years I've seen probably nine out of ten deer hunters discard them. It's just a habit—a wasteful one. I've never, as far as I can recall, weighed either the heart or liver of a deer, but I'd guess the two together would average at least 5 pounds. Figure that against a million deer. It's shameful to throw away such a tremendous amount of perfectly edible, nutritious meat.

Some years ago I hunted each fall in a deer camp in the Great Lakes region where none of the others saved deer hearts, although most took in the liver. I'd pick up the hearts or ask others to save them for me. My wife would trim them, slit and stuff them with dressing, and bake three or four at a time in a bread pan. They were superb. On a moose hunt I recall the camp cook all but demanding that whoever killed a moose bring in the liver and give it especially good care. We had great slabs of broiled moose liver for several meals. Couldn't have been better. If you see friends discarding hearts and livers of big game, con them into saving them for you. They can be wrapped and frozen like other cuts, if you have an overabundance.

There are no special instructions that I know of for keeping hair and dirt such as twigs, leaves, or even earth off big-game meat during dressing, skinning, and transport except the copious use of plastic sheets. Too commonly hunters butcher or skin deer in a rush, wanting to get the job over with, sometimes on the ground, or on a pickup tailgate, and during the process wallow the meat around until it is in horribly distasteful condition. To be sure, some hair may unavoidably get on most big-game meat, but careful, patient handling will avoid most of it. Dirt of various kinds is all but impossible to remove, even with water, from fresh, moist meat. So, the "cure" is not to get it on the animal in the first place.

KEEPING THE MEAT CLEAN

Opinions vary about washing the inside of a field-dressed animal or the skinned carcass. I remember one time in Maine being appalled to see a guide chuck a freshly field-dressed buck into a river to wash it out. Many hunters hang a fresh-killed deer in camp and slosh buckets of water into the cavity, then let it drain. Some, where it's possible, squirt water from a hose inside. To each his own. We never put water on big-game meat. I will admit that a paunch-shot deer, which is often a mess inside after field-dressing, may have to be cleaned up with water. There's an easy way to avoid the problem: don't paunch-shoot one in the first place!

Water on fresh or still not fully cooled big-game meat is an invitation for an instant culture to form and grow bacteria. Moist climates are even worse for this than dry ones. Dried blood and the dried natural juices of meat are the best coating meat can have afield. Water washes them away or mixes with them to inhibit drying. The longer the exterior of the meat, or the body cavity, stays wet or moist, the longer bacteria have to get started. My advice is, except in "must" instances such as the paunch-shot animal, let the carcass cool and dry as is, hung or laid so air constantly circulates freely over and into it. Always hang animals in shade, skinned or with hide on. If the sun reaches the meat pole at any time of day, you've placed it improperly.

Keep meat as cool, or cold, as possible, but hopefully not frozen. In the high country of the West, I've seen a deer hung in camp coated within a couple of hours by a dry crust that seals it perfectly. With crisp nights, this seal keeps venison or elk in excellent condition for days at a time. The seal hardens on the outside so quickly that flies or other insects can't harm the meat.

Flies in many areas are an abominable nuisance, often even

in cool weather. This problem is easily solved, though, and no big-game meat should have flies crawling over it. Net game or "deer" bags are readily available in hundreds of sporting goods stores. They're cheap, and one can be carried in a coat pocket even while hunting. The best way I have found to use them is to hang a deer, cut the legs off at the hocks to get them out of the way, then gently pull the bag over the animal. The secret of keeping flies out is how meticulously you secure the bag around the neck or the base of the antlers, and at the rear end of the animal. Most deer bags come with inadequate tie strings. I carry plenty of spares. Make sure you don't puncture the net while pulling the bag on, and be certain every top and bottom cranny is tightly sealed.

These bags can be used on skinned carcasses, too. They can also be used to cover quarters of big-game animals. Because of the dry air in mountain hunting, they're not quite as important there as in moist or warm climates. Another fly-proofing approach is to carry a big can of coarse black pepper in camp gear or even in the field under some circumstances. I've skinned antelope out on the plains when flies would find it in a rush, covered the meat with pepper, and kept them at their distance. Pepper clings best when meat is moist. Coating camp-hung big-game meat with black pepper when flies are present is a help, as is heavily dusting the interior of the body cavity.

TRANSPORTING MEAT

I've touched only lightly so far on actually moving deer and big game from the site of the kill to its destination. The how-to of this, following field-dressing, is not only a part of correct meat care, but additionally requires specific knowledge, varying species to species, about how to do the job most easily and efficiently. Believe it or not, I once bumped into a perplexed and frustrated hunter who was actually trying in desperation to drag his first deer out of the woods *by one hind leg!*

As I have indicated, large animals such as elk or moose cannot be moved (or very seldom can be) without first cutting them up. Even then, if parts are to be backpacked out, the job can be strenuous. A hunter should be fully aware of what he is getting into. Inexperienced moose and elk hunters intending to carry out meat, hide, and antlers seldom realize how much their loads will weigh. The meat of a big bull elk totals about 450 pounds, occasionally even more. Moose may be larger. A whole quarter is too much for the average hunter. The antlers of a big elk weigh 40 pounds or more and are an awkward load. Those of a moose may weigh as much as 90. The green hide of either animal is a staggering load for the average hunter. Packing out by boat, float plane, or pack horses solves the problems, but the hunter who must carry the kill himself should know what he's up against.

Much hokum has been published and pictured about how to get a deer from kill site to camp or home. Contrary to much of it, only the smallest whole field-dressed deer can be carried by a hunter. Photos showing a hunter with a big deer over his back are trumped up, taken just before he tried the first step and fell over! It requires a very strong man to carry even a 100-pound deer. Besides, it's dangerous—likely to get you shot or trigger a heart attack.

Large deer out of vehicle range and long distances from destination can be packed out by mule or horse. Doing it properly requires a pack saddle and knowledge of how to lash the deer on it. Don't let antlers gig the mount! That can be disastrous. Additionally, a hunter must know his pack animal, or be with a guide. Some horses cannot be induced to pack a whole deer. An outsize deer (field dressed 200 pounds and up) can be quartered and carried out like an elk or moose.

A small field-dressed deer (75 to 85 pounds) can be carried

whole by a strong, healthy hunter, if necessary. Securely lash all four feet together, putting half hitches around forefoot, hindfoot, forefoot, hindfoot, in that pattern, then around all four. Get your rifle on its sling over one shoulder first, then lift the deer by the lashings onto the opposite shoulder, head toward the rear. Reach back with your hand on the rifle side and bring the head around to that side, arm around the neck. Tie a red bandana or vest over the antlers and hopefully more red or blaze orange on the body before lifting the animal.

When more than one hunter is involved, deer or even black bear can be carried on a stout pole. Most attempt this improperly, simply lashing each pair of feet together and slipping the pole through the two sets of legs. This allows both head and body to swing, throwing carriers off balance. The proper approach is to get the animal on its back, place the pole close down against the open body cavity. Lash the legs near the shoulders and hams to the pole, then the head also. The

To carry a small deer, tie four feet securely together.

Sling rifle over one shoulder; then lift deer over other
shoulder, rear end forward, head pulled around to rifle side.
Drape blaze-orange jacket over antlers (*continued*) . . .

Side view of carry, showing how left hand grips antler.

Wrong way to carry deer (or other animal) on pole is shown above. Tied at feet, with head hanging, animal will swing as carriers walk, and get out of control. Correct pole carry is shown below with bear. Pole is tied well down next to body and head is tied close to pole.

animal then looks almost as if it were on a spit, but it can be carried without swaying. Tie bright red streamers to the animal, and talk loudly as you go, so no trigger-happy hunter mistakes what he sees.

The most common way to move a deer is to drag it. If you know you must do this, make the body opening when field-dressing as small as possible, enlarging it later in camp. This keeps dirt out of the cavity. On snow or leaves a deer slides easily and the hair doesn't wear off much on moderate hauls. Over rocks and wiry grasses, patches of hair will quickly wear off the hide. On a long drag, a piece of tough canvas with grommets, carried for this purpose, lashed around the deer on the drag side and to the neck or antlers to hold it in place, avoids wearing the hide through.

One man can drag a fair-size buck, if he pauses to blow often, by seizing the antler on the *down* side. This keeps the head well up off the ground. Two men, one on each antler, can easily drag a big buck. To prepare for a long drag, particularly in brushy country, bring the forefeet forward, hook them inside the antlers, and lash them there. Lash the forefeet along the neck of a doe. This avoids having the forelegs catch on brush or trees. Unless the entire deer must be brought in for registration and weighing, cutting off the rear hocks lessens difficulties in brush. Simply feel for the joint, cut into it, break it down across your knee, then finish cutting it off.

One, or two, hunters can sometimes drag a deer more easily by using a rope and a cross-piece stick for a handhold. Lash the forelegs up forward as described. Tie the rope around the antlers (or the neck of a doe). A short piece of stick tied at its center to the other end of the rope offers a handhold. A lone hunter can double the rope into a kind of harness loop to go behind his neck and down under his arms. Most important in using a rope drag is to make sure the length from the deer's head to you is short enough so the upward angle is steep, keeping the animal's head well up off the ground. Otherwise,

To drag a deer, first place forefeet inside antlers.

Tie rope around feet and antlers (*continued*) . . .

Grasp upper antler and drag deer.

it'll catch on everything or plow a furrow through grass or snow.

Once a deer is out of the woods and you have to transport it a long distance home or to a locker with the hide on, it must be well cooled out before you start the trip. Whole deer, or any big-game meat for that matter, should be as cold as possible, clear through, when you start a long drive. Never pack

Two-man drag using stick tied to end of rope, which should be short enough so deer's head is off the ground.

it where heat from exhaust—as in a car trunk, or on the floor of a pickup bed—can raise the temperature. If weather is at all warm, never stack one deer atop another in a closed vehicle. It's a good way to ruin meat.

Do your best to place an animal where air will continually circulate. If flies may be a problem, leave a deer bag on it. By all means, avoid dusty roads; if you must drive on them, wrap the deer well in a tarp early in the morning, while it is as cold as it will get. Proper field care, plus correct carrying and transportation of big game, requires patience and hard work. But it also greatly enhances the quality of the cuts that finally appear on your table, as well as very often saving much valuable meat from spoilage.

11

Skinning and Rough-Butchering Deer and Big Game

Surveys show that the majority of country-dwelling hunters skin and at least rough-cut their own deer and big-game animals, but that urban hunters usually take theirs field-dressed to locker plants to have them processed—that is, skinned, cut up, wrapped and frozen. Among both groups are numerous hunters who compromise, doing a part of the work but letting the locker processor make the final fine cuts and do the wrapping and sharp-freezing.

On hunting trips out of state, especially to distant places where they must fly, hunters can't very well take home their animals in a field-dressed state. They are more or less stuck to have processing done where the hunt ends, and the meat shipped to them, or they fly it home. There are, naturally, hurdles in this, to make certain it arrives in good shape. And regardless of where commercial processing of field-dressed animals is done, it is nowadays notably expensive.

Deer and antelope can often be transported home by vehicle either simply field-dressed or rough cut and in leakproof, heavy-plastic bags, well iced, or with dry ice. Large animals present obvious problems. One of the scenes I recall with great pleasure from my years of big-game hunting was a trip I made one fall into northern Ontario on the Algoma Central railway. I later wrote a magazine article about the trip and the railway, which runs up through the Canadian bush. At that time it was a true wilderness railway, servicing numerous settlements that had no other contact with outside. I dubbed the Algoma the "Moose Meat Special." Seventeen moose were aboard, in the baggage car, on the trip down from where I boarded after my hunt. Amazingly, several of them, loaded from small isolated waystops, were whole, simply field-dressed.

That was a different age and time. Yet many hunters who spend $50 or $60 or more, to have modest-size animals such as deer taken care of by commercial means could just as well do their own, depending on how "fine-cut" they want the results. I would guess that over the past few years between my two boys and myself we have skinned and rough-butchered afield or at home close to a hundred whitetail deer. Admittedly, we don't always get the neat steaks and chops that one gets from a locker, but we eat mighty good venison, nonetheless.

I therefore believe that every hunter ought to know the basics of skinning a big-game animal and of getting it at least started toward the freezer. If he learns how to handle a deer, he can handle anything else. Some big-game species are smaller, some larger, but the approaches are the same. If you want beautifully cut steaks, chops, and so on, then you can have the final cuts made at a market that does this, or take the meat to a locker. My purpose here is to instruct basically how to manage in the field, and, if you're a down-to-earth game handler, how to get meat in large pieces to your processor or in smaller pieces ready for your own freezer. Because deer are the most numerous of big-game animals, I'll use them as examples. With other animals one follows the same general procedure.

There's no reason why you can't skin your own deer, as I've suggested, at the kill site, or in camp, or at home. Why pay someone $15 or more to do the job, plus giving them the hide? You can sell the hide yourself, or you can give it to some charity (several organizations—veterans' hospitals in our area—accept deer hides and have them tanned for patients to work with). You can also have them tanned or tan them yourself and have jackets, moccasins, billfolds, or gloves made. Skinning a deer that is hung up shouldn't take you more than thirty minutes if you know the rudiments.

SKINNING A DEER

There are two schools of opinion about how to hang up a deer for skinning; by the antlers or neck, or by the hind legs, at the gambrels. Lockers, as a rule, use a kind of trough made like a pair of oldfashioned X-shaped sawbucks, with boards forming a long V between them. They lay the deer on its back in the V trough and skin it swiftly, cutting down the inside of each leg, peeling skin off the legs, then down the sides, turning it in the trough as needed. It's quick and clean. Few hunters have such a "skinning sawbuck," however.

We hang deer by antlers or neck. They're a bit less stable this way than when hung by the gambrels because the deer tends to turn around as you work. This is just habit on our part; I prefer to hang a deer that way to drain and cool. The first cut, when you hang it this way, is just below the head, a circular cut of the skin around the neck. Next you slit the neck skin on the underside from the chest to chin.

The hide on each foreleg is now slit on the inside of the leg, from the knee joint up to intersect the slit you've made up the underside of the neck. Don't make the mistake of cutting off and discarding the lower forelegs before you get the skin off; they give you handholds. Work the skin back from the cut on the underside of the neck, and down from the sides and back of the neck. Obviously, you pull and cut gently with the knife blade to help get the hide free. When

One man can hoist a deer for skinning with this strong, compact winch.

Lacking a winch, two men can hoist a deer by merely
throwing rope over tree limb.

working a hide down, the best pulling grip is to reach your left hand up under loosened skin, on the hair side, grip, and pull from beneath. You can hold better that way. If hair comes loose and sticks to your hand, don't get it onto the meat.

Once the hide is worked down from the neck, and away from the forelegs, from which it should be cut free at last at the knee joint, you now work along the edge of the upper body cavity with the knife, pulling the hide back, to loosen it from the brisket on each side. Following this, you can reach both hands up under the hair side and pull strongly down. You may need to cut some tissue here and there, being careful not to cut the hide or cut into the meat. With a strong pull and help from the skinning knife you can strip the hide clear down to and off the top portion of the hams.

You'll now see where the tail attaches to the back. Your knife easily cuts the tail bone at this point. Now turn the deer and slit the hide down the inside of each ham clear to the hock. Start to free the hide a bit along these slits, helping with the knife. Then pull the whole hide from below, and it will strip off the rest of the haunches. Cut it free at the rear hocks. If you use a meat-and-bone saw, simply saw off all four legs just above the hocks or knees. There is no useable meat on them.

If you prefer to hang your deer by the rear legs, simply reverse the procedure of the whole skinning process. First slit the hide on the insides of the hams and cut it in a circle around the legs below the rear hocks. Strip it down from the hams, cut the tail bone, work the hide off down the back, and so on. Skinning a deer this way, you come to the head last. You can cut the meat in a circle around the neck, then saw through the neck bone. Or with bucks, because the rear legs are secured so the deer won't turn, you can sharply twist the head around by gripping the antlers. The neck joint near the head usually breaks easily and the head and hide can be removed with your knife.

SKINNING A DEER

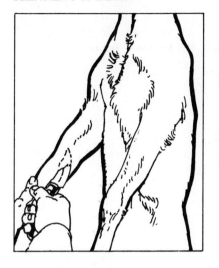

1.   Cut skin from foreleg knee joint (both legs) up leg to intersect with body opening where deer was field-dressed.

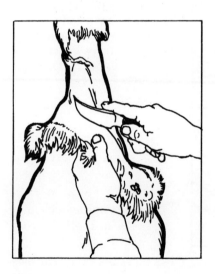

2.   Cut skin in circle around neck, then begin to peel it down, using knife as needed but taking care not to cut through skin.

3.   Continue to peel skin downward, off shoulders and back. Note left-hand fingers grasp hair side underneath, to get good grip. Skin can be forcefully pulled downward, with gentle assists from knife to loosen tissue.

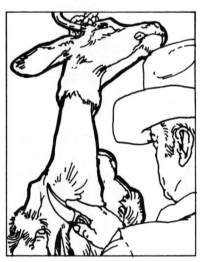

4.   Deer is turned as skin is loosened and peeled downward, and here knife helps loosen skin from upper part of shoulder.

5. As skin is removed from each side of foreleg, fingers are worked through. With grip as shown here, strong pull will peel hide away from leg.

6. Lower foreleg is now bent, knife seeks mid-joint and separates it, cutting or twisting it free. It is to be discarded. If bone saw is available, it can be used to saw off front hock.

7.   Slit is now made on inside of each hind leg, from hock joint upward along ham to intersect with field-dress opening.

8.   Pull hide down and off upper hams, until tail shows. Knife cuts through tail at end of backbone.

9. Next, pull hide downward from hams to hock joint. Then cut it away from each leg. Deer is now skinned.

10. Raise one leg at a time and insert knife point into hock joint to separate joint. If bone saw is available, it can be used instead to saw above hock joint.

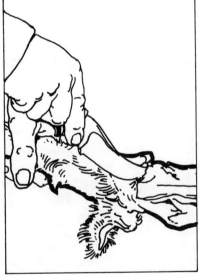

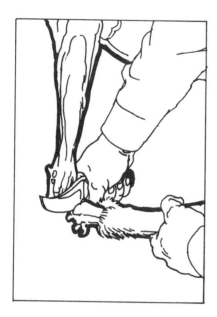

11. Cut off hind hocks and discard them. Deer is now ready for rough butchering.

As I said earlier, one advantage of skinning a deer right after killing it is that the hide comes off very easily then. In severely cold weather, big-game animals hung overnight are hard to skin, and if they are allowed to become partially frozen they are extremely difficult to handle.

It has long been my opinion that getting the hide off a deer or any other big-game animal as quickly as possible makes better meat. Admittedly, this is arguable. Often it isn't feasible Nonetheless, big game cools out far faster with the hide immediately removed. That is bound to help. There is, however, the matter, also arguable, about whether or not to hang a deer carcass for some days, hide either on or off, to "age" it, as beef is aged. I know hunters who won't touch a deer until it has hung at least a week. Conversely, some wouldn't eat one hung that long.

In chilly weather a deer can certainly hang, hide on or off, for several days with no harm. But aging venison in the same way beef is aged is, as most processors who handle hundreds of deer will tell you, a waste of time. Venison and other big game does not have meat marbled with fat, as beef does. Very little fat, often none, is intermingled with the muscles. The fat is put on and lost swiftly, invariably in two places: larded around the entrails and inside the lower body cavity; padded over the rib cage and the back and haunches.

You should consider very carefully before you hang a deer for several days to "cure." It should be kept at a steady temperature if hung. Contrary to popular opinion, locker plants in areas where hundreds of deer are handled don't hang them at a 32° or 34° F. temperature. They are kept in storage as a rule at about 38° or 39° F. Further, unless you specifically request hanging for some days, the reason most are "hung" in lockers is that so many are brought in during deer season that they get behind. Deer hang simply until the skinners and butchers can get to them.

If you've transported a field-dressed animal several hundred miles in a vehicle, leaving it hung for some days may be a questionable decision. I recall a season in western Texas when I killed a big mule-deer buck, and people I hunted with sent two of theirs home with me, asking me to drop them at a locker near us. The deer had hung in nippy weather for two nights at the ranch where we hunted, but the days had been warm. Even though the animals were in shade, in a screened building, they were exposed to broadly fluctuating temperatures, a bad way to handle meat.

When I started home, driving a 4WD Bronco hardtop, I had no choice, because of limited space, but to stack the three big bucks inside in the back. I didn't like it. I had 300 miles to go. I even drove with the back window raised and the front windows open much of the way to let air blow through. The next day the owner of the locker called me. He told me they had skinned the deer, but he did not want to process the one that had ridden on the bottom. It was starting to spoil.

At any rate, if you elect to hang your deer, do so as soon

as possible after it has been killed and cooled out. Most lockers with vast experience in handling wild meat hang deer for about three days, five or six at most for a fresh-killed animal. That's a far cry from what can be done with beef. Though most hunters may not know it, the real reason lockers hang deer at least a day or so after they're killed is that it's almost impossible to properly fine-cut meat that hasn't had time to become cold and firm.

Often a hunter brings a deer at midmorning, is in a hurry, and wants it skinned and cut up so he can leave for home middle of the afternoon. Any locker will tell you that trying to handle venison under a saw when it is slick and soft, not firm, is all but impossible. A locker will also tell you that meat this fresh should not be wrapped and frozen. It should be thoroughly cooled and chilled, and firm, before being wrapped for the freezer.

The system that has worked well for us for years now is as follows: If we skin and rough-cut a deer at the kill site or in camp at our ranch, we let the chunks of meat cool thoroughly, hung out in the crisp night air, which we invariably have during deer season. Or, if we hang a deer with the hide on, it still gets a night to cool thoroughly, then is usually skinned the following day. If weather happens to be warm in the daytime, we place the rough-cut pieces of meat in heavy-plastic bags the second day and ice them, making sure no water from melted ice can seep into the tops of the bags. Late that day or the next, we cut the meat and wrap it to be frozen.

ROUGH-BUTCHERING

What I mean by "rough-butchering" or "rough-cutting" is getting the meat off the carcass in sizable chunks that are easy to handle and transport, and doing the job swiftly and efficiently. The meat can later be cut by a professional, by an electric meat saw, into precise steaks, chops, or roasts. Or, you can cut it yourself into less professional pieces. At our house we never cut venison into the types of steaks and chops many lockers do. We eat it in roasts or in backstrap fillets, and find these without question yield tenderer, far more delicious meat. We treat elk, antelope, and other big game the same way. However, by following my rough-cutting directions, you can choose to proceed on your own or have a commercial place do it.

Rough-butchering a deer or antelope after the hide is off shouldn't require more than about twenty minutes after a time or two of practice. It can all be done with an ordinary, sharp hunting knife. However, I advise that you outfit yourself, for both camp and home use, with a bone saw. Especially for tyros, this makes the butchering far easier.

Again, let's presume the deer is hung by the head. Hide and hocks have been removed. There is no shoulder joint; deer shoulders are attached only by muscle. Lift one front leg at a time and slice under it, pulling the leg aside as you do. On small deer you can slice the whole front leg and shoulder off by just continuing to cut. On larger deer you may also need to make a cut from the back, lifting the shoulder blade. That's all there is to it.

For easier packing, you can now remove the lower leg portion from the shoulder proper with a knife or saw. If you use a knife, cut into the meat of the joint from the front. Probe a bit, and you'll see how the joint goes together there. Cut into it, and you can take the leg portion off. Or, if you use a saw, cut about at or just above that joint. The lower joint makes good hamburger or chili meat. Shoulders of small deer are, in my opinion, almost worthless as steaks. Shoulder roast is far better. If you are hurrying and don't want to take time to remove the lower leg from the shoulder, simply cut into the joint, then fold the leg against the shoulder. It packs easily this way.

If you want to go one step farther toward final packaging, on a large deer remove the lower leg as described, then lay the whole shoulder on a clean board, a plastic sheet over a log, or a camp or home table. Cut crosswise with your knife through the meat about at the middle, then saw the bone. Result: two good-size shoulder roasts.

Next cut is to slice off the flank meat. This is the loose, boneless flesh from just below the rib cage, along the belly, down to the top of the hams. Actually; on most deer this meat doesn't amount to much. On small deer it is all but worthless. It can be saved for hamburger if you wish. If you intend to use it as such, and the front legs cut off from the shoulder will also be boned out for burgers, put the pieces in a pile or bag by themselves. Cutting flank meat free is just to get it out of the way.

Now consider what you want to do with the saddle, the whole middle of the back from the base of the neck to the top of the haunches. If you want chops, or a loin roast with the bones in, cut with your knife into the sides or the lower back barely above the hams, then saw crosswise through the backbone. You need help for holding up the hams so that the whole rear end of the deer doesn't fall into the dirt (assuming you're doing this with the animal hung up by the head). Set the hams aside.

Saw off the whole middle of the body just at the base of the neck. You now are holding, in that big chunk, the whole rib cage and saddle. Lay it on one side and saw the ribs free up near the loin. Turn it over and repeat. The slabs of ribs can now be sliced in two pieces each, with a knife cutting between the ribs in the middle. You can also saw vertically through them on each side and fold the slabs together. The long loin can be left whole for transporting, or it can be cut in two pieces with a knife and saw. These are now roasts, or they can later be cut into chops.

ROUGH-BUTCHERING A DEER

1. Make cut under fore-leg as leg and shoulder are pushed aside. There is no joint in a deer's shoulder. You simply cut under the blade and shoulder is freed, whole.

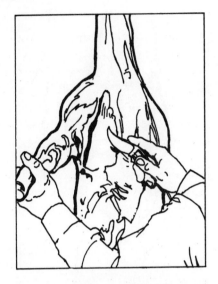

2. To bone out back-straps (tenderloins), cut from base of neck to top of ham on each side of backbone.

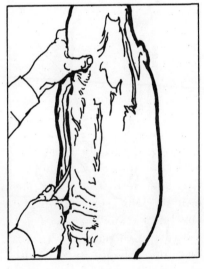

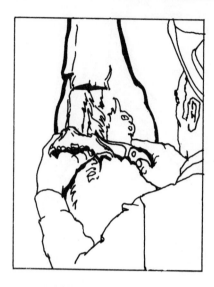

3. To bone backstrap, make crosswise cut at base of neck; with knife work loin free at top, then slit down along ribs on outside of loin.

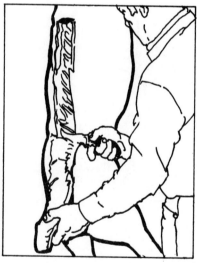

4. Cut closely along rib and free entire backstrap clear to top of ham. Repeat on other side. Backstraps can be cut in two for easy packaging, or in smaller pieces for serving.

5. There are several methods of removing hams. This one, devised by knife-maker Jim Barbee, is fast and easy. With heavy knife, make cut upward on each side of tail.

6. Make deep cut inside ham where it meets body.

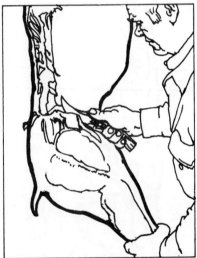

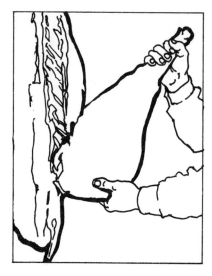

7. Grasping hock and ham, bend sharply upward. Joint will crack. Ham can then be cut free.

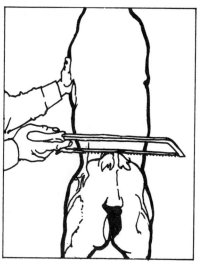

Another easy way to handle hams, if you have a meat saw. Saw backbone about where shown, removing both hams in one chunk. Saw cut should be at base of loins. Then . . .

. . . stand double hams on end and saw down through center, separating them whole.

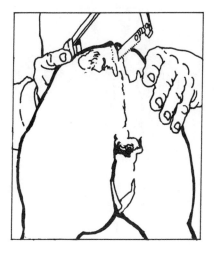

8.   Inside body cavity at lower end are the two small tenderloins. If hams are removed separately, these will still be intact. Remove them from along each side of inner backbone.

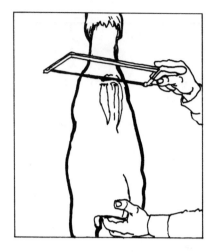

9.   If you elect not to bone out backstraps, and have a saw, after hams are removed by sawing through backbone (shown here), then saw across backbone at base of neck, removing entire midsection of carcass. Ribs are then sawed from carcass on each side . . .

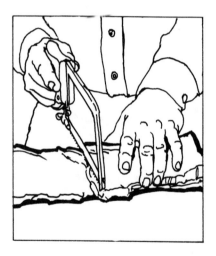

10.   . . . leaving the whole double loin with backbone in. It can be cut in two pieces if you wish, or left whole to transport. Ribs can be split down center (each slab) with hand axe and folded over for easier packaging. Ribs on small deer are hardly worth bothering with.

11. Whether you bone
out backstraps or cut with
saw at base of neck, the
neck can now be sawed
off. A knife can do it if
you find joint properly—
and it can be boned out
later for a roast, or
trimmed for ground meat.

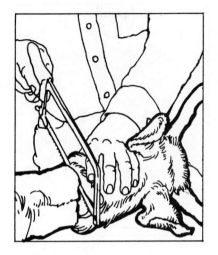

12. On large deer, the
flank meat is worth saving
to be ground. On small
ones it is not very desirable. It can be cut away,
as here, as a first rough
butchering step, if you
wish, to get it out of way.

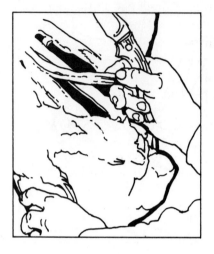

13. If you bone out backstraps, odds and ends of meat, such as between ribs, can be trimmed and saved while carcass is still hanging. By trimming thus, ribs are discarded when you're finished with the meatless carcass.

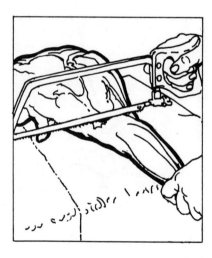

14. Saw (or knife if you properly find joint) cuts hock away from whole ham. Same can be done with shoulders. These leg portions can be trimmed and the meat used for grinding.

My own system is far different. I don't cut off the ribs, the twin hams, or the loin. After the shoulders are off, I bone out the backstraps, or loins, with the deer, of course, hanging. Start with a cut across the very top of the loin at the base of the neck. Cut lengthwise now right against the backbone, from the base of the neck to the top of the ham. Do this on each side. Work the knife in at the top of one loin and start freeing the big piece of boneless meat. By keeping hold of it in your left hand, and cutting deftly with your knife, you free the backstrap from backbone and ribs, all the way down, cutting it off above the ham where it ends. Repeat on the other side.

The two boneless backstraps from a big mule deer will each be almost 2 feet long, if you start high and go clear to the end. The backstraps can be transported whole, or cut in two. They are the most delicious portion of any big-game animal. We use backstrap for broiled roasts over coals, which is superb, or cut it into inch-thick fillets for broiling or pan-frying until only the middle is still pink. For a family, half a big backstrap can be wrapped in one package for freezing. For two people, a quarter or a third of a backstrap to a package (depending on the size of the deer) is enough.

So now the shoulders and backstraps are off. Whether or not you have sawed the two hams off together makes little difference. I seldom do. If you have done so, set the big chunk up on end, tail end down, and saw down the middle to separate the hams. If you've boned out the backstraps and the hams are still attached to the deer, you can go either route. I usually take them off with a knife. Cut around the back of each ham up high, making sure to waste no meat. Cut inside each to free it somewhat until you locate the joint. The knife point then can probe into the joint, cut the holding tendon, and the rest of the meat can be sliced through to free each ham.

The hams can be left whole for transport, with only the lower hock removed, same system as with the shoulders. Or, they can be cut and sawed, crosswise, in two. I very seldom do this even on large mule-deer hams. A big mule deer has hams that weigh 20 or more pounds. Barbecuing one whole is a delicious approach for a big party. I never cut hams into steaks. I commonly cut several boneless ham roasts of moderate size by cutting *lengthwise* the way bone runs on each side of the main bone.

Inside the body cavity of any big-game animal, low down in the back above the hams are the twin "tenders," or tenderloins. If you saw the whole saddle out, they'll remain attached. If you bone out the backstraps, you reach inside the deer and gently cut them free and pull them out. These will be two small, boneless pieces of exceedingly tender meat.

Some people like deer ribs to barbecue. Frankly, small deer have so little meat on the ribs they don't roast very well. Slabs of ribs from large deer, however, can be roasted or barbecued. Most butchers take meat off the ribs to grind into hamburger. If you have boned out the backstraps and removed hams and tenders, what is left hanging at this point is just head and neck, rib cage and backbone. A few minutes spent now while the deer is in a handy position will allow you to slice between each pair of ribs and remove all the usable meat.

While the remaining carcass is still hanging, saw through the bone at the base of the neck, above the now-clean-picked rib cage and backbone. These can be discarded for predators. The rope can now be removed, the head and neck brought down, and the neck sawed off. Some hunters bone out the neck later and use it as a roast; some use the meat for grinding.

If you prefer to hang deer by the hind legs, there's no difficulty in reversing the rough-cutting process. Backstraps can be boned out starting at the bottom as well as top, shoulders removed as easily in one instance as another. This rough-cutting manner of handling deer, antelope and the medium sized game animals is roughly similar to the manner in which the large ones like moose and elk must be handled because of their size. My theory is that if you have your game partly ready for freezer wrapping in the field or at camp, or even if you do it at home, you save a good deal of money. And, you get it started just the way you want it. There is often far less waste, too. Further, if you still want commercial cuts of steaks, chops, roasts, you can still get them. Game can be transported long distances from field to home far better, and well iced, if rough-butchered on the spot than it can be brought home in the whole animal with the hide on.

There is one caution always to keep in mind. Game laws differ widely state to state. Undoubtedly, whether you bag a buck or doe, you will have to transport the head with the meat, if you do the cutting up afield or in camp. In some states the tag for a doe must be placed on a foreleg. In that case, you'd have to keep a lower foreleg that you'd ordinarily discard, plus the head to identify sex. There may also be regulations here and there concerning tags or written notes attached to the meat. Be sure you understand all the regulations so you don't unwittingly get into difficulty.

12

Field Care of Birds and Small Game

At the end of a hot afternoon during bird season one year I ran into a quail hunter who had just arrived at his parked car after the hunt. He looked frazzled and sweaty. He was removing from the plastic-lined game pocket of his hunting vest a limit of quail he'd shot. The windows had been rolled up in his station wagon, and with its large areas of glass it was boiling inside. He was pitching the birds onto the rear floor, where the sun streamed in.

The birds looked unusually large. In fact, they were: they were bloated from their several hours of enclosure in the plastic game pocket of his hunting vest. I was glad I was not going to share them at his table. They were already about as close to ruined as they could get, and they were due for more of the same during his ride home.

Over the years I've seen hundreds of such instances. Game birds and small game commonly receive extremely inept treatment afield and during transport. Sometimes this actually results in the loss and waste of portions of the kill. More often it results in poor-quality meat for the pot. There's no need for it. Each time I witness such handling of game it impresses

174

upon me the fact that correctly caring for, carrying, and transporting the smaller game species is apparently an area of hunting lore about which the average hunter is not very well informed.

Much poor field care of birds and small animals stems from impatience, and some of it from lack of planning. Few like to pause, when heady action may be in progress, to administer temporary correct care to the kill. Yet if you think about it, the action on any bird or small-game hunt is intermittent. You pop a couple of squirrels from a tree, say, and that ends the flurry until you move on to the next undisturbed site. So why not take care of your kill on the spot so it at least will begin to cool out, rather than hemming it in so that it can't possibly emit body heat?

CARRYING GAME PROPERLY

As I've tried to emphasize in earlier chapters, it isn't just the hunt action that's important. The meat should balance that out on a 50–50 basis. With that kind of hunting philosophy, being prepared to carry game properly should be as much a part of the hunt plan as what size shot to use and where to go. Hunters who fail to plan properly for game care or to carry game so it stays fresh and in the best edible condition are cheating themselves. Besides, they may never have tasted it the way it *should* taste. Who'd eat a chicken from the market, for example, that had been killed and left with the feathers on and entrails in for most of a day, in a warm, airless place?

Curiously, big game is field-dressed immediately after it hits the ground, yet birds and small game usually await this process for hours. Fur and feathers are excellent insulators, invariably thickest during hunting seasons. They severely inhibit release of body heat even in cold weather. *All* game should be handled so the bulk of body heat can escape as soon as possible. Too commonly the way game is carried does just the opposite. Meanwhile, juices from shot-punctured crop, paunch, or entrails (especially of shotgun-killed birds and small game) seep into the body cavity. Crop contents lie against breast meat, and even if the crop is not punctured, at least mild tainting is too often well started before the bird receives further attention.

A rubberized or plastic-coated game pocket, common on so many garments, compounds the damage, holding in its airless and airtight compartment what little body heat manages to ooze out. The more birds or animals loaded into a game pocket, the worse the problem. Some hunters triple the desecration, once back at their vehicle, by transferring game from such pockets to plastic bags so no stains get on the carpet.

Old-fashioned ways of carrying game, contrived many years ago, were and still are best. One is the steel-wire carrier, two metal game holders connected by a canvas strap to throw over a shoulder or hang from your belt. The top of each holder is circular, large enough to poke bird or small-game heads through. This circle tapers away at bottom into a long, narrow U-shaped slot, down which the necks slip. Similar to this is the duck strap, a length of belt-wide leather with each end having several tabs with slits in them, through which heads of game are thrust and thus secured. Though little used nowadays, both are still available. Or, you can make your own.

Belt carriers are even better. Though you probably can't buy one these days, you can make one in a few minutes. Punch holes at intervals along an old belt long enough to go around you over a hunting jacket. From a leather boot lace make and secure in the holes short slip nooses from which to hang game by the head. All these carriers keep the kill out in the air, and your walking motion assists circulation, breeze or none. It's true that carriers that hang birds and small animals by the head for carrying can at times be troublesome, especially if a head pulls free. Belt carriers, at least, can just as efficiently carry game by the feet.

One of the best of all carriers is one probably not even made today, the plain old-fashioned washable game sack. I vividly remember when I was a youngster watching neighbors hunt rabbits with hounds. Each man was outfitted with the traditional sack looped over his head and shoulder. These were not commercially made. Hunters' wives simply cut out two rectangular pieces from some tough material and sewed them into a sack, then sewed on a carrying strap of similar

Steel-wire game carriers, connected by a canvas strap, can be hung from belt or thrown over shoulder.

material to go over head and shoulder. I remember them so plainly, because I used to look excitedly, occasionally from a country-school window, to see if I could detect a bulge in anyone's game bag. That meant, of course, that they had been successful, and I imagined myself out there proudly shouldering a game-heavy sack.

Even though you probably can't buy such a simple article in today's world of plastic and endlessly "improved" designs, anyone can easily make one or have it made. The sack should be fashioned from some material that breathes. Heavy nylon net is excellent; so is loosely woven light canvas, washed several times to open up its pores. Even fine-mesh, tough fish net makes a good game sack, although it is inclined to catch on brush. Loosely woven burlap is another good material. A strap of canvas long enough to go over your head and across your chest and back completes the rig. The game sack rides at belt level on the opposite side from your gun shoulder.

A great advantage of this simple carrier is that if it is bloodied after a hunt, it can be washed. It is virtually impossible to properly clean the plastic-lined game pockets of most hunting jackets and vests. If for some reason a game sack becomes smelly, run a bucket of water, pour in some household bleach, immerse the game sack in it, soak it for a couple of hours, then rinse and dry. Admittedly, the old-fashioned game sacks don't look natty—if that's important to you—but they treat game well.

Game vests and hunting jackets with nonbreathing game pockets are abominable creations. A few are available without airtight game pockets, although most have them, lined with some allegedly bloodproof material. One made of loose-woven canvas or comparable material is suitable, especially in cool climates. Sure, you'll get some blood stains, maybe even through it onto your hunting pants. Cold water takes blood out most of the time, and, anyway, a spotted pair of hunting pants is better than eating tainted meat. Besides, you look more like a hunter than a catalog model.

I have an ancient canvas hunting vest that I no longer button (I won't explain why!) that has been washed scores of times, is faded and pliable, and breathes well. The game pocket is simply a part of it, no lining of any sort. It has carried game birds from northern ruffed grouse to Mexican quail, always with respect for their table qualities after the hunt.

Carrying a wild turkey can be difficult—or easy. Try this. Make a slip noose in one end of a leather boot lace and another about 4 inches up from that one. Put one over the head, or the feet, of the bird, the other over your gun barrel. Carry the gun over your shoulder. The turkey hangs down your back for an easy carry.

REMOVING THE CROP

Carrying birds and small animals so that air circulates is only one part of proper field care and carrying, however. The first act as you pick up any upland bird you've shot, regardless of weather, should be to pull out the crop. It makes no difference whether the crop is full or empty. The crop of a bird is a moist, expandable sack for holding food. It lies against the most important meat area, the breast, bloats swiftly when warm, especially when full, and can taint the breast meat. Simply break the skin at the base of the throat, get hold of the crop with thumb and fingers, and pull it free. Only seconds per bird are required. You can remove the full crop of small-game birds such as quail and doves, especially when full of seeds, without first breaking the skin. Simply grasp the bulging crop, skin, feathers and all, hold the body of the bird with the other hand, twist, and pull.

Game that under certain feeding conditions takes a high percentage of soft vegetation may have the crop overstuffed with it. I have often shot ruffed grouse in fall when the birds had located a clover patch back in the woods. Their crops were bulging with this soft, green food. It deteriorates quickly, becomes juicy, heats up swiftly, and quickly taints the fine breast meat. It may not spoil the bird, but removal of the crop immediately after the kill certainly improves, or rescues, the delicate flavor while aiding air circulation.

DRAWING BIRDS

All game that takes much soft vegetation in its regular diet—rabbits, grouse, quail, waterfowl—are also "guttier" game than squirrels, woodcock, and jacksnipe, for example. They should be drawn just as soon as possible after they're killed. This doesn't mean hours later, after they've been carried around with the entrails in, but hopefully within the first hour.

All hunters pause for a breather now and then. After a drive for pheasants in a big cornfield, for example, it's traditional to find drivers and blockers standing around a few minutes, hashing over the action and plotting the next drive. This time can be put to good use drawing birds just killed. In a duck blind, it is no trick to pull the entrails out of birds between flights. Invariably there's water nearby to clean your hands. I carry a few of those small, individually packed wet towels available in almost any grocery store for this use. Afterward they can be stuffed into a pocket and carried back to the litter bag.

To draw birds quickly and easily, part the skin across the belly with your fingers or a knife, below the lower point of the breast. Make the opening wide, and pull out the entrails. Trim away liver and gizzard and lay them to cool out while you work. Leave the heart attached in the body cavity, a handy way to carry it. Run a thumb along each side of the backbone to remove the lungs.

If you use a game sack, toss the giblets back into the body cavities. Or, if need be, since they are now partially cooled, you can put them into a plastic bag carried for that purpose until you get to the ice chest at your vehicle. (I repeat, carry in your pocket a few small, sealed, wet towels for wiping your hands.) For drawing waterfowl, forget the metal "duck hooks" sometimes used. They leave the body cavity almost closed. Open it wide as for all other birds. Be sure to pull out the windpipe and the gullet of waterfowl. I run a finger down the neck into the body cavity on large birds, to make sure an opening goes clear through. This allows just so much more cooling out and air circulation. During a ten-minute rest period every half hour you should be able to draw all the birds you've killed.

Rabbits bloat quickly and should be gutted as soon as picked up. The commonly touted method of squeezing the entrails out the rear won't do: air won't circulate, and besides it's a repulsive procedure. Slit the belly from rear to rib cage, seize the animal by its hind legs and ears or head, hold it belly down, and give it an abrupt snap, throwing out the entrails. Cut away any that cling. Detailed dressing can be done later. This step allows body heat to drain swiftly.

Squirrels' diet during winter is more solid than that of rabbits. During spring, however, squirrels gorge on soft foods, and once in the game bag may bloat and taint quickly. One June I was on assignment to do a spring squirrel-hunting article in the Mark Twain National Forest in southern Missouri. Coincident with the opening of the spring squirrel season, the wild mulberry trees bore heavy loads of ripe fruit. The squirrels ate it eagerly, and all we had to do to find them was locate a bearing mulberry and, wearing camouflage, sit below it. We had to clean the squirrels as soon as we collected them, however, because they bloated quickly from the soft, sweet fruit. We didn't bother to skin them then. The best way to handle squirrels afield, if you'll be hunting for some hours and carrying them, is to slit them about the same as recommended for rabbits and take out the entrails and lungs for quick cooling. That spring we gutted each squirrel as soon as we picked it up. In fall or winter, with food habits changed and weather cool, the field-dressing chore can be done after every two or three kills, or within an hour.

KEEPING BIRDS COOL

Pheasants and the various grouses are mostly shot in cool weather. With crop removed immediately and entrails drawn shortly after killing, they can be carried to destination with little further attention. Quail, and sometimes waterfowl, may require different treatment, because quail in particular and waterfowl commonly in the South are often shot during warm weather. Kills of quail during any day's hunt should be skinned or plucked at intervals. Commonly hunters are out for an hour, then back at a vehicle to change locations. During the vehicle stops for a cold drink and a rest, it's a simply matter to skin or pluck birds so far collected, and put them on ice in a chest.

I don't like to coop birds up in plastic bags until they are thoroughly cooled out from body heat. If you plan ahead, you can be sure to have enough ice so birds can be laid out on it, well separated, during these interludes, but not in bags. There should be ample ice so there is no danger of the birds getting into water. On the next round, the iced birds, thoroughly cooled, can be put into plastic bags if you wish.

Actually birds don't have to be skinned or plucked to be put on ice. During a fall sage-grouse hunt in 1980 in Colorado I witnessed what I consider a good scheme, one not often used. It was mid-September and, though at 8500 feet altitude we'd had a light frost at night, by midday, as usual in the high country, out in the sun it was hot. These hunters had killed several big blue grouse and several sage grouse. They had drawn them and removed the crops, as I've suggested, in the field. We saw them back at their vehicle middle of the day, and they showed us their kill. The drawn birds still had feathers on and were laid out on plastic sheets on ice in a couple of big chests brought for that purpose. When the hunters finished for the day, they cleaned the birds, encased them in bags with zip-shut tops, and buried them in ice for the trip home. It was a good plan.

Whether or not you pluck waterfowl soon after they're drawn depends on how you intend to handle them later. Down efficiently holds in both heat and cold. On warm days when you'll be out many hours, take the time to pluck the birds as well as draw them during lulls. If it's cold, drawing is all they require. If you must transport drawn, unplucked waterfowl long distances to get home, they can be chilled thoroughly overnight by hanging them (by the head) in crisp air. Then, wrapped in a hunting coat or covered similarly in a vehicle trunk, their down and feathers keep the meat cold. Even in the rear of a car with the heater on up front all day, the chilled-out birds will stay cold if they are well wrapped.

In fact, one of the very best ways to make certain birds remain in prime shape, if you must be out overnight, is to hang them. Most bird seasons, in most places, fall when nights, at least, are cool to crisp. I remember hunting sharp-tailed grouse and prairie chickens in the western Upper Peninsula of Michigan years ago when we'd stay long enough to get (or try for, at least) a possession limit each of birds. We'd draw the birds, crops also removed, of course, and hang them in bunches of two or three by the head from a limb well off the ground. No varmints could reach them from below, and we dangled them far enough below the limb, using wire, so no raccoon or other animal could reach them or cut them down. The frosty nights chilled them, they drained well, and were in shade with excellent air circulation all day. If you are on an extended trip and can't get pheasants or other game birds dressed, frozen, and held in a locker until you go home, hanging at night, feathers on, and icing by day if weather is warmish will keep them in good shape for several days.

Doves present special care problems afield because most

dove hunting is done in hot weather. Crops should be pulled as kills are made, and the birds laid out separated, not piled, in shade, even in your own shadow, if necessary. Check every few minutes for ants, and move periodically if they appear. Because dove diet is 90-plus percent seeds, and the feathers are thin, drawing them quickly is not quite as crucial as with most other birds. Never, as you are shooting, drop them into a plastic bag to "keep the ants off." Keep them out in the air in shade.

Many wild turkeys also are killed when the weather is warm. Turkeys have an astonishing store of body heat. Never take one home as killed if the trip is more than a few minutes. Because one bird is ordinarily a limit, it can be cared for immediately. Part the lower-throat feathers and remove the crop. Lay the bird on its back and pluck some feathers from near the anus and across the belly. Slit the skin and tissue clear across the belly, that is, below the lower point of the breast. Pull out the entrails and cut out the anus. Hang the bird for a few minutes from a limb to drain, using a leather boot lace carried for that purpose. Let the giblets cool meanwhile in shade; it's all right to put them into a plastic bag until you reach your vehicle, which is seldom very long. Or, if you intend to carry the gobbler out of the woods by its feet, the bird thrown over your shoulder, simply drop the giblets inside the body cavity. An excellent way to cool out a fresh-killed turkey or other large birds such as geese during transport by vehicle is to fill small plastic bags with ice, tie the tops, and stuff one into the body cavity of each bird.

When you think about it, the proper care and transport of game birds and small game from kill site to your home amounts to nothing more than plain good sense. Just do what seems logical. When you bring meat home from the store, you don't let it lie around in the sun in your car for several hours before getting it into the refrigerator. That meat has been refrigerated, and still you care for it immediately. You can't expect game fresh-killed, poked into an airless game pocket for hours, treated to more of the same in your vehicle on the ride home, and even left until you get rested up some before it is cleaned to amount to much. Sure, taking care of it as you bag it requires a little extra work, but in the end you get a lot of better quality in the meat you eat. You finally know what each species *really* tastes like!

Part II

Fishing for the Pan

13

Ethics and the "Meat Fisherman"

There has always been a stigma, sometimes valid, sometimes not, about keeping "too many" fish when they happen to be biting eagerly. One might be forgiven once, but a certain type of angler who habitually carried enormous catches home from lake or stream was invariably dubbed a "fish hog." Sometimes the derogatory term was richly deserved by a supergreedy fisherman, and sometimes it stemmed from jealousy. The inept angler was simply venting his frustration upon a more expert member of the clan.

Subsistence fishing was taken for granted by early settlers and pioneers. When "luck" was extra good, naturally then was the time to gather the manna. In many cases in the past, no harm was done. Waters, some of them, were stiff with fish, and it really didn't matter how many one took for consumption. Indians, remember, commonly put a fish in each hill of corn, as fertilizer. Eskimos fed beautiful, big Arctic char to their sled dogs, and in some places still do.

I recall reading about how fishermen from Saginaw, Michigan, used to go, way back in the 1800s, by rail up into the northern part of the Lower Peninsula, hire a team and wagon, outfit with wooden barrels and sacks of rock salt, and make annual trips over to the Manistee River, where they camped and fished for grayling. Old accounts relate how, using a cast of three flies, they would routinely have three grayling on at once. They cleaned and salted down their catch, and when the barrels were full, headed home.

Were they fish hogs? Viewed by today's so-called environmentalists, they certainly would be. Viewed against their own time in history, probably not. They were having heady sport, and using an abundant resource that received virtually no fishing pressure.

The fact is, however, that the Michigan grayling has been extinct since some time in the 1930s. It is common nowadays among some conservationists who see only blacks and whites to assume that overfishing accounted for the decline in whatever species is under consideration. "Overfishing—the greedy meat fishermen—extirpated the Michigan grayling." Is that true?

Certainly, if such pressure had continued on a steady scale by numerous anglers over some years it would have been. The actual fact is, anglers never got a chance to bring the grayling low. The heyday of the logger in both peninsulas of Michigan, it has been concluded, was chiefly to blame. During the 1800s vast log booms and free-floating logs went chuting down the Manistee and every other Michigan river as the tremendous stands of pine and hardwoods were cut. Enormous forests were stripped away. Spring was the time when the rivers were high enough to transport the hundreds of thousands of logs downstream to mills. It was also the spawning time of the grayling. The gravel bars where their spawning took place were scoured clean by logs riding spring torrents.

In only a very few years of the heaviest logging, the grayling was almost gone. Denuding the land of timber then allowed incessant, swift runoff and endless habitat damage year after year. By the time the modern sport fisherman arrived on the scene, he wouldn't have known what a grayling was. There were no more.

So, how many fish can one keep to eat without being a fish hog, an overconsumptive, destructive user of the fishery resource? That's a ridiculous question to which there are as many answers as there are fish species and states in which they are found. One measuring stick, perhaps, is the daily bag limit set by fish and game departments in each state. Fish management is a most intricate business these days, and trained biologists know quite well how many fish of each variety can be taken without harm to the population. In former times, when there were no limits, undoubtedly here and there some overfishing resulted. Certainly commercial fishing, especially in freshwater, harmed numerous species. So today the varieties that are less prolific can be taken legally only in limited numbers, while the superprolific species can sustain more pressure (higher daily and possession limits) without harm.

Certain species today are under worse pressure from deterioration of habitat than from fishermen. Obviously these cannot be considered as legitimate "meat fishing" targets. Probably the most striking example is among the freshwater trouts. There is immense sentiment today toward catch-and-release for the trouts, especially in streams. Some of this is a legitimate concern. It can be predicted that the time will surely come when most of the nation's classic trout streams will be hard put to sustain a catchable and keepable trout population.

This is by no means the fault of "meat" fishermen—or any other fisherman. Stream habitats are swiftly deteriorating from pollution, misuse and changing uses of the land, and overuse by the general public. It is curious that the millions of the new crop of recreationists who think of themselves as nonconsumptive users of the environment, as opposed to consumptive users (often their term for hunters and fishermen) commonly are among the most resource-damaging segments of the population that use the lakes and streams. And most of them don't even know it.

The fact is, there is no such human being as a "nonconsumptive user" of natural resources. Every act of every person in some way touches the environment in some deleterious manner. Consider as a striking example related to fishing several of Colorado's once most famous trout streams, on which over past years the tube-float and inflatable fad has erupted. Few of these people fish. They just float. How can that possibly "consume" any resource, especially fish? They litter both water and banks, scour the gravel bars, pollute with human waste, disrupt the trout environment of both banks and water to such an astonishing extent—thousands of them over a summer—that trout biologists cannot hold back trout declines due to lowering levels of stream quality. Trout populations diminish in alarming proportions as the fad grows. Nonconsumptive? Hardly! The fisherman who takes a legal limit of trout from such a stream to eat is a miniscule consumer compared to the tremendous degradation caused by the so-called nonconsumers. There are scores of comparable instances.

One of the interesting slants, especially with trout and on the affirmative side, again argues against all-black/all-white, even among the catch-and-release enthusiasts. For example, in New Mexico the brown trout was introduced many years ago. It not only thrives there in waters where rainbows and other trout do less well, but since it's also a difficult fish to catch, most anglers pass it up and try for rainbows. The result: an overabundance of browns, which become, from management's viewpoint, an underutilized resource. The rainbows are, by comparison, overutilized. The answer, New Mexico found, was to place on many waters a so-called bonus limit on browns. You can keep a regular trout limit, which might be mixed, and in addition you can take—if you can catch them—a specified extra number of browns.

The department *wants* these fish removed, to help balance the trout fishery. Is the angler who helps, who learns to catch browns and receives this bonus for his table, unethical—a fish hog? By no means. He'd be silly not to take advantage of the opportunity to put a few extra meals on his table.

There is a similar situation in some states, mentioned in the introduction to this book, concerning the brook trout. As I've already said, trouts in general cannot be considered, because of difficulties they are having in general, meat-fishing targets. Yet there are exceptions, and these are bright spots for those who fish both for sport and for the pan. The brook trout is a singularly nonprolific species. Egg production among the females is quite low, compared to many other fish. Throughout roughly the northeastern quarter of the country and on into Canada, where the brook trout was native, it is not doing very well today. It probably never will again—there.

A good many years ago, however, brook trout were transplanted into the West. They were stocked chiefly in the cold, small streams of the high country in the Rockies. These waters they readily adapted to, whereas other trout species were not nearly as suitable. The catch was that all those creeks way up in the mountains, with blue droplets of countless beaver ponds scattered along them, got little attention from fishermen. Although the brookies didn't grow very large in those cold waters (only 6 to 10 inches), the habitats were perfect. Soon they swarmed. Soon, too, fishery managers began to realize that here was an overpopulous but drastically underutilized resource just going to waste. Trout fishermen preferred the larger streams and lakes of lower elevations, and the bigger trout that lived in them.

As an inducement to utilization of this enormous sport and eating potential, several states added a so-called bonus limit of brook trout. During the late summer of 1980, I fished a creek in Colorado at about 10,500 feet that had more than twenty beaver ponds strung along it. These waters, both creeks and ponds, swarmed with small brook trout. We camped there in a mountain meadow for a week and saw not a single other fisherman. The delights of this uncrowded wilderness, where elk, mule deer, beavers, and whistling marmots were our resident companions, are indescribable. And the fishing was tremendous.

I was allowed by regulations to keep eight trout of any or of aggregate species, and I was allowed to keep *ten* additional brook trout up to, but not over, 8 inches long. In other words, I could have in my creel eight brookies, the only species there, of any length, over or under 8 inches, and I could have ten more that did not exceed 8 inches. As trout fishermen know, a 6-inch brook trout is a meaty and delicious little fish.

I have no guilt feelings whatever when I tell you I caught and kept my eighteen trout per day. We simply love to eat them. We ate trout for breakfast every day, and for supper, and sometimes for lunch. We packed some in ice and brought them clear back to our home in Texas, for the freezer and future wonderful meals. Was I a fish hog?

I talked to one trout fisherman later and told him about taking so many. He was incensed. Trout, he reminded me, were a resource in difficulty. In many places they certainly are, the brook trout especially. But *these* brook trout aren't in difficulty; they needed thinning. They were still swarming in overpopulous numbers when we left. Later on, I wrote a magazine piece and mentioned taking eighteen brook trout a day in that location. The editor asked me to delete it—the readers might be furious. In this specific case, the ethics of keeping those trout should not have been in question. Meat fishing for them was a management tool.

Ethics and meat fishing thus are related not only to species, but to place and circumstance of each species. My own feeling is that some severely purist trout fishermen of today are simply too finely focused on the popular catch-and-release idea. There certainly can't be a general concensus that you should gather in all the trout you can get, to eat. On some waters, catch-and-release should be in force. On others, it isn't needed and would serve no useful purpose.

For example, in my home state of Texas we now have a minor trout fishery. Each year the department stocks a few thousand catching-size rainbows and occasionally some browns, below two or three dams where outflow and a few miles downstream are cold enough to sustain them, at least through the winter. These trout cannot spawn. Very few live into a second winter. They're put there to be caught. If all of them were, let's say, caught and then released, most would simply die. If all were caught, released, and lived, and more were stocked each season, they'd all run out of food and living room.

In some situations, a certain species should be viewed as only moderately a candidate for the pan; in others, the same species legitimately can be a bonanza for the pan, with no guilt qualms on the part of the angler. This is as true in saltwater as in fresh. Time was when everyone, sport and commercial fishermen alike, seemed to think the vast reaches of bays and oceans could not possibly be depleted of fish. Today all know better, although many are loath to admit it or reluctant to learn.

In the huge expanses of bays along the Texas coast, as an illustration, the sea trout, or speck (spotted weakfish), beloved by sportsmen and commercials alike, and the reds, or channel bass, have long been the backbone of the catch for both groups. Biologists over recent years have proved without doubt that today pressure is far too great on these fish, *in these Texas bays*. Something has to give. The species are coming under regulation and have been temporarily removed from commercial fishing. Yet there are other locations along our coasts where these particular species are not in any difficulties.

In general, the fish species that are ethically candidates for heavy use in the skillet are those that are the most prolific, or those stocked without much chance that they will spawn and thus purposely cultured on a put-take, or utilization, basis. Location, as I've illustrated, also is related to ethics. In other words, there is nothing whatever unethical about being a meat fisherman, even one looked upon by some as a "fish hog," if you simply are guided by conscience and good sense and adhere to the laws scientific management has recommended. Within this logical framework, by all means take advantage of every opportunity to add both to your enjoyment and your larder.

14

Abundant Freshwater Species for the Pan

When a fisherman begins thinking in terms of fishing for the pan as well as for the fun of it, he's certain to find that his fishing emphasis and aims will change to some extent. He doesn't need to quit fishing purely for sport on, say, a trout stream where a catch-and-release rule is in effect. But he will begin to *broaden* his views on fishing, specieswise, and that is advantageous.

You may find to your surprise that a species you never paid any attention to is lots of sport to catch, that it hits eagerly and is easier to catch than what have been your favorites. The new species thus becomes a day saver at times, adds new zest to your scope of angling, and meanwhile provides valuable food in substantial quantity.

Most of the species you'll go after will generally be the abundant ones, the kinds that reproduce so successfully they can be taken in quantity without twinges of conscience. In addition to these mainstay candidates for the meat fisherman there are also a few freshwater denizens far less well known generally, some of them with quite restricted ranges. Not many anglers consider them sport fish. Fewer still eat them.

And a good many anglers aren't even aware of them. These seldom publicized freshwater orphans I have purposely held out of this chapter, wishing to focus special attention on them by dealing with them in a chapter of their own—"Myriad Unsung Eating Fish," Chapter 17.

Like hunting, fishing is of course governed by regulations. Some states have daily limits and possession limits on all freshwater species. Some have no limits. Some set day and possession limits on certain species, but have none on others. There are instances where a possession limit may apply not only to fresh fish but also to how many you may have packaged and put into your freezer. By and large, however, fish possession limits differ in most states from those on game, in that you can put away your legal limit—in the freezer or your locker plant—and then if you go on another fishing jaunt the next week you can still take home a possession limit and process it for the freezer. In other words, processed frozen fish don't count against a possession limit, so, in effect, you can have all you want, as long as you adhere to whatever limits are stipulated for *fresh* fish.

Let's assume you go largemouth bass fishing on a two-day trip, are allowed ten bass per day, twenty in possession. You clean your catch and fillet them at the end of each day. You ice the fillets and take them home. If you already have a possession limit of bass packaged and frozen from the previous weekend, in the majority of states you have no problem. Conversely, hunters who hunt where there is a one-deer limit of course would be in violation for having more than one packaged and frozen—quite another matter. I note these restrictions, and in some cases lack of them, because the first thing the pan fisherman should do is familiarize himself with his state's regulations, or those of any state where he goes to fish.

Once one knows how many fish of each species he is allowed per day, how many he can have in possession for transport to his residence or locker, and whether or not it is legal to possess limits from former trips, he can begin to plan what will be his best species bets for "meat" fishing, limitwise. The third step is to look down the freshwater game-fish list in the state where you'll be fishing, and note which species will be your most valuable targets strictly from a pan-fishing point of view—the most surefire, best tasting, and abundant. Happily, you don't have to fret about the fun quotient. Catching any species of fish, it has been said, is fun; catching a lot of them is just so much more.

Fish size is, of course, a consideration, but it must be related to chances of success. If the daily limit in your state on largemouth black bass is ten, and the daily limit on crappies twenty-five, certainly you *might* catch ten bass that would outweigh twenty-five crappies. However, your chances of stringing ten *big* bass in one day are by no means as good as for putting twenty-five crappies in the boat. Crappies gang up in schools, and when they're biting the action is fast. Bass are more whimsical and difficult, seldom in schools.

Further, the average bass worth keeping, or legal (depending on size regulations, if any), will weigh perhaps 1 pound. The average bass caught will weigh from 1 to 1½ to maybe 2 pounds. The crappies will average around a half pound, with one-pounders not at all rare and often the rule; a few may run 1½ to 2 pounds. There's a lot of weight waste in black bass. Overall, thinking strictly about the eating, crappies are your best bet and catching gamble. A good scheme, if you're torn between watching bass jump and catching fish for the kitchen, is to pick off the crappies while they're ganged up and eager, then spend whatever time is left on the bass.

Looking down the list of freshwater species, you will discover that quite logically, where limits are in force, as a rule the larger the species the smaller the limit. Large fish require more individual living room; thus there are never as many of them as there are of the smaller kinds. It's a law of nature. The big eat the little. The little are in turn and of necessity

invariably more prolific than the big. This is another of nature's astute arrangements. Therefore, the little (a comparative term) need and are given the least protection by fishing
laws, and for the most part will be the chief freshwater targets
of the angler fishing for the pan.

CRAPPIES

The crappie, mentioned above, is a classic example of a
truly great pan fish. Its range is enormous, throughout the
entire interior of the United States, and it has been widely
transplanted elsewhere. It comes in two quite similar varieties: the predominantly northern black crappie and the predominantly southern white crappie. Because crappies usually
are found in large groups, when you happen upon them your
chances are good of catching them fast. Plus they are delicious
eating. Some states record crappies around 4 or 5 pounds, but
most, as a general rule, average less than a pound, as I've
noted.

In Texas, looking at current regulations as an example I find
that in counties under regulatory authority of the state fisheries department, there is no daily or possession limit. In
nonregulatory counties, the daily limit is twenty-five, but
without possession limit. In a great many states, there is no
limit on crappies. One time I was passing through Oregon
into Idaho and stopped to visit well-known writer and fisherman Ted Trueblood. He took me crappie fishing. He had
in his vehicle an old-fashioned wash boiler, for transporting
our fish (we hoped!) back to his home. I stood in one spot on
the lakeshore and, as I remember, caught forty-five big ones
as fast as I could cast, hook them, and get them ashore.

We did indeed come home with that wash boiler brimming.
There were no limits, and these prolific pan fish sustain themselves so admirably all over the country that no one needs

feel guilty about taking as many as he can use or legally possess. Ted's family and mine had an enormous meal of crappie fillets. He packed the rest for his freezer, with the exception of an ample supply I took along in our trailer when we left, to make meals for the next couple of days.

Like other fish species, crappies grow larger in some lakes than in others. They seem to do best in large impoundments, often reaching prodigious numbers. But within any given area certain lakes seem consistently to produce crappies of large size. This is true of other "meat" species of freshwater as well.

Crappies are abundant and delicious. In most states there is no legal limit on the fish; if there is, it's very high.

For example, the Game, Fish, and Parks Department of South Dakota keeps track of "trophy" catches of all its game-fish species week to week. For years I have been receiving releases from South Dakota, and I often run down the list of big fish caught to see where they came from. Certain lakes invariably show up with trophy crappies, the same lakes often with several busters caught each week. The avid pan fisherman should make it a point to find out which lakes in his area produce the largest crappies, or other meat-list candidates, and if a choice is possible it's smart to fish the spots that consistently produce the heaviest fish. Obviously, there are several more meals—as well as more fun—in twenty-five 1½-pound crappies than in twenty-five half-pounders.

SUNFISHES

Crappies belong to the fish family *Centrarchidae*. This is the same family which contains the black basses and the various sunfishes. Several of the better bets for the meat-conscious angler are in this family. These are among what can be called the true sunfishes. There are some thirty-odd species of these, but the important ones for both sport and eating are the bluegill, dubbed "brim" in the South, the redear sunfish or shellcracker, the yellowbreast sunfish, the common sunfish, and the green sunfish. These are the ones of largest average size. Of the five, far and away the most important, largest at maximum, and abundant are the bluegill, the redear, and the yellowbreast.

Undoubtedly, most readers are thoroughly familiar with one or more of these species. The bluegill has the widest range, natively and by transplant—practically the entire country. Bluegills of ½ to 1 pound are the rule in better habitats. The shellcracker is predominantly southern, but is present from southern Indiana all the way to Florida and Texas. It is a bit larger than the bluegill when fully adult. The yellow-breast is most abundant from the Midsouth eastward and down the coast, throughout Florida, and westward into Texas. Maximum size vies with the bluegill.

These and the other sunfishes are usually sensationally abundant. The bluegill in particular is so prolific and adaptable that it often becomes overpopulous and stunted. So there is no need for any stigma attached to taking as many bluegills, or other sunfish, as the law allows or as you can conveniently care for. I don't suggest keeping, frozen, any of the freshwater fish for much longer than six months. Not that they'll spoil after that period, but they won't be as tasty. Thus, if you are in a situation where you can catch a lot of bluegills, or red-ears, and intend to keep them all yourself, use some restraint.

A nice catch of bluegills and, at far left, sunfish. These fish are so prolific that if they're not caught in quantity they become overpopulous and stunted.

You won't harm the population by sacking up all you want, but it makes no sense to take more than you can use to best advantage.

As with crappies, some lakes become famed for their big bluegills, shellcrackers, or other sunfish species. I used to fish a small lake in northern Michigan where bluegills that would weigh a full pound were common. I caught smaller ones, of course, but I'd cull them, keeping only the slab-sided, thick specimens. At that time in Michigan, there was a bag limit of 15 bluegills. I was in an area where trout were the big thing, and locals paid little attention to other species. I talked a group of friends into bluegill fishing, though, and they learned to love catching them. Of the four anglers who regularly fished with me, however, not one wanted to bother cleaning or eating them. This suited me fine since they turned over their catch to me. I remember evenings sitting in our yard under a light cleaning bluegills until I was worn out. But seventy-five big bluegills made a tremendous amount of food for my family, and in those days (just as many find it today, with food prices sky high) the extra meals were a most worthwhile boon to our slim budget.

Very few states have limits on any of the sunfishes. They need catching to keep the populations in check. I've seen shellcracker strings in Louisiana containing a couple hundred fish that didn't even dent the local population. Several years ago I made a trip to Toledo Bend Reservoir on the Texas-Louisiana border for a fishing vacation focused on bluegills and shellcrackers. I brought home a big ice chest with 100 of them packed in ice, all large as your palm when cleaned. These and other sunfishes are extremely flavorful and firm. As quarry for pan fishermen, they and their relatives the crappies are at the top of the list.

I want to emphasize here that fishing for the pan is not a grim business of flailing away just to haul in meat. Quite the contrary, it is a delightful *expansion* of fishing interests, and it offers more, not less, sport and enjoyment. If you have long been an avid black-bass fisherman, you don't need to sacrifice your hobby for the sake of putting food on your family's table. You simply make it a point to learn about some of the other fish in your bailiwick, You switch emphasis a little, or begin perhaps to *balance* your fishing interests as they broaden, to expand what has been your tunnel vision focused on bass. Begin to spend some time with the overpopulous species. You'll discover that you haven't diminished your enjoyment, but enhanced it.

The sunfishes, for example, are truly excellent game fish in their own right. Their very abundance and willingness has all too often caused fishermen to consider them inconsequential so far as heady sport is concerned. So has the manner in which they're so often caught, with a heavy cane pole or tackle too stout to give them a chance to exhibit their sporty qualities. A 1-pound bluegill, shellcracker, or yellowbreast is capable of far outfighting a largemouth bass of similar weight. If bluegills grew regularly to 4 or 5 pounds, they'd put bass so far back in the shade that bass would be inconsequential.

PAN-FISHING PLUSES

All you have to do, so far as great sport is concerned, is match the tackle to the stature of the fish. The fisherman after supplies for the pan who switches to ultralight spin tackle or a fly-fishing outfit for sunfishes, crappies, and other small, abundant pan species creates a whole new field of sport for himself. He may even discover that he'd rather catch big brim this way than to spend so much time on his beloved bass in the same waters. Again, he doesn't need to quit bass fishing. Whenever opportunity is presented for a mop-up of a pan species, he simply seizes it, temporarily interrupting his pursuit of bass, or other favored species, meanwhile enlarging his overall angling interest and activities, and gleaning the satisfaction of putting valuable food in the freezer.

And believe me, it *is* valuable. I made a point while writing this chapter of checking prices in a supermarket in our town on various frozen and canned fish. Nothing was less than $2 a pound. Some kinds were double that. The variety is limited, too. If you are a seafood lover and have to settle for such items as breaded shrimp, or canned crabmeat (impossible for most to afford), you're talking about anywhere up to $7 or $8 a pound. Canned salmon runs, by the pound, around $4 or more; lowly old tuna fish, well above $1 for a mere 7 ounces. So you see, a couple of pounds of bluegills is easily worth five bucks. In many budgets it may be worth much more, because if it weren't for the fun-caught fish there wouldn't be any on the table!

Fishing for the pan differs substantially from hunting for the pot. Seasons on game are relatively brief, and limits comparatively smaller, although of course the big-game animals furnish a lot of meat compared to catches of fish. But fish populations don't fluctuate radically year to year, except in rare instances; seasons run all year in many places; and most waters contain a variety of large and small sport fish, often saving the need and expense of making extra trips for additional varieties.

Black bass, both largemouth and smallmouth, can be considered to some extent legitimate candidates for pan fishing. However, bass do receive enormous fishing pressure nowadays. There is sentiment among bass fishermen, particularly because of the hundreds of bass-fishing clubs, for catch-and-release. Nonetheless, many bass lakes are heavy producers of fish and stand up under pressure; sometimes you can find bass lakes that get little fishing or need harder fishing. In such instances, taking daily limits of bass does no harm, and bass fillets packaged and frozen should give you no twinge of conscience.

By and large, the trouts, as I explained in the previous chapter, aren't in today's world abundant enough nor do they sustain themselves well enough to come under fishing-for-the-pan rules. But, as I also pointed out, there are exceptions. The bonus limits I mentioned on both brook trout and browns in some western states make these, in such circumstances, legit candidates for pan fishing. There are also numerous locations across the country today where put-and-take trout fishing is all that's available. In these instances, where stocked trout cannot spawn and eventually die if not caught, there is no stigma attached to their consumption.

KOKANEE

There are some places, too—notably the Great Lakes— where various salmon (the big Chinook and the Coho) and trout species are stocked on an annual basis, but do not have proper spawning locations in tributary streams. A tremendous bonanza for the pan, along with fantastic sport, can be gleaned under such conditions. One of the finest opportunities among the salmons now in freshwater, for those within reach of it, and one about which little is heard, concerns the kokanee. This is the landlocked form of the saltwater sockeye salmon. Its original range was small, chiefly in the Northwest, but over past years it has been widely stocked down the Rockies and in a number of places eastward.

The kokanee grows to an average maximum of 2 pounds. In a few lakes 3- and 4-pounders occur; in others, the fish seldom attains at adulthood more than a half-pound. It consorts in large schools, usually has richly orange-colored flesh, and it is a superbly delectable fish either fresh or smoked. Kokanee where present from stocking do not sustain themselves. Like all Pacific salmon, when adult they attempt to spawn, and whether or not it is a successful attempt, they die.

Thus each year-class of adult kokanee, fisheries managers hope, will be used by anglers rather than wasted. This is a resource easily renewable yearly by the hatcheries.

My first kokanee fishing was done in Montana, at Lake Mary Ronan. I fell in love with this diminutive freshwater salmon. It is a doughty battler and utterly delicious. We had a big batch of kokanee smoked to take with us in our camper, and we ate them fresh daily while there. In most states where kokanee are present limits are high, at least ten fish. In some places there have been fifty-fish limits. In most lakes where they're stocked kokanee do not have proper spawning territory in tributary streams. They're fall spawners, and gather in vast schools attempting to make the upstream run. Because this is the end of the line for that year-class, several states—New Mexico, for one—allow a snagging season. During this time it is legal to use a weighted snag hook to haul out fish from the packed schools. Limits usually run at least twenty-five daily. Needless to say, the kokanee either in the summer or during fall-winter runs where snagging is legal is a very special candidate for the pan.

WHITE BASS, YELLOW BASS, WHITE PERCH

The sea-bass family includes some very prolific species. Chief among these is the white bass. Two others, of lesser importance because their range is not as great, are its close relative the yellow bass, and the white perch.

Interestingly, as little as fifty years ago the white bass was not an especially important U.S. species. When the building of large impoundments on our major rivers all across the nation began, the white bass, given all this immense acreage of new water, which formed optimum habitat for it, had an unbelievable population explosion. It is an extremely prolific fish, gathers in large schools, and is a willing, aggressive striker. Because it colonized so successfully and became popular with fishermen, it was soon transplanted far past its original range. Today white bass are found in large manmade lakes, and some others, almost nationwide.

Certainly the white bass is not overlooked by anglers. Millions of pounds are caught annually. In Oklahoma, where the white bass, often called "sand bass," has been named the official state fish, it is estimated that each year fishermen string at least 2½ million pounds of them. Even though white bass are popular, it is mostly among only a modest percentage of anglers. The majority pay little attention. In many states there is no limit on the species. Where limits are stipulated, they are high, usually at least twenty-five fish.

White bass weigh anywhere from a half a pound to 3 pounds or more. The record is 5-plus. They are excellent table fare. No matter how you like best to fish—with bait, fly rod, spinning tackle, or casting rod—white bass can be caught. Further, they are within easy range of most anglers and are usually most abundant in the large impoundments so popular with bass fishermen and others. Thus white bass are also on tap for the black-bass addict, and almost everybody. For those who have not focused attention on this species, it is a prime contender for high rating in the pan, and it is great sport to catch.

Its close relative, the yellow bass, is by no means as common or abundant. But in lakes where it is present it is usually abundant, as eager as the white bass, and just as good to eat. Your fisheries department can tell you what lakes, if any, in your area contain yellow bass. The white perch averages roughly the same size and is also excellent eating, but its range is restricted to the states of the Atlantic Coast, roughly from the Carolinas northward, where it is often extremely abundant in both fresh and brackish ponds. Anglers within white-perch range substitute it for white or yellow bass. It is one of the abundant species for the pan.

As most anglers are by now aware, the burly saltwater relative of the white bass, the big, powerful striped bass (sometimes called "rockfish" in the East) has been adapted to freshwater and is now found all across the southern half of the nation. Obviously, the striper is a big-time sport fish, but fishermen also thinking about the food aspect should take a close look at this inland version. The fact that it could live in freshwater year-round was discovered accidentally in the East, when some became landlocked. The freshwater striper was so successful that states all across the country began experimenting. Now landlocked or freshwater striped bass are present all the way from the Carolinas to California, and as far north as Nebraska.

In only a few instances are stripers able to spawn successfully in their new homes. So, most of them are stocked annually as fry or fingerlings by the numerous states that are culturing them. There is therefore no reason not to catch out the big fellows. To date, strict bag limits exist almost everywhere. However, most states already have an abundance of stripers in the 5- to 10-pound classes, and year by year records reach higher. It is now not uncommon to catch striped bass in the 20-pound class in a number of states. Some have records of 40 pounds or more, and as high as 60. Most of the stripers are in the large impoundments, and they inspire much interest among sport fishermen. Needless to say, a single fish in the 20- or 30-pound class or a pair or half dozen 10-pounders add up to a tidy bounty. The inland striper should therefore get the attention of all pan-oriented anglers.

It and the white bass are also responsible for another excellent, manmade "meat" fish now swimming numerous impoundments across the lower half of the nation. Fishery

Transplanted far beyond its original range, today white bass are found in lakes almost nationwide. It's a willing, aggressive striker.

biologists a few years ago tried crossing stripers with white bass; the two are closely related. The resultant hybrid has been extremely successful. Not all the states that have stocked stripers have gone for a hybrid program. Those that have find this a perfect fish for stocking. It grows to a maximum of 12 to 18 pounds, but so far as is presently known does not reproduce its own kind. Thus it can be perfectly controlled. Like white bass, these husky hybrids are school fish, as are stripers to some extent. Table quality is the same as for the striper. From the pan fisherman's point of view, the hybrid is an excellent quarry because no matter how many you catch, you are not harming the put-take population. They're intended to be taken, and sporting qualities are dramatic. Your fisheries department, or those of other states you may visit, can tell you where to find these fish.

YELLOW PERCH, WALLEYES, SAUGERS

The family *Percidae*—the perch family—contains three U.S. freshwater species that rate high on the pan angler's list of possibilities. The most wide-ranging and abundant is the smallest, the ubiquitous yellow perch. This pan fish has been dubbed for many years a "kid's fish" because it is so easy to catch and so common. Yellow perch range all across the country, chiefly the northern half, and live in lakes of all sizes, from the Great Lakes to thousands of small ponds. They are so prolific that they sometimes overwhelm a small lake and become stunted because they do not receive enough fishing pressure.

Tens of thousands of U.S. anglers never bother to fish for perch. Yet here is one of the most delicious of eating fish. It has been claimed that after a week of eating trout every meal most people would be unable to face another one but that the white, flaky, sweet meat of the yellow perch can be eaten every day for a month and still leave one ready for tomorrow's table. In a few places there are limits on the perch catch, usually high—twenty-five, fifty. In most places there is no limit, nor is any harm done to the perch population by taking all you want.

Some of the fondest memories of my long fishing career center around yellow perch. I recall fishing along Lake Huron in early spring, in dredged ditches or canals where perch swarmed in thousands. We filled whatever containers we had

The author displays a stringer of yellow perch on Michigan's Lake Huron.

with us to the brim and quit only because we had no place to put more perch. On fall trips to the Upper Peninsula of Michigan after ruffed grouse, we'd get out early and hunt until mid-morning, then go perch fishing in the bays around the vicinity of Les Cheneaux Islands.

Two or three of us in a boat would set a big washtub in the middle of the skiff. Dressed in wool jackets against the crisp fall weather, we'd go at perch fishing as if it were a business. We shared many laughs and wonderful good times, and if the weather was too cold on occasion, there'd be a modest nip to warm the inner man. We would set about locating one big perch school after another and filling that tub. When it was level, we'd quit.

A couple named Rudy and Flo Rolfhs ran the camp where we stayed, near the village of Centerville. In the evening we'd have platters heaped with fried perch Flo had cooked. Yellow perch run anywhere from 5 to 12 inches long, exceptional ones a bit larger. They are thick bodied. Half-pounders are the rule when you hit a school of older fish. Sometimes you get into 1-pounders. At Flo's table if you didn't eat more than a dozen big ones, you were a piker. The remainder of the tubful were packaged and frozen to take home. Wherever found, the yellow perch should be one of the chief interests of the pan fisherman. Granted, they're not much for fight, but they are always good fun and superb eating.

Though not as abundant, the much larger walleye, relative of the yellow perch, and its relative, the somewhat smaller sauger, also fit into the meat-fisherman's plans. Both are top food fish. Both are schooling species, not likely to be harmed by overfishing. Both are subject to limits everywhere, but limits commmonly as high as ten a day. Ten 2-or 3-pound walleyes, with their delectable white meat, make a very worthwhile contribution to the freezer. The walleye over the past few years has been widely transplanted. Once considered a northern variety, today it can be found almost everywhere across the nation.

CHANNEL CATFISH

The tasty channel catfish is another species that should get close attention from those who accept the new philosophy of fishing both for sport and for the pan. The large catfish varieties—yellow and blue—are to some extent game fish for specialists. The smaller and exceedingly common channel cat, a fish of clean waters and abundant over a vast range, is for everybody. This fish needs special emphasis, not because it has no following, but because though thousands of fishermen claim it is their favorite fish, the rest of the angling clan pay it little attention.

In the South, channel cats are caught on trotlines, on lines hung from floating jugs, by bank fishermen and boat fishermen using countless kinds of stink baits and others, from angle worms to cheese. In all of the restaurants across the country that feature catfish, the channel cat, often commercially farmed, is the species. For the meat fisherman, even if his first love is the black bass or the rainbow trout, acquaintance with the channel cat can be most valuable.

SMELT

Last on the list of common freshwater pan fish so abundant they are prime freezer material is the tiny smelt. This silvery little fish was once a saltwater variety that also long ago became landlocked in the northeast, and successfully sustained itself. A good many years ago it was introduced to the western Great Lakes. It has been transplanted to a few other places also, but all its transplants, even to Lake Michigan, were originally as a food fish for some transplanted game fish. However, the smelt thrived in most cases, and became a commercial as well as a quasi-sport fish.

Not everyone gets a chance at smelt because of their modest range of abundance, from New England to the Great Lakes

region. For years, though, they have been gathered eagerly
by ice fishermen in winter and by smelt "dippers" during
their spawning runs. During my days in northern Michigan,
a group of us always went smelt dipping when the runs began
out of Lake Michigan and the Strait of Mackinac.

Unless you've experienced it, you might wonder how haul-

Smelt dippers fill buckets with the little fish during a
spawning run in a stream tributary to Lake Michigan.

ing a fine-meshed dip net of fish out of a creek could be any sport at all, but it was dramatic and wonderfully exciting. The dipping occurred at night, when the streams tributary to the big water would be stiff with moving smelt. Snow was usually still patching the ground. Ice had just gone out. Water temperature was in the mid-40s. Bonfires flickered on the banks, drawing lacy shadows across stands of white birches and evergreens. Lanterns and flashlights flared. Some people dipped commercially. We took a few bucketsful and headed home. Then came the cleaning, interspersed with swigs of hot coffee. A 10-incher was a giant; most were 5 and 6 inches.

You can scale smelt simply by rubbing them together in water. We snipped off the heads and cut off the belly skin with shears. We zipped out the entrails with a toothbrush. When fifty to a hundred had been cleaned, my wife Ellen, and whoever else's wife was present, began frying smelt. We ate them bones and all. If someone was finicky he pulled out the backbone. Fried smelt are among the most delicious of freshwater fish. It was a contest to see how many each person could down. The rest were cleaned and wrapped for freezing.

The fisherman balancing an interest between sport and pan comes to realize that fish are rather short-lived creatures. A white bass four years old, for example is not likely to be alive another year. Fish are swiftly renewed resources, particularly the more prolific varieties. There is no harm looking upon them in monetary terms, in taking them within legal limits for food. But food is the by-product. The average angler all across the nation talks mostly about bass, or trout. Finding new interest in varieties that he has not paid much attention to greatly expands enjoyment, results in a much wider variety of sport, and certainly a catch that is extremely valuable in today's world. Dovetailing fishing for the pan with fishing to which you are addicted chiefly for recreation vastly broadens your horizons, makes you a more expert angler—and pays high dividends in freezer and skillet.

15

Abundant Saltwater Species For The Pan

The world of saltwater is far more varied in species of edible fish than is freshwater. That makes it somewhat more complicated from both the sport and pan points of view. Also, the distinction here in saltwater between what most consider game fish and those of little consequence is more emphatically drawn. For example, there are several dozen small saltwater varieties that seldom wangle their way into the "game" category, but they also aren't labeled, as are many freshwater varieties, "panfish."

An additional number of saltwater species, just as in freshwater, receive little attention as either sport or eating fish. Many are all but unknown to the average marine angler, yet are by no means rare or scarce. To avoid confusion and an overwhelming number of species in this chapter, I have held out the smaller species not generally tagged as "game fish" and grouped them in the following chapter, "Saltwater Panfish for the Pan." Also, to give proper attention to some varieties too often spurned by saltwater fishermen, I have placed them, along with their freshwater counterparts, among "Myriad Unsung Eating Fish," Chapter 17.

In saltwater, because we deal with oceans on both sides of the continent and a Gulf to the south, there are wide gaps in anglers' knowledge of the species that are available. Even though the domain of the freshwater species is vast, the chief game fish are much the same coast to coast and border to border, especially because of so many transplants. Some saltwater species are wide-ranging; some are abundant only along the northeast coast, or the southeast and the eastern Gulf; others are most abundant in the western Gulf. On the Pacific coast, species in general differ quite radically from the Gulf and the Atlantic. There are Pacific varieties abundant along the northern half of our coastline that do not appear at all along the southern half, and vice versa.

These widely separated marine domains make looking at the abundant candidates for the saltwater meat fishermen a bit complicated. Some close relatives along all shores, however, are enough alike so that for our purposes here they can be lumped together. Likewise, just as in freshwater, some of the most popular game species cannot always be considered acceptable quarry.

In an earlier chapter I mentioned the speckled trout, or spotted weakfish, of the southeast Atlantic and the Gulf, and the channel bass, or redfish, of generally the same range of special abundance. In some places they are presently in difficulties. The striped bass has been an overfished species along the Atlantic in some areas. The marlins, swordfish, and sails cannot remotely be thought of as fish for the freezer; nor can the larger tunas. As trophy incidentals, some of them certainly furnish a large amount of valuable food. But no one goes after them, or should, just for that purpose. They aren't abundant enough; additionally, catching them today is an extremely expensive proposition.

SHARKS

Odd as it may strike some readers, one of the most important groups of meat fish to be considered here is the sharks. Of late there has been a great outcry from the saviors-of-everything, most of whom have never been face to face with a shark, or anything larger than park pigeons, to be kind to these creatures. On the other side, the spate of shark movies egged a lot of people on to catch big sharks and sell the teeth, hide, and jaws at high prices. From a less emotional or faddish point of view, the fact is that along our coasts shark meat is seldom used by average anglers, yet many sharks of moderate size are caught by anglers not purposely fishing for them, and a good many large ones are caught by a specialized clan of modern anglers who are mesmerized by the awesome battles that ensue. Shark *meat* is definitely underused.

There are a great many species of sharks, and I do not intend to attempt any separation of them here. But the fact is, most of them are not only edible, but excellent. Many other countries have utilized shark meat—and the Orientals their shark-fin soup—for centuries. I recall fishing from piers in Florida, California, and Texas, when every now and then a shark would be caught. Most of these, caught from pier railings or from bridges across narrow bays, were small to moderate in size. Their usual fate—because they were difficult to release and received no respect, anyway—was to be bopped on the head or killed in some other manner and dumped back into the water. No one even considered *eating* a shark.

A couple of years ago I was on a big party boat out of Port Aransas, Texas, some 40 miles out in the Gulf, on a magazine picture assignment. There were at least fifty fishermen aboard. Every so often someone would hook a shark. Most were 2 or 3 possibly 5 feet in length. Each time, the deckhands, or the skipper making rounds of the rail, would suggest that the angler have the shark iced and that he take it home to eat. Each time, the fisherman would look at him as if he were kidding. No one wanted shark. But the skipper, and some of the old-time deckhands, kept insisting this was the best meat we'd catch that day. No sale.

Fishery biologists handling marine matters for the Texas Parks and Wildlife Department did an extensive survey several years ago, trying to get people to make use of sharks, in an attempt to establish a viable shark fishery along the Texas Gulf. Within the department, a home economist works full time developing recipes for, and publicizing the use of, various saltwater fish and shellfish. The Department oversees the commercial use of marine products, as well as sport fishing; it concocted methods of preparing several kinds of shark, set up booths in various population centers, and got people to taste various morsels of fish, shark and standard commercial species included. The questionnaire tasters rated the quality of the different species, and guesses were made as to which was shark and which wasn't. Interestingly, overall results gave shark meat a high-edibility rating. To date, however, the hoped-for commercial shark fishery along the Texas coast has failed to develop.

That's not to say shark meat is not sold commercially elsewhere. For many years there have been commercial shark fisheries of varying importance along the southern Atlantic, and sharks have been rather highly utilized by commercials along the Pacific. Shark also has often been sold under "assumed" names. Nonetheless, only a very few sport fishermen use shark to any extent.

The party-boat angler, the pier and surf fishermen should keep in mind that shark *is* edible, good tasting, nutritious, and valuable. Sport fishermen annually waste tremendous amounts of it. In some instances, anglers will find themselves able to fish purposely for sharks of moderate size without any specialized tackle, and take home a big bonus of meat. This is true for all our coasts—Atlantic, Gulf, Pacific.

It is the meaty strips along the back that make the prime cuts of shark meat; these can be fried, baked, or broiled. Startling as it may seem, the various rays are also palatable. It's the muscular "wings" that should be processed. Rays are common everywhere, in various sizes and species. Also, in the Pacific, several members of the ray group, called "skates" along that coast, have for years been important commercially.

I recall that when I first fished from a Pacific beach in the late 1930s, one of my first catches was a big, curious-looking critter that someone told me was a guitarfish. Its shape was mildly similar to that instrument. This creature is actually a member of the ray family. I asked a native fisherman on the beach if I should eat it. He thought I must be balmy. The fact is, the flesh of the guitarfish is perfectly edible. The entire group of sharks and rays, if anglers will just put away their prejudices, can furnish many pounds annually for the larder of those who fish saltwater.

KNOW WHAT'S AVAILABLE

One of the big differences in angler approaches to saltwater fishing is that thousands of inlanders make only occasional trips to a seacoast or know very little about what they are likely to catch. They go out on party boats, or fish from piers, or the beach. Often they are unsure about what is edible and what is not. Curiously it is not difficult to find party-boat skippers who in some instances don't know, either. Sometimes a tremendous bonanza of delicious eating is passed up for lack of knowledge.

To illustrate, my wife and I were fishing in the Gulf off Texas once on a big party boat, and she caught a fish that was obviously of the tuna family. I had not seen this species previously; it was a blackfin tuna weighing 22 pounds, and, as it turned out, rather unusual in the western Gulf. We questioned the skipper and deck hands about its general edibility (some of the tuna and mackerel families and their relatives— the jack crevalle, for example—are rather strong and bloody). They had never tried blackfin tuna and were skeptical. I cleaned the fish, removed the leathery hide, and the fatty dark meat along the lateral line (on most such fish, this is strong), and we pan-broiled steaks from the fish. If ever there was a supergourmet flavor, the blackfin had it. We rated it just possibly the best fish we'd ever eaten.

The general rule for all visitors to saltwater and all marine-fishing tyros is that practically all saltwater fish are edible. Some obviously are better than others, but a bonus catch such as that blackfin should always be tried, whether or not you know how it tastes. Otherwise, you lose many a valuable addition to the pan.

TUNA AND MACKEREL

In fact, in the tuna family and closely related families are some abundant species that should be among your pan fishing targets. Some of these are the bonitos. Oddly, few fishermen purposely fish for these handsome fish, which are found in several varieties along both coasts and in the Gulf. Of the tunalike fishes, bonitos are not among the most desirable taste-wise; they are palatable, although they're inclined to be a bit strong. They have over many years had some commercial importance, but I recall that years ago it was not legal, in California at least, for commercial processors to label bonito "tuna."

Of the large group of tunalike and mackerellike fishes, possibly the various mackerels should stand highest on the pan fisherman's list. Although mackerels are found along all our coasts, the species differ widely from place to place. The Atlantic mackerel, the fish of the wooden casks full of salted fillets, traditionally famed as broiled mackerel in eastern cities such as Boston, is one of the most abundant. Farther south, and throughout the Gulf, schools of somewhat larger Spanish mackerel, superb eating fish, abound. And on the Pacific coast their relatives, especially the small Pacific mackerel, are present.

I suppose one either loves to eat mackerel or doesn't. The meat is dark and has a distinctive flavor. Especially when broiled, fresh mackerel is delicious. Salted, or smoked, it is just as good. Because mackerels are tremendously abundant school fish, pan fishermen should make a point of going after them. They are also great sporting species.

A word is due here about the king mackerel, or, as sportsmen in Florida and Texas invariably call it, the kingfish. This

The author cooks Atlantic mackerel fillets over a campfire, using a grill made of green willow sticks.

These Spanish mackerel were caught on flies in Sarasota Bay, Florida.

large member of the mackerel family, weighing anywhere from 5 to 40 or more pounds, is also a species consorting in large schools. It is one of the most dynamic and popular of saltwater game fish. But a curious situation occurs especially along the Texas coast in regard to eating it.

I remember that when I used to spend six months a year—fall through spring—in Florida, the kingfish was a most important commercial food fish, as well as sport fish. When we settled in Texas I found the kings there, but nobody took them commercially. You couldn't buy kingfish steak in any market, and even the people who loved to catch them wouldn't eat them. It was, and still is, common along the Texas coast to see boats come in with large catches of kings, and hear the fishermen who've had their sport tell the skipper to give the fish to some charitable institution.

The fact is, kingfish steaks, broiled or pan-broiled, are delicious. The meat for several inches behind the head is somewhat fibrous, so I steak the ones I catch by making inch-thick cross-body slices beginning behind the head about one-third of the way back into the forward low portion of the dorsal fin. Because the kingfish is generally at least seasonally abundant, and such excellent eating when cut up and cooked properly, any freezer-bonus angler should make a point of gathering a few. Fish of this size furnish a lot of food. We don't like to freeze kingfish steaks for any long period, but for a few weeks they are fine.

I mentioned before that the meat fisherman's views of saltwater are quite different from fresh, because of the expanses of oceans, and the variety of species. There are several fish that need coverage here that may not be as abundant as the mackerels are, but in a relative and usually seasonal way they should be prime targets for the pan. Two of these are Pacific species, the albacore, and the Pacific yellowtail, the latter a close relative of the Atlantic amberjack.

Both species are at the top of the list of popular Pacific game fish. Nevertheless, there are hundreds of visitors and natives who've never fished for them. Both are excellent table fare. Both are seasonal, and run in large schools. Party boats depend heavily on them. A fisherman who is aware of these species, and who makes a long-range plan to book himself to go out after them, not only will enjoy great sport, but may well bring in the prizes of the year so far as the freezer is concerned. Both fish average 5 to 25 pounds. The albacore is what you may well be eating when you open a can of tuna.

COBIA

Another husky game fish prime for the pan, of relative abundance, but invariably scattered in small pods of individuals over much of its range, is the cobia, or crab eater, sometimes called ling, or lemonfish. This big, brownish and cream-colored distant relative of the mackerel clan weighs anywhere from 5 to 50 or 60 pounds or more. It ranges from summers in Chesapeake Bay clear around and through the Gulf, but is most abundant along the upper Gulf and along the Texas coast.

Possibly because cobia are scattered, and require some specialized hunting down, they are not broadly popular. They are a kind of specialist's fish—and it is worthwhile becoming a cobia specialist. What few saltwater anglers realize is that the cobia is an extremely excellent table fish. They are not difficult to catch, once you locate them, and are, in fact, rather unwary and dumb. Some Gulf Coast anglers have discovered that gangs of cobia often hang around oil rigs.

Ever since we've lived in Texas I've tried to catch one or two each time I fished the Gulf. To illustrate the sort of bonus you get, I once caught a cobia that weighed 52 pounds, and I steaked it. The head is rather large, and the skin like leather, so you have to skin it. That big fellow was too big to steak whole, crosswise. So, after skinning it, I made slits lengthwise on either side of the backbone, then cut steaks from each side. Cobia steaks, even taken from fish of 10 or so pounds and cut whole across the fish, contain a minimum of bones. The meat is a beautifully, flaky translucent white when broiled—one of the best of the sea's offerings. So few anglers realize this that concentrating on cobia puts you in a very select meat fisherman's class.

DOLPHINS

One other gamester that needs attention here as a pan candidate is one few marine fishermen might guess: the dolphin. This beautifully colored game fish is found in southern Pacific Coast waters, in the Gulf, and off the eastern U.S. coast chiefly along the Gulf stream. For the most part, it is considered a trophy fish for mounting. Anglers have a great penchant for bull, or male, dolphin with their steep forehead and brilliant colors. The dolphin has never been handled commercially to any extent in this country. Nor do sport anglers very often eat it.

The first time I ate dolphin was in Key West, Florida, where Cuban commercial fishermen often brought them in on their boats. It was one of those fishermen, in fact, who explained to me that the meat of the dolphin, which is quite red, is delicious. When Hawaii became one of the states, tourists from the mainland began flocking there, and came home singing the praises of a Hawaiian seafood specialty called *mahi-mahi*, which is none other than dolphin. The species is an important commercial fish there.

I suggest that dolphin be considered by U.S. meat fishermen because anglers in the Gulf or the southeastern Atlantic occasionally run into large dolphin schools. These as a rule are fish in the 5-pound class, from 3 to 10 pounds at most. They love to hang around any floating debris out in open water, from a single plank to drifting batches of weed. A friend of mine once got into a school and with ordinary freshwater bass tackle he and a companion "jumped" and released well over 100 fish. To be sure, dolphin schools are too scattered and sporadic to make regular forays after them logical. But because the school-size fish are almost entirely unused, they should be kept in mind by the pan angler as prime candidates for his purposes.

WEAKFISH, CHANNEL BASS, CROAKER

There are certainly locations along the Atlantic and the Gulf, as I've mentioned, where weakfish (of all varieties—common,

Wading the flats for redfish is a popular sport in shallow Texas bays.

spotted, sand) and channel bass (redfish) can legitimately be considered species for packing into the freezer. Off the Louisiana coast, for example, around the Chandeleur Islands, at times trout (weakfish) and reds simply swarm. There is no harm whatsoever in keeping enough of these fish in such places, or up along the Carolinas and northward, to make a substantial contribution to your freezer. They are among the most delicious and abundant of inshore marina fishes.

Related to these fish is the golden or Atlantic croaker, a smaller version of the channel bass and just as tasty. Two-pounders are about maximum. Croakers are usually overwhelmingly abundant. Along Texas there is annually a brief period when hundreds of fisherman catch them by the thousands. They are caught in similar fashion along the Atlantic. Other croakers—spotfin, yellowfin, corbina—are popular and abundant along the Pacific in the surf, and should get the focus of any pan fisherman's plans.

SHEEPSHEAD

Certain saltwater species have their select clan of admirers but get scant attention from the majority. If you intend to balance your fishing interest between sport and eating, it is worthwhile to pay close attention to some of these. A classic example is the sheepshead, the vertically striped, deep-bodied common inshore denizen of southern Atlantic coastal waters and throughout the Gulf. Hardly ever does one see sheepshead on a restaurant menu, and almost never in markets. When they are found in markets, they are one of the cheapest varieties offered. This is because the majority of saltwater anglers simply do not believe this tough-scaled, buck-toothed, stiff-boned species is worth eating.

The truth is, the sheepshead is a delicious fish. It is common, invariably abundant where present, ridiculously willing.

Often neglected by anglers, the sheepshead is a delicious
fish. It is also abundant and easily caught.

We scale, gut, and remove the gills from sheepsheads of 2 or
3 pounds, freeze them whole, and broil them whole. The skin
peels off easily with a fork, and the big, hard bones stay in
place while you scoop out the excellent white meat. A catch
of sheepsheads is a gold mine of good eating. From roughly
Cape Cod to the Carolinas the tautog, blackfish, or oysterfish,
is a somewhat similar proposition. Beloved by a small clan of
enthusiastists, it is scorned by many, yet is abundant, un-
harmed by hard fishing, and fine eating.

COD, POLLOCK, FLATFISHES

All of the marine species so far dealt with are only a part of the great bounty saltwater holds ready for the angler as much interested in his food budget as in sport. Jot down a note, if you live in the Northeast, or will fish there, that there are times when both cod and pollock, the most important commercial species here since colonial days, can be taken in fairly shallow water by average anglers, and even when they're deep the many party boats along this coast make gathering a catch of them a paying proposition.

There are also the abundant flatfishes—flounders, soles, sand dabs, and others—ranging along both coasts and throughout the Gulf. You can go down to the Texas coast during certain periods and see at dusk, and afterward, scores of gasoline lanterns and other lights winking along the bay shores. Here eager "giggers" wade the shallow, sandy flats and watch for flounders lying flat and immobile. The gig stabs downward, and up comes a 2-, 3-, or 4-pounder. If you want to think in terms of dollars, a 3-pounder is worth about $7.50 on today's market. Scores of giggers take home six to a dozen or more flounders for an evening's recreation. Numerous flatfish species can be had from inshore and shallow surfside waters, caught on bait, or even with lures. These are among the best of the abundant species for the pan.

BLACK DRUM

Some species of saltwater get short shrift from both sport and meat fishermen, for no logical reason. A classic example is the black drum. This large member of the croaker family is closely related to the channel bass but does not have its status. Admittedly, it is a sluggish, though dogged, fighter. The flesh, especially of large specimens from 15 to 40 or more

A planked flounder being cooked on the beach. All the wood, including the plank, was found nearby.

pounds, is inclined to be tough and, though palatable enough, is by no means in the class with the redfish.

This is another fish seldom handled commercially to any great extent. Like the sheepshead, when they are in a market, they're the cheap fish of the day. However, black drum aren't all large oldies. *Young* black drum, instead of being gray to gray-black overall, have quite distinct vertical stripes of light and dark. In some places these are called "butterfly drum." Typical specimens weigh 1, 2, or 3 pounds. We have eaten lots of them, and in our opinion, they are, like the sheepshead, fine fish for the pan. Often they gang up over shell beds and can be caught by the dozens on almost any kind of bait. Such a find is indeed a bonanza.

RED SNAPPERS

For those who live near or vacation along any of the Gulf Coast, or along the middle Atlantic, periodic trips after red snapper should be planned with a tilt toward stocking up on food fish. The red snapper has long been an extremely important commercial species. It is a deepwater fish, usually found some miles offshore over hard bottoms of banks and reefs, down anywhere from 100 to several hundred feet. Most of the snapper party boats are based along the upper Florida Gulf Coast and on across to several Texas coast ports, from Galveston to Port Isabel. It is necessary, unless you have a seagoing craft of your own, to book on one of these party boats that specialize in red-snapper fishing.

One of the most delicious of all saltwater commercial species, it averages 2 to 5 or 6 pounds on many banks. Larger fish, of 8 to 15 pounds, are also common, and those of 30 and up are by no means rare. Most small snappers are broiled. Big ones make marvelous, thick fillets. Some large ones are cut up into boneless strips or "fingers" that are fried. It is routine, when you go out for a day of snapper fishing, to bring in a dozen to twenty or more fish. The fishing's great fun, and the catch often more than pays in value for the trip.

My wife and I once went about 40 miles out into the Gulf on the big Scat Cat, an 85-foot, 22-knot snapper boat berthed at Port Aransas, Texas. The skipper anchored over deep banks in about 200 feet of water. On this boat, and some others, stiff rods equipped with electric reels are furnished to the clients, the rod fixed to the steel rail by a swiveling device. In free spool the baited hook is let down to bottom. When a fish grabs the bait, you set the hook and push the button which turns on a tiny electric motor. It does the reeling. To hand-crank a big, tough snapper up from bottom would be a long-term proposition.

We each came in with ten snappers, some caught two at a time on double-hook rigs. Our catch ran from 3 to 10 pounds each. Scaled, gutted, and gilled, we had some 70 pounds of fish for the freezer. The population of these abundant commercial fish is not harmed by the scattering of party boats. I'm sure most anglers along saltwater are aware of the snapper trips available, but it is amazing how few fishermen have actually tried this fishing. Granted, it's not the same kind of sport as catching a sailfish. But it's very enjoyable, and with numerous clients all excited and hauling up snappers, an interesting experience. You might say, too, that with a good catch it's often costfree.

ROCKFISH

Along the Pacific a somewhat similar situation exists with the numerous varieties of rough-looking rockfish native to the coast, and almost always found in deep water. They range from British Columbia to Mexico, in one species or another. In numerous locations several kinds are taken during one fishing session. There are the black, blue, orange, vermilion, rosy, greenspotted, starry, speckled, whitebelly, yellowtail, and olive rockfish, the chilipepper, the bocaccio, and several other varieties. All are caught on bait, on bottom. Numerous party boats take people after rockfish. All the species are excellent eating. They are rough-scaled, sharp-spined creatures, but top-notch members of the abundant list for the pan. Often scorned by the more purist sport-fishing clan, they are a delight for the man after meat.

The overwhelming variety of species in saltwater can at

times be confusing as to which are the "abundant" ones for the pan and which are not. Sometimes it all depends on circumstance. I think the angler should first be aware of what is available. Surprisingly, many are not, even those who habitually fish saltwater. They get used to one kind of fishing and don't bother learning about or trying new categories. Even the Pacific Coast salmon rate as pan species on occasion.

For example, one time my family and I were traveling in a trailer up the West Coast. We stopped at Monterey, and I booked a trip out into the ocean on a party boat, after chinook salmon. That was some years ago, and the cost was, by today's standards, extremely low, around $10, as I recall. There was a three-fish limit in force, and, of course, a California license was needed; it also was cheap. I actually went on the trip to shoot photos for a magazine story. After I'd shot a good many photos, I fished with the clients, and caught my three salmon. Each weighed between 15 and 20 pounds.

I shared my catch with a neighbor in the park where we had put up, and estimated that the salmon we packed away to eat along the road north was worth far more than my trip cost. We ate salmon steaks, baked salmon, salmon patties, and salmon salad all the next week. Had we been where we could have processed the big fish for a freezer, this would have been a supply for several months of once-a-week salmon meals. Certainly the average angler wouldn't think of salmon as a prime, day-to-day pan candidate. But if you are aware that this fishing is available—particularly if you are an inlander who visits the coasts only occasionally—you can grab opportunities when they are present.

16

Saltwater Panfish for the Pan

As everyone knows, the term "panfish," as one word, has long applied to the small, or pan-size, species of fish, invariably of freshwater, that are abundant, also sometimes dubbed "kids' fish," and thought of by many sport fishermen as rather inconsequential. It has been said that the only respectors of panfish are people, by the millions, who love to catch them and eat them.

At any rate, "panfish," and "fishing for the pan" are two different concepts. You may be fishing for the pan when after big fish, but a panfish is one that, in the early-day terminology where it was born, will fit, whole, in a skillet, or is of a size that allows the average skillet to hold several. The bluegill, the yellow perch, the crappie of freshwater are classic examples of what "panfish" always has meant. Perhaps I'm fond of the term because way back in 1947 the first of some twenty books I've written to date was titled *Panfish*. It dealt with the so-called less consequential, small freshwater fishes, and was perhaps the first book to give these species just due as authentic game fish as well as superb table fare.

Curiously, the term panfish has seldom if ever been applied to saltwater. Further, perhaps because so many saltwater fish

237

are large and powerful and therefore attract attention, the small saltwater species are somewhat neglected. To be sure, there is a quite numerous scattering of coastal fishermen who have fun catching what might be called the saltwater panfish. Most marine anglers, however, aren't interested. In fact, the small, less consequential saltwater species are unquestionably the most overlooked resource of sport and good eating in the world of recreational angling.

The saltwater fisherman who fishes for the pan, therefore, should obviously not neglect the panfish. For the average angler there is probably more good eating easily accessible at virtually no cost among the numerous small species than among all of the large ones combined. It would be impossible to list and describe all of them here. But if you are aware of the presence of at least a few, their abundance, and the fact that in almost all instances there are no limits on them, it's not very difficult to track down others. Awareness is the key.

Most of them are easily caught with bait. Most inhabit bays and channels or the surf, thus can be reached from shore or by wading with a small skiff. Many swarm around piers and bridges. But oddly, lots of these get no attention at all because the fishermen who happen to catch them shake them off and don't realize they're ignoring excellent, and valuable, food.

Another great advantage of making a whole new fishing habit out of the saltwater panfish is that you seldom have much competition. It's no shoulder-to-shoulder proposition. And, they are so common—one or more anywhere you fish— and so abundant, that you can really load up without any twinges of conscience. Most of these smaller species receive neither heavy commercial nor sport-fishing pressure. Putting away a catch of thirty or fifty periodically does no harm, and is simply a matter of using a resource of the sea that receives miniscule recognition. My main point in reviewing all these panfish is that most anglers, even widely experienced ones, are barely aware of their existence. Further, if you make a point of fishing for these smaller species, you can match your tackle to their fighting abilities, actually have just as much fun as with larger fish—far cheaper, sometimes at no cost at all—and more of it, more sustained. Make no mistake, all saltwater fish are stronger fighters than their freshwater cousins, even the pan-size ones.

SPADEFISH

I remember standing with my two boys, when they were kids, on a pier jutting into the Gulf of Mexico. The rails were lined with people trying with large hooks and stout tackle to catch big fish. Below us, gyrating round and round several pilings, I could see closely packed schools of small fish with thick but deep, compressed bodies, almost round in general broadside outline. I couldn't tell what they were because of the broken water surface.

The shape of the fish suggested to me that they must have very small mouths. I peeled a shrimp tail, broke the meat into tiny bits, tossed it in, and let it filter down into a school. They swarmed into it, gobbling the tiny pieces. I then rigged a limber spinning rod with light line, a tiny hook, and one small split shot, the size I'd use for bait fishing for bluegills in freshwater. I let it down and instantly had a fish. To my astonishment, it fought unbelievably. When at last I flopped it up onto the pier, I recognized it as a spadefish. I'd guess it weighed half a pound. I got the two boys rigged up and we caught about a half bushel of the little fish. The largest, a prodigious fighter, might have weighed a pound.

Onlookers smiled indulgently. I smiled back, indulgently. I knew something they didn't. Spadefish are absolutely delectable eating fish. Although they are common along the lower Atlantic and all of the Gulf Coast, and move in large schools, the smaller ones are seldom caught because almost nobody offers them a bait they can handle, or even cares about them, or in fact knows they're there. Spadefish are gray with striking vertical black bands; one band runs upward across the eye. They are commonly called "anglefish" and confused with the anglefishes, to which they are not closely related. Occasionally spadefish grow large, up to 15 or more pounds. One that size is an awesome battler. Most usually, however, one catches fish of the size we were catching, and on up to perhaps 2 pounds. This is an excellent example of a saltwater panfish that gets almost no takers, yet is truly in the gourmet class.

SURFPERCH, SEAPERCH

Along the entire length of the Pacific coast the most important group of panfish is that of the so-called perches. They are not perch at all, but belong to a family of their own. Some are called surfperch because they're found there most often. Others are called seaperch, and inhabit deeper water, sometimes around rocks. There are fifteen or twenty species of them within our waters. Oddly, all bear their young alive. All are reminiscent in shape of the freshwater sunfishes. On the average they measure from 8 to 15 inches long. All are delicious table fish. Some are important commercially. They're abundant, gather in large groups, and are easy to catch on various baits.

Examples to keep in mind and track down are the rubberlip perch, the barred, walleye, redtail, and calico surfperches, the striped, white, rainbow, and pink seaperches, the pile perch, black perch, and kelp perch. One or more can be found almost anywhere along the West Coast. Actually, they're doughty little gamesters, astonishingly sporty, as are most of the saltwater panfish. Getting a fix on these abundant perches is a sure key to a freezer full of quality eating, and the relaxed fun aspects of the fishing makes the taste all the better.

GRUNTS

Some of the most enjoyable fishing and best eating I can recall from all my years of angling occurred one winter in Florida when I decided to spend some time learning about the grunts. Thousands of people who've fished coastal Florida don't know what a "grunt" is. There are numerous species, averaging a half pound to 2 pounds. They're most abundant along the lower Atlantic and Florida coasts and across the Gulf.

I caught scores of them, under bridges, around the mangroves, near pilings, over shallow reefs, and in the bays. Invariably they were consorting in small groups. All were eager to seize bait. Grunts make small sounds, which gives them their name. Some varieties have a habit of rushing up to one another, opening their mouths, the interior of which in some is gaudy crimson, and "kissing." Just what this is supposed to mean, no one is certain.

Among the common species are the yellow or French grunt, the blue-striped, white, and margate grunt. The yellow-and-silver porkfish found along the Florida Keys is a grunt, and so is the common pigfish of the Atlantic and Gulf coasts. In the Pacific, the sargo, or "china croaker," abundant along the California coast, is one of the grunts. All of them are prime saltwater panfish.

PORGIES, CUNNERS

Along the northern half of our Atlantic coast, a species that perfectly fits this category is the locally much loved porgy. There are several varieties, most running from half a pound to a couple of pounds. Their finest attribute, perhaps, is their swarming abundance, abetted by their willingness and their excellent table qualities. Scores of sport fishermen disdain the lowly porgies, but for those who think in terms of fish in the pan, in quantity, they are hard to ignore. In shape, the porgies are deep and compressed, with a high, humped back just behind the head. They are, in fact, shaped much like the sheepshead, to which they are related.

Another northern panfish of saltwater that is at times despised by anglers after other species is the cunner. Usually it is small, half a pound, a pound, 2 at most. It can be an exasperating bait stealer if you're after other fish. The tautog, or blackfish, mentioned in the preceding chapter, often lives in the same habitat favored by the cunner. So tautog fishermen have to put up with what they call the less desirable cunner, and aren't fond of it. Nevertheless, it is extremely abundant, a good eating fish, and it is a standby of party-boat skippers and shoreside anglers who are eager to catch just anything. The pan fisherman eager to put fish into his freezer can have a lot of fun fishing for it.

WHITINGS, SNAPPERS

The species I suggest in this chapter, I want to emphasize, are simply samples of the countless small fish found in surf, bays, channels, and the vast areas of inshore, protected saltwater. The whitings, of which there are northern and southern varieties, are good examples. They are members of the croaker family, good table fare, willing biters, and commonly found along sandy shores and in the surf. A big specimen may be 18 inches long. The average is a foot.

Among the snappers there are several common and abundant small varieties, and many more found occasionally. The majority are fish of the southern half of the Atlantic coast and throughout the Gulf. All are superb eating fish. Some grow fairly large, to 5 pounds or so, but the average is much less. I've caught mangrove snappers, for example, in southern saltwater that were all pan size. The schoolmaster and lane snapper are other examples of abundant southern panfish from this family. One of the most handsome and abundant in southern waters is the yellowtail snapper often found in large groups along Florida and the Keys. Its deeply forked canary-yellow tail and the yellow, blue, and sometimes pinkish stripes along its body make it the dandy of the group.

FILEFISH, MOONFISH, LOOKDOWN

It is true that the greatest number of marine panfish are southern species, from the mid-Atlantic southward, along the entire Gulf coast and the California coast. When casually fishing any of these waters, the angler who is quick to try almost anything will turn up many surprises. During my first winters in Florida, years back, I fished a lot from the causeway running from Sarasota out across the bay to the several keys there. A common, odd-looking fish often seen around causeway pilings was the filefish. Most were about as big as my palm. They are extremely thin-bodied, compressed, but deep, with extremely small mouths. I caught them with small baits and hooks, and couldn't resist trying their eating qualities. The skin is rough enough to scratch matches on, but when I skinned them, I discovered pearly white meat. They were excellent.

Here was a case—and it happens regularly—of a small, peculiar-appearing saltwater fish that receives no attention because it simply doesn't look good to eat. But what does "good to eat" look like? You won't know if you don't try. Lots of small saltwater species would hardly grab an angler and cause him to think, "That looks delicious!" Some that come to mind are curiosities that make one wonder if they wouldn't serve best as oddities in an aquarium. Yet in truth they are fine little sport and eating fish that nobody even tries purposely to catch.

Two of these I immediately think of are the moonfish and

the lookdown. They're found along the Atlantic and into the Gulf, with largest populations the farther south one goes. Both belong to the jack family, both are thin, extremely deep bodied, with steep foreheads, that of the moonfish strikingly concave. The lookdown has long filaments streaming from the dorsal and anal fins. Both stand on their heads or tilt downward much of the time. The lookdown is exquisitely hued with a pearly iridescence tinged with greenish overtones; colors and brilliance change with flashing reflections as you turn a fresh-caught specimen.

The lookdown especially is a wonderful little panfish. It usually weighs less than a pound, rarely may go up to a couple of pounds. It consorts in schools, hangs out under and around bridges and pilings, usually over sandy bottoms. It readily takes small baits of shrimp or bits of fish, puts up a startling protest, and is a simply grand little fish for the pan.

LEATHERJACKETS

Some years ago when I was spending much time along all three of our coasts, I was always eager to try anything I caught, and especially to find out what it was I had caught. One day, fishing from a causeway for Spanish mackerel, I brought up several small fish, each about a foot long. They were mildly similar in shape to the Spanish mackerel, but distinctly different. Other anglers intent on mackerel were catching them, too. They pitched them back and told me these were "young mackerel." Obviously, that was not true, but I kept both my counsel and my catch.

I remember the incident in great detail for two reasons. First, I took a number of the fish back to the travel trailer in which I was living (in fact, I had had poor luck with the mackerel) and I spent a long time trying to identify them. I was rather new to saltwater then and I was still unacquainted with many of the smaller fish. These turned out to be the leatherjacket, a mackerel-shape member of the jack family. The second move I made was to get out the skillet. The fish were so good it was downright sinful. Just because they were small, and thus presumably inconsequential, the mackerel fishermen had been throwing away better eating than they were determined to catch!

BLUE RUNNERS

Then there are the instances of unwarranted prejudice. The classic one of all saltwater prejudices, I think, concerns the blue runner. This is a common, abundant, schooling member of the jack family. It is more greenish and silvery than blue, ranges most of our Atlantic and Gulf coasts, averages a pound, goes fairly commonly to 2, rarely to 5 or 6. It is an absolutely fantastic fighter. But because it looks mildly similar to the jack crevalle or yellow jack, a common fish of the same range that is inclined to be bloody and strong and thus is seldom eaten, the blue runner, or blue jack, is tarred with the same brush.

In my early days in Florida I caught scads of them, and was told always that they were not fit to eat. I watched boat skippers throw them overside by the bushel. When we moved to Texas I listened to coastal residents without fail telling me blue runners were inedible. Even the most knowledgeable of party-boat and charter skippers commonly agreed. But all this time I knew better. For in Florida I had decided it was foolish to listen to others when I could as well settle the question via the broiler. My wife broiled a couple of Spanish mackerel I'd caught, and with them a couple of blue runners caught incidentally. We love broiled mackerel. The blue runners, however, their flesh much paler and bland, put the mackerel to shame.

It amuses me to recall that the last blue-runner session I

had was on a boat working the tide rips off a jetty on the Texas coast. We really got into them. I wound up with fifty-two. Because I was keeping them, the skipper thought I was, for sure, an uninformed inlander, and probably a snowbird Yankee, to boot. I just smiled and later carefully cleaned every one for our freezer.

The species I've covered here are the cream of the lot, but there are many more. You have to find out what is available to you before you can concentrate on catching them. Make it a point to seek out new species and try them. The saltwater panfish are undoubtedly the most numerous and varied of all U.S. fish species. You won't read much about them in the sports pages of coastal newspapers. You won't see many anglers concentrating on them. Among these small gamesters, however, is the greatest bonanza for the pan that any angler can discover.

17

The Myriad Unsung Eating Fish

"There is no accounting for tastes." Where the palate is concerned that may not be true. Perhaps there's a very basic reason why certain tasters like something and certain others don't. Back in the early days of this country (and many another) staple foods were invariably items that were abundant. If something edible was abundant, it was sure to be less expensive than something in short supply.

Taking this thought one step further, a food item of abundance in any locality was likely to be easily available, and because it was cheap it was used not only by the poorer members of society but also the average citizen. Gourmets started at the top of the taste scale and moved downward to a point where their trained palates yelled "Stop!" Ordinary folks started at the bottom, discarded the thoroughly unpalatable, but never yelled "Stop!" They just ate what was abundant and cheap, and, delightfully, they discovered many fine food items that kept body and soul going. A few of these, almost comically, eventually *became* faddish gourmet items. The world of fishing is laden with examples.

When I was a small boy, an immigrant Jewish fish peddler came through our small-farm community a couple of times a summer, driving a wheezing Model T of pre-1920s vintage. He had a little tin squeeze-bulb horn in this topless, rickety vehicle with its big wooden fish box on back. We could hear the racket of the vehicle as it chugged and uncertainly snake-tracked along our dusty one-track road. But he *beep-beeped* his tin horn anyway, and we all knew as we ran to see the car (we always ran out to see *any* car go by, they were so rare) that it was Sammy the fish peddler. He bought his fish along the Lake Huron shore in lower Michigan and made rounds of the countryside. He obtained ice as he needed it from ice-storage places in small villages where it had been put the previous winter, cut from local lakes, and covered in an ice shed with thick sawdust.

If we had been any poorer when I was a kid, we would, in today's world, have had at least six federal government agencies filling out questionnaires on us, sending people to study us, redesigning our diets and our lives, and helping to haul us into the century well regimented. But we didn't know what terrible shape we were in. We had an abundance of delicious food, which we took from the soil by dint of pure old-fashioned sweat. When Sammy came by, however, we scraped up twenty or thirty cents and eagerly bought some lake herring, which my maternal Irish grandmother always called "heron," and whitefish, which was a cornhill fertilizer from Indian days. Seven cents a pound for whitefish, a nickel for herring.

CISCOES

The herring weren't herring at all. They were so named because to settlers in the Great Lakes region long ago they had resembled the saltwater herring many of their ancestors had known. They were actually ciscoes, smaller relatives of the Great Lakes whitefishes. Later, of course, Great Lakes whitefish became a gourmet delicacy throughout the region and over much of the East, but "lake herring," except locally, remained cheap, common fish, and the last I knew whatever were caught were mostly made into fertilizer. Even in modern times commercial fishermen were receiving maybe five cents a pound for them.

The whole point of this tale is that smoked Great Lakes ciscoes, a popular local item for years around the lakes, are simply delicious. My Irish grandmother knew how to slip the bones out of the fresh ones and cook double fillets of "heron" that were marvelous. Years ago, small eateries along the southern Lake Erie shore served fish sandwiches made from a bun containing a cisco (herring) fillet. Much later, maybe thirty years ago, I learned to catch ciscoes with dry flies in spring along the northern Lake Michigan shore when enormous mayfly hatches brought these deep-water denizens into shallows to gorge on this bonanza of nature. Dynamic in sporting qualities, they tasted just as good. But modern anglers know almost nothing about them and how delicious they are. Yet here is one of the myriad unsung eating fish that can be, within its range, a tremendous find for the meat fisherman.

WHITEFISH

From here let's go west clear to the Rockies. A majority of our famed trout streams are in the West, and in many of these streams also dwells the Rocky Mountain whitefish. It is a close relative of the ciscoes and Great Lakes whitefish of my boyhood. Probably 90 percent of the fishermen who flail the western trout streams take the purist view that the mountain whitefish is a "trash fish."

Oregon, Washington, Idaho, Montana, Wyoming, Utah, and Colorado all have abundant mountain whitefish in certain of their streams. They are troutlike in general outline, but with prominent scales, and the tough, tubelike mouth is very small, designed for grubbing aquatic nymphs from gravel and rocks. I've watched sophisticated trouters battle a 2-pound whitefish, which is a big one, faces wreathed in delight—until they saw what it was. It fought as well as a trout, even though it didn't leap. But it was considered undesirable. Once a ranger in Yellowstone Park told me with great satisfaction that there was not a trash fish in the famed Madison River. He was referring to whitefish, which I happened to know abound in the lower few miles of the river within the Park. I've caught and eaten dozens of them.

Mountain whitefish, studies have shown, sustain themselves far better than trout, but they are far underutilized. Consequently, limits are usually high, and there is no harm whatsoever in taking limits. A select clan of locals in the Rockies fishes for whitefish in winter, usually using long cane poles and bait. Most smoke them. They are a delicacy prepared this way.

We eat them fresh, slipping a slender fillet knife under the ribs on either side, finally pulling out backbone and ribs, splitting each fish clear to the tail. With fins cut out, this leaves a big double boneless fillet, exactly the way my grandmother prepared the ciscoes. I have never frozen any and don't know how well they would freeze. But, either fresh or smoked, Rocky Mountain whitefish are a wonderful bonus. Often when we have gone to the mountains to fish, I try to pick a stream that contains whitefish as well as trout. It's a wise scheme for the meat fisherman. You can fish for both, add to your eating take, or, if you wish, you can release the trout and still keep the whitefish.

One of the reasons anglers pass up so many of the unsung species (and many others, too) is that we are all such creatures of habit. One is a trout fisherman, another a bass fisherman. One concentrates on walleyes, another on outsize catfish. It would pay any fisherman to go down the list of fish species native or transplanted to his bailiwick or to a state he visits for fishing, and to make sure he knows *all* the kinds that are available. You don't have to give up your precious trout. But you might find something in the same area, such as the white-fish just mentioned, that will add variety and interest to a trip, and maybe once in a while even *save* a trip from becoming a debacle while producing a return in great sport and good eating.

GOLDEYE

I got mixed up with a trout-fishing disaster one summer in Montana and had to start home practically empty-handed. We camped overnight at Fort Benton, on the Missouri River. I had heard that the goldeye, a small, sprightly, distant relative of the shads, was abundant here and on into Manitoba and Saskatchewan, as well as erratically elsewhere (in the Missouri River system). I decided to give it a try.

The goldeye averages about a pound maximum. For many years, it was smoked in commercial quantities by a company in Winnipeg and served as a gourmet delicacy in the fine dining cars of the Canadian National Railway. My boys and I caught goldeyes by the score, on flies, on small spoons and spinners. They are great leapers and most interesting as sport fish. They saved the day for enjoyment, that trip. Since then I've caught them on several other occasions. We've tried them fresh, and I can't claim they are anything special, but smoked they are superb. Here is a species that quite literally gets no attention at all from sportsmen as a catching or eating fish, yet any angler who comes within its range might put up a large quantity of smoked goldeye without a tremor of conscience.

Smoking does surprising things to many otherwise so-so species. In some areas—North, South, Midsouth—various kinds of suckers are considered by their small groups of fans true delicacies when smoked. There are many sucker species. The large ones such as the redhorse, and the big white sucker, are avidly fished for, especially during their spawning runs in spring, by enthusiasts here and there.

Friends of mine in northern Michigan used to smoke quantities of big suckers taken from the clear, cold trout streams in early spring. They'd score the flesh deeply on both sides before smoking. The scoring and smoking softened the bundles of bones so they were not troublesome. The result was delicious.

SUCKERS, CARP

One spring I was producing a portion of a TV film on the Current River in Missouri when the sucker run was on. Natives made a regular festival out of gigging suckers from a floating skiff or canoe at night. This local sport was followed by a huge fish fry on shore. Not all suckers are tasty, to be sure—those from muddy waters often are not very palatable—but suckers from clear water make good eating, and some fans even can them. Canned, they taste much like salmon.

There are quite a few states where spearing, or gigging, for suckers, carp, or buffalo (the so-called "rough fish") is legal. Many followers of this sport enjoy it, and eat their catch, smoked, fresh, or canned. The buffalo is taken commercially in some places as a food fish and is quite good. Carp have long been caught commercially. I recall that carp farms were launched a few years ago in the Midwest, and the fish, which are predominantly vegetarian in diet, fattened on corn. Bow-and-arrow carp and buffalo fishing is a popular spring sport in many areas during the spawning runs of these species. I certainly wouldn't claim that a buffalo is as tasty as a brook trout, but all of these rough fish are abundant, and with some special attention in the pan, extremely palatable. There are millions of pounds of food represented among these species that is barely nibbled around the edges.

Just why all of the rough-fish species should be so looked down upon in general as eating fish is puzzling. A carp caught in clean water is probably one of the most amazing fighters found in freshwater, both for strength and tenacity. Well cleaned, and thoughtfully prepared, it can be delicious. On my bookshelf is a compact little cookbook, published by the South Dakota fish and game department, titled *Cooking the Sportsman's Harvest*. South Dakota has plenty of carp, suckers, and others, and a heavily rural population, and this cookbook offers such tempting dishes as carp chowder, baked stuffed carp, and instructions for canning suckers, for pickling rough fish, and making fritters. So you see, where unsung species are abundant and available, people do contrive to make hearty food from the perhaps less desirable.

PADDLEFISH

Interestingly, the paddlefish is mentioned often in recipes from this book. Down the chain of huge impoundments on the Missouri that reach from eastern Montana into Nebraska, this large, ancient, odd-looking species is present in substantial numbers. The paddlefish is equipped with a long, broad, spatulate "paddle" extending from its snout. It also has enormous gill covers. It lives chiefly on plankton and small items of forage strained through its gill rakers. Seldom is a paddlefish caught on hook and line, but several of the central states have a snagging season. Some specimens weigh 50 to 100 pounds or more.

This is an example of a species that might be the object of

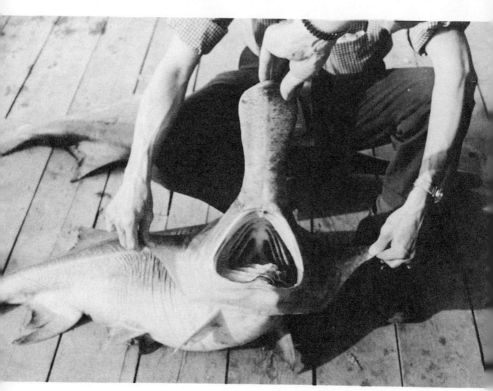

The paddlefish, found in the chain of impoundments on
the Missouri River, is considered a delicacy by a small clan
of enthusiasts.

a special fishing trip. Catching one is a new experience, I can
assure you. I've done it, and for a long time I was not sure
whether I was fast to the fish or it was fast to me. One large
paddlefish is a lot of good eating. Among the small clan of
paddlefish enthusiasts, the flesh is considered a delicacy. The
cookbook mentioned above also includes recipes for baked
paddlefish squares, baked paddlefish with rice, paddlefish fritters, and paddlefish strips in deep fat. Perhaps, after all, there
is an accounting for tastes!

FRESHWATER PANFISH

Even among the smaller freshwater fish—the panfish—are several that receive very little attention; yet here and there they are extremely abundant, easy to catch, and good eating. The rock bass is one of these; so is its southern counterpart, the warmouth bass, both colloquially called "redeye," "goggle-eye," "goggle-eye perch," and even "Molly." In some waters they are extremely abundant, with almost no one fishing purposely for them.

Sometimes small species with very restricted range offer a bonanza for the angler with his ear bent. I can think offhand of two in the state where I live. The Rio Grande perch is not really a perch but a member of the Cichlid family, the numerous species of which are found throughout the tropics. The northernmost fringe of range of the Rio Grande perch reaches into southern Texas and as far north as the Guadalupe, Comal, and San Marcos rivers. It averages from half a pound to 2 pounds occasionally and cannot tolerate waters that drop below about 50 degrees in winter. Few local anglers make any attempt to catch it. Yet it is sporty, abundant, and just as palatable as any of the more highly regarded sunfishes.

The second Texas panfish that badly needs more catching is the tilapia. These also are Cichlids, with many species in Africa especially. They are not native to Texas, but accidental transplants. Others are found, purposely established, in Florida and Arizona. The Texas variety is the blue tilapia. It is in shape reminiscent of the native sunfishes, handsomely colored. Average weight is around a pound. Tilapia are what are called mouth brooders, the eggs held in the mouth until they hatch.

From ancient times tilapia of varied species have been raised as food fish in ponds throughout much of the warmer parts of the world. They were once heralded as potential providers of protein for the world's hungry peoples because they multiply with astonishing swiftness. Unfortunately, there are many reasons in most U.S. waters *not* to let them get started. They are present in some of the power-plant impoundments in Texas, where warm effluent allows them to remain all too populous. They cannot tolerate low temperatures. Texas fishery biologists would, and do when possible, welcome the harvest of any amount of these not very desirable fish. Regardless of their poor biological reputation, as table fare they are delicious.

BULLHEADS

A few wide-ranging freshwater fish are well thought of in one area and scorned in others. The most striking examples are those small relatives of the catfishes, the bullheads. In the introduction to this book I told how I went as a small boy with my father while he caught a mess of bullheads for our table. That was in Michigan, where bullheads are considered desirable, though not classed as game fish. In New England, the brown-bullhead species has been a well-loved panfish since early settlement days. There it is called the "horned pout." But move down into the Deep South and on into Texas, and you'll find if you mention "bullheads" few anglers know what you're talking about. When you explain, they'll say you're talking about "pollywogs"—and they'll say it most often in disgust. Not fit to eat.

This, of course, is ridiculous. It's simply regional tradition. Four bullheads can be considered worthwhile panfish. The brown bullhead is chiefly in the Northeast. The yellow bullhead spreads over most of the eastern two-thirds of the country and has been transplanted elsewhere. The flat bullhead is found most often in streams of the Southeast. The small black bullhead ranges widely, usually in small streams and ponds. All of the bullheads, when taken from clean waters, are fine eating. No one will quarrel with the idea of stringing a lot of them. They're fun to catch, though no great shakes for fight. Among the unsung, they are definite candidates for special attention.

DRUM AND GARS

Perhaps the most unique of all regional uses of freshwater fish not thought highly of over most of their range occurs in the Cajun country of southern Louisiana. Here in many small towns and cities you will see signs outside small seafood markets that read: "Goo & Gar." The "Goo" part comes from "gaspergou," the Cajun name for freshwater drum. Sometimes these drum are simply called "gasper." The other word, "Gar," means just what it says—the market sells drum and gar meat.

The silvery-gray freshwater drum ranges from portions of the Missouri River drainage eastward to eastern Canada, and is found from the Great Lakes where it may be called a "sheepshead," to Texas. It is often abundant, commonly fished commercially. At one time Lake Erie produced several million pounds annually. These drum grow to large size, but average from a pound to 5 or 6 pounds. A few old-fashioned anglers catch them here and there, but very few modern sport fishermen pay them any attention. They are known as trash fish or rough fish. Most fishermen have never even tried to eat one.

The fact is, freshwater drum can be caught on bait or lures, and they prefer habitats that are clear and clean, both lakes and streams. They are astonishing fighters, and modest-size drum are simply delicious. Yet if you read numerous books about fishing, you will discover barely a mention of freshwater drum, except perhaps that they aren't much for catching or eating.

I make a trip each year over to a certain stretch of the Pedernales River about 60 miles from our home purposely to catch drum. The river there is swift and clear, the average drum rather small, although there are big ones. Sometimes I bring home fifty or more, and we package and freeze them. They are one of our favorite eating fish. Frankly, I'd far rather have them than black bass.

I noted in the beginning of this chapter that poor people and country folks—maybe because many of them, past and present, are not well off—always seem to discover good items to eat from the land and waters simply because they are abundant, available, and if purchased in markets, cheap. Blacks in the South have been eating freshwater drum ever since they've been here. Cajuns, many of whom have always been poor, learned long ago that bounty from the lakes, swamps, and river bottoms would admirably sustain them.

Although there are in this country several species of gars (longnose, shortnose, and the huge alligator gar) and they range from the Great Lakes throughout most of the eastern two-thirds of the nation, they never have been eaten except in rare instances by recreational anglers. At one time the specialized sport of catching enormous alligator gars, up to 200 or even 300 pounds, had a fair following in Florida and other Deep South states and in eastern Arkansas, where rivers such as the White joined the Mississippi. There was also, years ago, a substantial commercial fishery for gars along the Mississippi and elsewhere. They were skinned, the head lopped off so the bill wasn't present, and the meat sold to poor people in New Orleans and elsewhere in that region under other names.

All the gars are prodigious fighters. The longnose and others of the smaller gars are difficult to hook, but over past years anglers have discovered that frayed nylon floss used as a pulsating type lure will elicit strikes, the gar's fine teeth become tangled in it, and the fish cannot get free. Especially in some southern waters, gars gather in swarms in quiet areas of lakes, canals, and slow rivers. The sport of catching them is dramatic, and the flesh very good. Prejudice and the tough job of getting the hard "shuck" off discourage most anglers from using them. One caution: gar eggs should never be eaten; they're poisonous to humans as well as other animals.

SALTWATER VARIETIES

Saltwater has just as many—indeed more—unsung eating fish. Here again is the curious situation of fish avidly eaten in one area that go untouched in others. In Florida fried mullet and broiled mullet are standard restaurant fare, and mullet is a common fish in markets. Along the Texas coast, a fisherman would have to be on the verge of starvation before he'd try one. Mullet are not easy to catch with hook and line. Sometimes they're snagged from compact schools. Occasionally they'll take a hook baited with a bit of moss or seaweed. Most of the time they're caught in cast nets, often to be used as bait. Any angler who has access to mullet from clean water and over clean bottoms and doesn't use them is passing up dollars by the handful.

On the West Coast there is a superabundant fish called the jacksmelt, not really a smelt but a member of the Silverside family. It is smeltlike in its slender shape. Large specimens reach a length of 16 to 20 inches; many are smaller. For many years jacksmelt have appeared, fresh, in coastal markets, but sport fishermen pay little attention to them. They are dynamic little fighters, can be caught from massive schools on all sorts of lures and bait. These, and several others of the same family, are tremendously abundant Pacific Coast species that are well worth some attention.

One of these most readers have at least heard of is the little grunion, caught by hand during its spawning ritual as it rides waves up onto the sand and rides others back out. There are also several of the true smelts, among them the whitebait smelt, that are excellent bets for the pan. The little tomcod, a member of the codfish family, is a ready biter along the Pacific, is often caught from piers and by small-boat fishermen. Not much to look at, and only about a foot long, it is nonetheless a very good table fish that is spurned by most sport anglers.

There are so many of these "inconsequential" species all along our coasts that a book might be written just about them. Probably the classic of all scorned and wasted saltwater fish are the sea catfish. I've watched anglers on piers all along the Atlantic and Gulf coasts whack sea cats onto the planking to stun them so they can be removed easily from the hook without a wound from a spine, then kick them back into the water. Admittedly, sea cats are not gourmet tidbits, but the larger specimens are meaty and palatable. Moreover, they're invariably abundant.

A relative, the gafftopsail catfish, grows much larger, ranges from the New England coast clear to and around Florida and on to the western Gulf. These cats, with long anterior dorsal spine that trails a long filament like a sail, average 1 to 2 pounds, with many specimens going to 4 or 5. Maximum weight is about 10 pounds. I've gotten into large schools of gafftops quite often. They are ready biters and fight hard. The gafftop is a quite slimy fish; for that reason, many fishermen dislike it and don't want to handle it. However, when skinned and made into white, thick fillets, the fish is truly superb eating.

Certainly the fish, of both fresh and salt, that I have mentioned are by no means all of the unsung species excellent for the pan. But they give you a good start toward discovering

Often ignored by saltwater fishermen, the gafftopsail catfish is an excellent table fish.

others. The main thing is to be aware that almost all fish are edible, that many which look odd or make you suspicious of their culinary appeal at first glance may turn out to be far more pleasantly palatable than you imagined. When you're fishing for the pan or your freezer, it pays to do so with a curious palate and dollar signs lurking in the back of your mind.

18

Best Times and Places to Fish

All species of fish can be caught, of course, most of the time during the year. But there are certain times when practically any species is likely to be concentrated in numbers, and in places where an angler can reach it with the least difficulty. When fish are concentrated, for whatever reason, competition among them for food becomes severe, and the chances of catching each fish are heightened.

Obviously, it is not possible to list every lake and stream here and tell you when and where on each one certain fish can be taken in quantity. There are tens of thousands of individual waters. What I can predict, however, for at least a moderate number of the more abundant varieties, are the *kinds* of places to look for concentrations, and at what times of year. Most, but not all, such large gatherings of any species occur because of spawning. Where less abundant or extremely hard pressured species are concerned, some states keep a closed season during the general spawning season, to allow them to reproduce without population loss to fishermen. Many varieties are not harmed by fishing in spawning areas. They are extremely prolific, inclined to overpopulate, and occasionally to stunting from overpopulation.

Any astute fisherman who keeps one eye on the available space in his freezer should make at least a mental list of the species in the areas where he fishes, and when accessible concentrations (for spawning or other reasons) occur. He can then plan his fishing time to take advantage of as many of these as possible. Or, if he is one who likes to go every week-end, rain or shine, concentration or none, at least he knows from his "meat list" when special occasions are at hand. He can make a point, say, of attending the white bass run on a certain stream, or getting in at least one heavy lick when the bluegills or shellcrackers are bedding.

Not all fish spawn in spring. Some are fall spawners. This is true in both fresh and salt water. Certain fish, some of them deep-water species, move into shallow waters in spring even though not for spawning, giving average anglers a good chance at them. One of the best examples is the lake trout. Lake trout are wonderful eating fish. They grow large. They are, however, spotty in their range as to which waters they inhabit. Some of the best lake-trout fishing is found over northern and southern Canada and in the Great Lakes, and in some large lakes of the West to which lake trout were long ago transplanted.

These fish live in deep water, often at 100 or more feet. This presents difficulties to anglers. Although lake trout are fall spawners and come upward and inshore at that time, they still may spawn in 20 or 30 feet of water. Right after the ice goes out in the spring, however, when the water temperature near shore in shallows creeps up to 45° F and goes no higher than 55°, this fish moves up and in over the rocky and gravelly shoals in the lakes where it is abundant. Small forage fish are also abundant here at that time, and the lake trout gorge on them.

During this period, which occurs in most lake-trout waters sometime from about mid-May to mid-June, fishermen can catch lake trout from small boats or even from shore by casting spoons, bait fishing, using streamer flies, in water from 3 to 10 or so feet deep. I have had experiences in southern Canada when on practically every cast a trout 3 to 5 or 6 pounds would hit. In most places there are strict limits. Even so, a few big lake trout add up to some marvelous eating, and if you had to buy them, you'd pay a small fortune.

TIMING

Although I didn't mention the lake trout earlier as an abundant meat fish, which it is not except in specific waters, it is an excellent example of time and place related to filling your freezer. Although both time and type of place are important, the timing is the crucial part. This also applies to all spawning concentrations of all species. Water temperature is the key. Each variety spawns within a certain range of water temperature. Movements to spawning beds begin when water temperature reaches a certain level, can be shut off by sudden cold snaps, and frustrated at times by unseasonably hot weather. Each species has its own key temperature range.

Bear in mind that spring, when the majority of fish spawn, is an erratic time for weather. Weather obviously controls water temperature. Thus during a "normal" spring a certain species will arrive on the spawning grounds right on the dot. Years ago the white-flowering bush, so common throughout the East, that is commonly called "shadbush" got its name because when it bloomed the shad "run" in the streams was in progress. People who liked planked shad and shad roe watched the bushes for blooms, which burst forth before leaves form. When that occurred, they knew it was time for the shad to appear. Interestingly, around the central area of the Great Lakes where this shrub also is common, no one ever heard the name shadbush. There aren't any shad. There, as in much of its wide range across the United States, this small tree is called "Juneberry." That's when the fruit begins to mature.

In spring the pan fisherman watches the weather and keeps

tabs on when to make his pitch for the big mop-up on whatever species he has in mind. I mentioned earlier catching large numbers of big bluegills from Toledo Bend Reservoir on the Texas-Louisiana border. This huge impoundment is a top producer of big bluegills. During any normal spring, May 15 is the date to work around. If you have to go far, you try to have a contact in the fishing territory, to let you know when things are right. The lake trout are a good example again. When I was going to go way up into Canada after them, I'd stay in touch with a guide up there who, in turn, kept tabs on lake-trout movements. When they were in, he let me know that it was time, and to hurry before things changed.

Thus, timing is most important. Even if you can't keep actual track of water temperature, which differs lake to lake and stream to stream, you be aware of the general period of the run, then watch the weather, and work from there. Quite a few state fishery departments now have toll-free telephone numbers which one can call to find out if a run has begun.

SPAWNING HABITS

The reason spawning concentrations of fish are so commonly called "runs" relates to spawning habits. Certain species move from lake habitats into streams and spawn in the streams. So they are said to be on their annual spawning run. Most species that live year-round in streams also move upstream, making runs as they seek proper spawning beds. Many other species that live for the most part in lakes do not make runs up tributary streams, but simply move inshore and spawn along the shore in shallow, protected water. Some of these do both—spawn in lake shallows and also run up tributary streams when they are available. The common yellow perch is one of these, but bluegills and other sunfishes are lake spawners. In saltwater, a number of species make runs up

streams emptying into an ocean or bay. They live out most
of their lives in saltwater but do their spawning and develop
as juveniles in flowing freshwater. In its pure state, before it
was also a landlocked species, the striped bass was (still is)
one of these. So are the Pacific salmons. These are called
anadromous fishes: they live in saltwater but run up freshwater streams and spawn there.

Thus it is mandatory that you make it a point to learn at
least the basics about the spawning habits of any fish you are
after. Some run scores of miles up streams. Their eggs must
float free, downstream, until they hatch. This requires a long
float. Again, the striper is one of these. Others have adhesive
eggs. As they are deposited and fertilized, they sink and stick
to whatever they touch. This is true of the white bass. Yellow
perch drape long strings of eggs in a filamentous material over
rocks and debris in shallows.

Some species, the sunfishes and black bass, fan out beds
in which the eggs are deposited. The males do most of the
bed fanning. Thus they come into the spawning area first.
After spawning, the male sunfish and largemouth bass stay
hovering over the nest, protecting the eggs until the fry are
hatched. Curiously, the smallmouth bass does not. Some
other fish—the trouts—make fanned-out nests, but after the
eggs are deposited do not stay to give any protection to their
young. And, of course, those such as white bass and yellow
perch simply drop and fertilize the eggs and then leave.

Several items have to be considered if you hope to gather
in large numbers of abundant fish during spawning time in
spring. I noted weather and the timing and quality of each
individual spring. Latitude is another consideration. May 15
may be just right, given a normal advance of spring, to catch
Texas bluegills, but in Wisconsin concentrations would be at
least two weeks to a month later. In the Midsouth timing
would fall somewhere in between. Each lake may differ from
every other to some extent. In big Toledo Bend the May 15

bluegill date is just right, as a rule, but I have caught bushels
of bluegills and shellcrackers in certain smaller lakes of northern Louisiana, and in similar ones in Florida, in April. Your
local situation is what will be most important, plus a good
basic knowledge of the habits of the species you're after.

As an example, some varieties make extremely long runs
that start several months before they spawn. One I think of
offhand is the Dolly Varden trout. This trout, a char, is a fall

Some species, like this big Dolly Varden trout caught in the
Flathead River, make long summer runs up streams to fall
spawning grounds. They are especially vulnerable during
such runs.

spawner like all the chars. But the big trout begin moving up certain western streams famous for their runs way back in June. In headwater spawning areas you'd fish in fall. In the Flathead River at Glacier Park, trout would be moving upstream, passing through, in June.

For all the species that make beds or nests, the angler must know what type of bottom each requires. The bass and sunfishes are again a good illustration. Largemouths will fan beds over sandy or fine-gravel bottoms, but in a pinch they will even make beds by fanning out with their tails the dirt from among roots of plants, if nothing more suitable is available. Firm bottoms, however, are preferred, to keep eggs from being smothered by silt filtering over them. The smallmouth, conversely, often fails to spawn unless it can find clean sand or gravel. The sunfishes such as the bluegill and shellcracker

In spring all over the continent, wherever sunfish and bluegills are found, concentrations gather for spawning. Wading a lake shore can often garner enough fish to fill the freezer.

prefor firm sand or fine gravel. The fisherman who tracks down suitable spawning bottoms can usually know way ahead of time where his quarry will be concentrated. Further, if a lake has certain stretches where numerous sunfishes are found on beds one year, they will continue to use the area as a rule unless some drastic bottom change occurs. So, you know year to year where to go.

Depth at which spawning occurs is also a consideration for the fisherman, else he may miss finding concentrations. Here once more, using bass for illustration, largemouths commonly spawn in water so shallow their backs almost show. But they may also make many beds much deeper. The smallmouth seldom fans beds in extremely shallow water. Possibly this is because most good smallmouth lakes are steep sided and exceedingly clear. It's routine to find smallmouth beds in 3 to 6 or more feet of water. The sunfishes spawn both shallow and about like largemouths, depending on what bottoms they find that they prefer. In some places (my own ponds) I've watched them fan beds in a few inches of water, where a patch of fine gravel showed. I've also found swarms of bluegills, and shellcrackers, concentrated over hard sand in as much as 10 feet of water.

The crappies, also nest builders, gather in large concentrations in spring, but they are seldom in shallow water. Depths to 8 feet are common, and 3 or 4 average. However, crappies have a preference for distinct cover. They get into weed beds, for example, to make nests. Their main hangouts in spring, all across the southern half of the country particularly, are in brush that is partly submerged. Here the abundant so-called button willow that rises in patches above the protected shallows is a magnet for large schools. Find the submerged brush in protected bays, and you'll find the crappies. In the North I caught black crappies several years from a small impoundment where submerged tree stumps were dense. Maneuvering a small, light boat around them was a chore, but crappies were simply everywhere.

Fishermen should know that wherever it is legal to do so crappie enthusiasts can make their own pay-off spots for almost any time of year by weighting and sinking brush in piles. Many southern crappie addicts build underwater cribs by thrusting stakes into the bottom, wiring them together, and filling the interior with weighted brush. In northern Wisconsin a friend of mine who owns a lake back in the woods built a long T-shaped dock, cribbed the sides down to bottom, and filled in under the dock with brush. The idea of these structures—and sunken brush piles—is to attract minnows. Crappies are predominantly minnow feeders. Once minnows have taken up refuge in the brush, crappies gather round to pick off any that appear.

In Oklahoma and elsewhere in the middle of the country these days, there are enclosed, heated winter fishing piers where owners sink weighted evergreens as cover for minnows. They even bait them with such small-fish food as grain and cattle cake that ranchers feed to cattle. Minnows flock to this and draw crappies after them. Some of these docks are amazing businesses. They have concessions, even TV. With a blizzard perhaps in progress outside, clients sit in a warm room and fish over the railing, along the sunken cover. Sometimes a big catch of crappies is worth more than the fee charged for the convivial fishing.

Among the free-spawning species that do not make beds, water type preferences may or may not occur. I've seen yellow perch literally by hundreds of thousands that had moved in from Lake Erie and Lake Huron, from clear, clean water (at least in those days!) into the long ditches we called dredge cuts that handled drainage from inland. Yellow perch run early, around the Great Lakes usually in April. It's still chilly, and so is the water. They'll gang up in any protected spot, without much regard for water quality or where the swaths of eggs are strung. On the other hand, in many lakes with slow tributary streams yellow perch practically pave the flowing water when they are on their spring run. Along the smaller

lakes they come in over gravel or rocky shoals much like their
big relative, the walleye.

White bass, caught by millions on spring spawning runs,
much prefer *large* streams tributary to lakes in which they
live, and often pass up the small creeks. In the large rivers
they'll lie in large numbers just out of the most forceful current. Because of their penchant for the bigger streams, a series
of impoundments on a river forms an excellent situation for
anglers. White bass move up from one lake and are stopped
by thousands in the tailrace of a dam forming another as they
attempt to spawn. Anglers should also be aware that the newer
landlocked striped bass has a fix on tailraces, too. Further, a
sharp fisherman will concentrate at almost any time of year
on power-plant dams. During the hours when they are generating, with ample water rushing out below, white bass and
other fish will swarm. Then as the plant shuts down and water
subsides, they'll drift on down to deeper water to await the
next generating period.

One should also be aware of what can be called "double
runs." Again, white bass make good illustration. The smaller
males start upstream as much as a month before the larger,
egg-laden females. In my state, runs of males often start as
early as February. Lake to lake the timing differs because,
obviously, lake and stream temperatures differ. Some anglers
get into male fish and think they're into the main run, are
irked because the fish average rather small. They simply are
too early for the run of females. I remember that in Tennessee
the main white-bass run, with both sexes intermingled on
spawning grounds, materializes as a rule about as the redbud
and dogwood come to full bloom. This is a pleasant way to
time it.

I mentioned that male sunfishes come into spawning areas
first, to fan out beds. So do bass. There is a very special
consideration here for anglers who want top-quality eating

fish. I always try to start a bit early, according to peak dates.
The reason: by doing so I begin catching a preponderance of
male sunfish. They're not difficult to distinguish from the
females, they're always much gaudier in color. (This is true
of bluegills, shellcrackers, yellowbreasts, all the sunfishes.)
Keep in mind that the most important period of the year for
all creatures is the period launching the production of progeny. Thus, given normally healthful living conditions during
the prespawning period, fish will be in the very best condition
physically of their entire year.

When you locate a big sunfish bedding area and begin catching mostly males, each one slab sided, thick, hard fighting,
colors fresh and bright, you know instantly that spawning has
not yet occurred. Within a brief time—a day or so, or a week—
the egg-fat females will begin to appear. The time to make
your heavy catch is before the fish are spawned out. Females
do not extrude all their eggs at once, nor does the male drain
himself entirely of milt at one time. The spawning continues
for a few days. The early part of it puts the finest fish on your
stringer. Because these species are abundant, no harm is done
by taking fish as spawning begins.

After spawning is complete, and the males are guarding
beds with eggs in them, they are not feeding and are thin
sometimes to the point of debilitation. Many of both sexes die
from the exhaustion of the spawning activities. I've caught
and released spawned-out male bluegills that were so thin and
compressed there was almost no meat on their bones. Any
fish species taken during the spawning period is far better
eating in the prespawn days or at the start of spawning than
in the immediate postspawn period.

Some fish pursue routines that make them vulnerable, concentrating them over special feeding areas, during the postspawning period. The walleye is a classic example. This
delicious eating fish spawns early in spring, while water is still

cold. In latitudes where lakes freeze, it spawns shortly after ice-out with the water temperature at 45° to 40° F. This is a first mop-up time for walleyes. Where large streams are available, many will run up them to spawn, just like their small relative, the yellow perch. Most will gather over gravel and rock-rubble shoals in clear, clean water 2' to 5' or 6' deep. This puts them where fishermen can easily get at them.

Following spawning there is a lull as the fish recover. However, the walleye and many other free-spawning species seldom finish the spawning period in such a debilitated physical condition as do those that make beds and stay with the eggs or young. Because walleyes finish spawning while the water is still cold, they commonly stay in fairly shallow situations for several weeks, gorging on minnows and crayfish found over the shoals and sand bars, swiftly growing fat again.

Some of my finest walleye-fishing memories bring visions of Munuscong Bay in extreme upper Lake Huron, where St. Joseph Island demarks the Canadian shore and the western one is in Michigan's Upper Peninsula. At this latitude, June is still chilly. This is tremendous walleye water. The fish have spawned earlier, but they rove in large killer schools along the shores of the numerous small islands, fattening while the living is easy. By end of June they will have drifted off into deep water for the summer, except for periodic daily migrations upslope to pick off unsuspecting forage. With friends I have caught big walleyes during the June fattening period when practically every cast brought a strike.

These postspawning feeding periods of game fish should be kept in mind. Not all species follow this routine, at least not where they can be found so easily. The bluegill, for example, will scatter after spawning, and may not be located abundantly again for some weeks. Then, during summer, knowledgeable fishermen will probe deep holes and may find scads of bluegills ganged up.

INSECT HATCHES

You should make a point of knowing, in your area, what special heavy insect hatches occur, when, and what feeds on them every year. Of the several sunfishes, bluegills do the most surface feeding and have the highest incidence of insects in their diet. If there are heavy mayfly hatches in your area, evening fishing in shallows with a fly rod and small bug, or dry fly, will put scores of fat fish on your stringer. In the South, mayflies are usually dubbed willow flies. The willow fly hatches on certain rivers are the times when enthusiasts of the "brim" have some of the season's best fishing.

I noted earlier how I caught ciscoes on flies during hatches. Even walleyes, on some lakes where hatches of large mayfly species occur, spend a few evenings each season taking them at surface, and can be caught on surface-bass bugs. Many trout streams all over the country are famed for hatches of certain aquatic insects and the wild feeding of trout during these periods. The Madison River in Montana is known nationally for its so-called salmon-fly hatch. The insects are actually stone-flies. They are also sometimes called willow flies in the West, as mayflies are in the South. Numerous western trout rivers have heavy stonefly hatches. The Madison hatch is a perfect illustration of what happens. The hatch begins far down the river, where water is warmest in late spring, and day by day moves a mile, a half mile, or several miles upstream, depending on weather and water temperature.

Lots of trophy-size trout are taken on streams where and when such tremendous hatches of large insects occur. Michigan's Manistee has long been renowned continentwide for its so-called caddis hatch in late spring. Again, the insect is misnamed. It is actually a large variety of mayfly. Big browns are the chief targets here. I recall fishing the Yellowstone in Montana during a tremendous hatch of big stoneflies. Cut-

Certain fly hatches bring out big trout in spring and summer. In fall trout often gather to gorge on minnows.

throat trout of several pounds were so easy to catch that it was just ridiculous. A comic incident from that experience, which illustrates just how easy, was that I ran into a couple from Texas, tourists who'd previously never caught a trout in their lives. They were fishing, believe it or not, with heavy cane poles, baiting hooks with fat stoneflies caught in their hands from nearby rocks and bushes. All fish seize any special opportunity to fill up on a temporary forage bonanza. If you acquaint yourself with those occurring in your area, you are prepared to grab your own chances at bonanzas for your freezer.

FEEDING HABITS

A few species have specific feeding habits that point an angler to unusual opportunities. The walleye, for example, is to a great extent a dusk and nighttime feeder. Walleyes often move up from deep water in summer as dusk draws near and slash into minnow schools or gobble crayfish from a shoal. Good examples of places to find them at these times are along the sloping, rocky rip-rap of an impoundment dam, around small islands or submerged humps out in a lake that slant steeply down into deep water, off rocky and gravel points that slope into deep water.

The white bass is another fish with a summer feeding routine that lays it wide open to a trip to the freezer. White bass travel in schools. In scores of impoundments their mainstay of diet is the gizzard shad, or, where present, the threadfin shad. Those fish also move in dense schools. The whites hunt like vast wolf packs. They come up from below a school of forage fish, surrounding them, driving them to the surface and slashing into them. This results in massive boils on a lake surface. These, when large on a lake calm, can be seen for long distances. In some instances, the whites pen a shad school in a bay and push it up along a shallow shoreline. The result is the same.

Anglers who are acquainted with this habit cruise a lake slowly watching for those "jumps." I've seen times when several acres of lake surface would be wildly boiling as shad tried to escape and white bass smashed into them by the hundreds. This "jump fishing" for white bass is mostly a summer sport, in hot weather. Very early in the morning, and again late in the day, are the two peak action times. Anglers rush a boat up toward a big feeding school, cut the motor well out away so not to disturb the fish, and make long casts into the feeding fish. After a brief flurry the school submerges, but soon will be up again at some other angle. Once my wife and I drifted a boat on a just-right small breeze parallel to the shore of an impoundment bay where white bass had shad penned against the shoreline. Casting as fast as we could and flicking caught fish off into the boat bottom, we counted over fifty white bass when the flurry was over and the big school had submerged.

AID FOR ANGLERS

The alert meat fisherman can avail himself of a lot of help from his state fisheries department, when looking for special opportunities. I think offhand of the enormous interest nowadays in the salmons and trouts (steelhead, brown, lake trout) that have put the spotlight on the Great Lakes during late years. For some time it was fish hunting by trial and error to find the fish all season. Now the movements have been quite thoroughly plotted. Biologists in Minnesota, Wisconsin, and Michigan know just about where each population of coho, chinooks, pink salmon, and the several trouts will be during any given month, not only roughly what water depth, but at what places in the big lakes. This information is easily obtainable by anglers.

Oklahoma offers another example. In the big impoundments there where landlocked stripers have done extremely well, fisheries people have plotted and mapped the general seasonal movements of the fish. They even have for angler use maps showing where most of the fish will be and when—that is, in what arm of a big lake and at about what depth, during which months. In Texas, the Parks and Wildlife Department provides a chart showing where and what times of year are best for most of the popular freshwater and saltwater game fish. All such clues—and all states have them—are enormously valuable to the angler keeping his own charts and making his own plans to keep his pan overflowing. I would warn readers, however, not to go on "fishing expeditions" that

request general information from a game-and-fish department. Ask specific questions about precisely what you want
to track down. The "tell me all about" queries go into the
wastebasket, which is what they deserve when poured upon
busy professional people.

Ultimately, the fisherman is responsible for finding out
what's going on in his state and surrounding ones. Has a new
transplant been made that is doing great? All sorts of experiments are currently being tried. That's why we presently
have walleyes, smallmouth bass, and pike along the Mexican
border, hundreds of miles from their ancestral beginnings.
That's why salmon are swarming the Great Lakes, and stripers
are found all across the country. Keep on top of developments.
A transplant that suddenly becomes successful in your bailiwick may be just what you need as a freezer filler.

ICE FISHING

Not much is said in popular fishing books about ice fishing.
I may have a soft spot for the sport, even though I now live
outside the ice zone, because years ago I wrote the first book
ever published on the subject. I learned during my long as-
sociation with cold weather throughout my boyhood and on-
ward that ice fishing is not only a lot of sport, it is also a
fantastic producer of good eating fish.

Not all fish are ready biters during winter ice fishing. Two
of the panfish, the bluegill and the yellow perch, are mainstays
of the sport. There were winters when I went almost every
afternoon to a small lake near where we lived, and always
caught a mess of bluegills. In some places yellow perch can
be hauled up, using a small jigging spoon let down through
a hole in the ice, as fast as you can get the spoon down and
flutter it.

A tip to prospective ice anglers is to do as many an old

commercial winter fisherman used to do around the Great Lakes bays: They used what was called a "Russian hook," a brass- or gold-colored spoon, narrow at the tail and wider up front, with a hook braised to the concave side. They filed off the hook barb. The angler jiggled the spoon near bottom and when a perch struck kept right on moving the spoon up until he flipped the perch out on the ice. As he let the line slack, the perch flopped off the hook because there was no barb to hold it. These men used a short jigging stick with a line winder on the side to keep slack up, depending on water depth. When they got into a perch school they could put dozens on the ice in this way in minutes, never touching a fish with their mittened hands.

Walleyes, lake trout, pike, crappies, rainbow and other trout (where legal), whitefish, and smelt are all eager biters under the ice in winter. They gang up in deep holes, spring holes, over or along weed beds, and off stream mouths. Ice fishing is a world of fishing unto itself, and none was ever better for attention of the pan fisherman in cold latitudes.

POND FISHING

If you are ingenious, you can concoct many ways to discover unusual concentrations of eating fish. I used to take summer hikes back into the forest, following small creeks, looking for new beaver ponds. I've done the same in the western mountains many times. As a beaver family grows, the progeny must move out and build their own homes. New beaver ponds are invariably swarming with brook trout within a year or two, wherever brookies are in the creeks on which beavers construct their dams. Keeping a checklist of pond locations is like having your own rearing ponds for abundant trout.

Another kind of pond fishing that deserves attention is farm pond fishing. I own property where for years we have had our own ponds, with bass and sunfish in them. Not everyone has this privilege, of course, but today there are in this country several million farm and ranch ponds, the majority stocked with fish. Many serve only for recreation and table fare for their owners, but thousands of farm pond owners are amenable to letting someone keep the fish populations under control. Bass, sunfish, and channel cats, the most common pond varieties, quickly overpopulate unless fished hard.

Many pond owners charge a small fishing fee. Sometimes you can catch enough to pay for several days of trying. In Texas, it is common for sportsmen to join in small groups and buy a lease. Mostly the lease is for hunting, because Texas has little public hunting land, but leases usually include fishing rights, or can be written that way. In some instances, a landowner leases hunting rights to one group, fishing rights to another. Whether you lease, pay a daily fee, or fish by permission, the farm-pond situation should not be overlooked. Sometimes, even where limits are in force for state-owned fish, there are none for farm or ranch pond fish. That's a real freezer special! If you happen to own a piece of property with a location suitable for building your own pond, you may want to pursue that idea—your own permanent fishing hole and pan filler (see Chapter 19).

SALTWATER FISHING

The where and when of saltwater related to fishing bonanzas is somewhat different from that of freshwater. The expanses of water are so vast and the species so diverse. However, spawning periods are as valid for catching large numbers of quite a few species. Just as in freshwater, spawning is triggered by water temperature. Hard storms along coasts may hold up or inhibit mass spawning activities. Latitude makes great differences in spawning *times*, of course. Also, some saltwater denizens spawn in the oceans or the Gulf; others spawn in protected inside waters, the bays and channels.

Saltwater striped bass make spawning runs up large fresh-water rivers all along the Atlantic and around Florida. These occur in spring, precise times depending on latitude. The abundant sheepshead spawns in southern latitudes in Feb-ruary and March, around rocky jetties and reefs of the Gulf and Atlantic. Great strings of them are caught during this period and on into April. When golden (Atlantic) croakers move from bays into the Gulf and Atlantic to spawn, a mi-gration that occurs after fall's first crisp nights, they can be caught by hundreds in passes, channels, and in the surf. Black drum make spawning runs in late winter through channels and passes and along the Intracoastal Waterway around the Gulf of Mexico. The spadefish I mentioned in an earlier chap-ter come inshore to spawn around piers, pilings, and rocks in the Gulf about May. So do pompano. These are examples of spawning movements or migrations that put large concen-trations of marine fish at one's disposal.

As important as spawning runs, or more so, are the mass movements of saltwater fish all along our shores that are sea-sonal migrations. Some of these are from warm tropical waters northward in spring, to summering grounds. Some are move-ments from protected inside waters (shallow bays) out into the oceans or the Gulf, where the species spend the winter. Many can't tolerate the low temperatures that often chill shal-low bays, and so they go into deep offshore water for the colder months.

Bluefish, cobia, king mackerel, Spanish mackerel, many of the tunas and bonitos, dolphin, Pacific yellowtail, albacore, and many other prime game fish migrate much as most birds do.

They spend the winter in tropical waters, then move north

progressively as the water warms. Some migrations cover vast distances. Bluefish, for example, rather erratic in their appearances in abundance, are found off Florida in midwinter as a rule, begin to be caught on up the Atlantic coast through March, April, and May, and by late May are off the coast of Massachusetts.

Any state fisheries department in any coastal state can furnish basic information as to when the various migratory species appear and when they leave. Many species make their northern migrations not only to stay within their comfortable range of temperature, but also for spawning, just as most waterfowl migrate north to nest. All the migratory species are usually in their more northerly ranges for several months. Track down the peak month for the ones you are interested in, and plan accordingly.

Some saltwater species present rather complicated routines to the fisherman. Channel bass (redfish), for example, spend their early years in protected waters of bays. The big, mature fish (four-year-olds and up) then move out into the open water of the Gulf or Atlantic to spawn. These large ones, in the 10-pound-and-larger class, usually spend most of their time from there on in the outside water. That's why large specimens are so often caught in the surf. However, when channels and passes offer ready access, many of these large fish move into bays in substantial numbers in fall for short periods. Then one can catch many of them over the grass flats and shell beds.

Meanwhile, most of the smaller and medium-size fish, not yet of spawning age, live in the bays. But when a cold snap strikes, depending on its severity, they head out into the big water, so they can find deep havens for protection. Anglers all across southern waters should keep this in mind: the more severe and unusual the sudden cold that strikes, the more the bay fish are affected. Weakfish and channel bass cannot tolerate extreme temperature drops. Occasionally many fish die from severe cold spells. They do not have time to find their way out into deep outside water if a severe weather change occurs suddenly.

What they do at such times, many of them at least that get caught in the shallow areas, is head for deep holes nearby. Most bays, even though generally shallow, offer a few havens—scooped out basins on bottom, or even dredged ship channels—that are at least a few feet deeper. Bottom water here is somewhat warmer. On several occasions I have fished with great success the Texas coast during cold snaps by studying depth contour maps and seeking these deep holes. Tremendous gatherings of fish gang up in them at such times. Boat basins are sometimes famed for this phenomenon.

Once three of us discovered a small stretch of freshly dredged channel that dropped off to 20 feet. The deepest hole probably wasn't over 50 yards in diameter. We discovered trout and reds by dozens lying in it. Low temperature, of course, slows metabolism at such times, but competition for food still is heightened. You must fish a bait (we used live shrimp) very slowly, right on bottom. Bites are weak, but large catches can often be had from this situation.

The chief rule to sift out from this chapter is to learn in detail the fishing potential of your particular area. Know what's there, and how latitude, normal and erratic weather, types of water and bottom all affect each fish that interests you. Make a point of studying the life history of each species, so you know when and where it spawns, whether it makes inshore and offshore movements, how it feeds after spawning and over what kinds of bottoms, what special forage situations occur that cause certain fish to concentrate, and when they take place. The times when any variety of eating fish congregates in a small area, and the times when any one makes mass movements through narrow waters such as up streams or through passes, offer the best freezer-filling opportunities.

19

A Pond of Your Own

The day is one I remember vividly because it brought our family a feeling of immense satisfaction. We all went out to the pond, carrying picnic supplies and fishing rods. While my wife, Ellen, spread a blanket and laid out lunch in the shade of a live oak, the boys insisted that I make the first cast. I aimed a surface plug near a willow growing in the edge of the water. There was an instant strike, and I fought in a bass.

It was not large, but it was the first fish from our very own pond. The picnic trip had not been a long one. The pond was scarcely 100 yards from our back door.

That pond, a small one, was our first. Since that time we've built and enjoyed several, two of them quite large. Our boys grew up catching bass and varied sunfishes in them, swimming in them, and having friends do likewise. Much of our family recreation for years has revolved around them. A great many meals have come out of them, too.

There is, indeed, tremendous satisfaction and enjoyment in having a pond of your own. It is there to use and share with friends as often as you wish for any water-oriented recreation that it is large enough to support. Unlike many public

285

waters, it is never crowded. To this day, Ellen goes swimming almost every afternoon during summer in one of our ponds. I've gathered frogs around them, picked mint we planted, and photographed a wide variety of wildlife that ponds invariably attract. I've hunted the deer and turkey trails leading to them, taken numerous ducks, and, of course, fished incessantly. I'm sure the amount of fish we've used over the years wouldn't pay the costs of the ponds. But the beauty, the solitude, the satisfaction of ownership and having created such an oasis—plus the fish and game—were all provocative reasons for having our own ponds. They are an all-encompassing hobby, as well as a pot and pan supplier.

In the nation today there are already over three million acres of privately owned ponds. Annually upward of 40,000 new ponds are added. More than half are farm ponds built

Before: Bulldozer shapes the beginning of one of our ponds.

primarily as stock-watering or conservation impoundments. More and more, however, farm ponds serve the double purpose of recreation and business. Some ponds—currently about 40,000 acres of them—are built for catfish farming, others for commercially raising trout or minnows.

In addition, a vast number of ponds are built by the tens of thousands of escapees from the cities who have acquired "a little place in the country." Many people already live on their country tracts, having built permanent homes there. Others have put up a cottage or fixed up a camping site to which they can flee temporarily from city stresses to picnic, fish, or camp away from the crowds. But there are also many thousands who own a piece of land, perhaps even live on it, who have never considered or discovered the fact that an excellent pond site is right there. They already have the potential for a pond and don't realize it. More thousands are contemplating buying a country tract, and should consider a pond, as well.

Building a pond costs a fair amount of money. However, the investment so enhances property values that it is a good one. You might say you'll get the fish and the fun for free, even *make* money. In addition to cost, ponds require care and management. These, though admittedly some work and expense, are challenging and intriguing hobbies. You'll also need patience. Waiting for a pond to fill, for its surroundings to become green, for fish to grow to catching size all take time.

How *much* time? This is the question always asked immediately by friends who have become enthused about building their own pond after fishing one of ours. There are endless variables influenced by geographical location, pond size, water and food quality, and so on, but I can give an example from my own experience that probably is fairly typical.

The last pond I built was constructed of necessity in the driest part of the summer. The water source was runoff. Rains would impede or stop work. It was finished in late August. The actual construction required only three weeks. Then we waited and hoped for heavy rains. We received drizzles. Grass, seeded around the edges, sprouted nicely, and surroundings began to look a little bit green. The pond did not catch much water, however, until into the winter.

I planned to get fish from the state for stocking—fingerling bass, sunfish, and channel cat. It was far too late that year (the fish were reared and delivered during spring and summer), so I applied for fish to stock the quarter-acre pond early in the new year. By spring the pond was beautifully full. Alas, there was a shortage of fingerling bass that year, so I got none, but tiny sunfish and channel cats went into the pond in August.

It was lower than I liked at the time, and I was worried. However, it overflowed during winter rains and went into the second spring in fine shape. I test-fished it in late June. The catfish, put in at about an inch long, were up to 4 or 5 inches. The sunfish had made somewhat uneven growth. Some were almost eating size even though still small for that purpose. Some were only 2 to 3 inches long. That summer I did get baby bass.

It was three years from the time the pond was finished until we began taking out mature sunfish and frying-size channel cats. The bass, a year behind the others, grew slowly and really weren't worthwhile until they were a full three years old. By then we had quite a green oasis and good fishing. So you see, patience is mandatory. You have to keep thinking of the future. If you prorate the financial and effort investment over the many years of use a well-managed pond will offer, cost per year is low indeed compared to enjoyment and return to the skillet.

Because of the tens of thousands of ponds that have been built in every part of the country, expert knowledge of the "how-to" is vast. The central storehouse of all this expertise is the Soil Conservation Service, a branch of the United States

Department of Agriculture. Fortunately for prospective pond builders, the SCS is intensely concerned with the building of these small impoundments. It makes a regular business, at the builder's request, of helping plan and lay out private ponds.

This organization has mountains of precise specifications for dam construction, offers expert advice about proper site, pond size, water source and quality, and, in fact, will help guide you step by step through the entire project. Further, all of this assistance is free. There are some 3000 SCS offices scattered throughout the country. One is certain to be near you.

Prospective pond builders invariably ask: will the SCS offer actual federal financial assistance? For all practical purposes, the answer is no. In the past, under certain specific circumstances, authentic farmers and ranchers have received some financial help. Rules now are tightened even in those cases. Nevertheless, the technical guidance available at no cost is actually worth a very substantial amount of money, if you had to pay for it from comparable professionals. Thus, the best advice you can possibly get is to use SCS services from the day your decision to build a pond is made, and to follow meticulously the procedures they set up for you.

Of course, you do need to acquire basic information and knowledge of fundamental options. For example, generally speaking, there are two kinds of ponds: one is an excavation scooped out where there is a water source to fill it and proper terrain configuration to get the water into it; the other is formed by a dam that blocks a valley or a stream. Dams of this sort usually form the largest ponds. Strategically placed, even a dam of modest size may back water over several acres, whereas excavating a basin that large would be a prodigious and expensive undertaking.

Most pond dams are of earth. They are the cheapest to build and fit the largest number of terrain situations. In some instances, however, dams are built of concrete, or rock and concrete. One of our ponds is a good example of a location where concrete is advisable. It was built on a stream with rock bluffs on both sides and a solid-rock stream bed. These made it possible to bond the concrete to the rock. An earthen dam would have been impossible here; it could not have been bonded to the rock and would have washed away on the first big rise. Another dam type occasionally used on streams of fair size is of earth overlaid with a concrete shield. This is a tricky design that requires expert engineering.

While considering possible pond sites, you should thoroughly research water laws in your state and county. They're highly varied, state to state. Some states may stipulate a minimum pond size. Many have laws pertaining to water quality, to water storage, even to certain specifications on ponds—for example, making an emergency drainage mandatory, or having your pond plan approved before building. Water-rights laws may pertain, depending on your water source. So may liability laws, and even, after your fish are catchable size, fishing laws, in some cases.

In my state no license is required to fish private ponds, nor is there any fish limit. Some states, however, require a license, and enforce limits as on public waters. Be sure also to look into any regulations that may exist about privacy. In some states which stock private ponds gratis, the public must be allowed to participate. In such case you're better off buying stock from a private hatchery. Here again, the SCS is your best guide. A local office will be familiar with the laws, or point you to proper counsel, perhaps a water quality or land-use zoning board. Further, SCS pond specifications will invariably adhere to existing local regulations.

Obviously, the most important pond ingredient is water. Chief sources are streams, springs, wells, runoff. Large creeks look appealing, but it's wise to avoid them if other water sources are available. Legal restrictions may be numerous; such streams require large, expensive dams, and they are subject to flooding, pond siltation, and entrance of unwanted fish species.

Sometimes a small amount of water flow can be diverted from a sizable stream to feed a pond basin excavated nearby. But this is expensive and also creates numerous problems. If you must use a stream source, a mere rivulet with a reliable, strong yearround flow is best. A good spring also is an excellent source. Again, reliability is mandatory. Any source that diminishes drastically in summer when surface evaporation is high may let your pond down badly. Also, many dams have moderate seepage. A well is a fine water source, but costly if you have to drill one.

A great many ponds depend on runoff water. Two of ours do. Runoff is by no means the best source, but we owned the land, wanted the ponds, and had no other supply. I checked average rainfall, plus the size of the watershed in each case, and tailored the size of the ponds to what water might reasonably be expected. Both have worked out quite well. A rule of thumb is that in areas of modest rainfall and/or barely adequate watershed, runoff ponds will have good and bad years, with water-level fluctuation. Where rainfall is high and stable, and the watershed fully adequate, runoff water is a good source.

Water quality is even more important. The watersheds feeding both our runoff ponds, for example, are grassy and forested. Those are the best kind. This eliminates possible siltation. There are no croplands that might pollute the ponds with sprays, no cattle feed lots or possible sewage pollution. This is the kind of situation to look for if you use runoff. Water running off tilled lands is seldom desirable.

If you plan to use well water, have it analyzed beforehand to be sure it is not low in oxygen (some well water is) and that there are no minerals that may be harmful to fish. By and large, a strong spring is top choice as a source. Springs seldom cause legal involvement, seldom are polluted, and ordinarily are well oxygenated. A reliable spring plus a site that will also catch watershed runoff is ideal. The spring is a surefire backup during dry weather.

An ugly, eroded gully is often a perfect spot for a dam. It indicates that water has been cutting it for a long time, and that ample water is probably assured. If you're buying land for a pond a gully comes cheap and can be transformed into a true beauty spot.

Pond construction costs are not easy to estimate. Pond size—and dam size and type—have much to do with dictating cost. Don't get grandoise ideas. For example, there is a beautiful 15-acre pond a couple of miles from my home; the dam, on a large-flow creek, cost $32,000 years ago. Ponds of one-fourth to one-half acre are the rule, with 1 acre average maximum. Those of several acres are expensive to build and maintain. At today's costs, few ponds are possible for "just a few hundred" dollars. It's best to figure on several thousand, but the minute the pond is full, property value is enhanced to probably double, and continues to accrue.

Once the pond is constructed, the intriguing business of managing it begins. The spillway of an earth dam and the dam itself should be seeded immediately. Good sod or a carpet of grass will keep it from eroding. Even though you want everything to look pretty, be careful what you plant. A friend of mine started water lilies. They just about took over, and the bulbs are difficult to get rid of. I made the mistake of tossing some ripened cattail heads on the shore of one of our projects. The next year green shoots sprung up abundantly, and we spent weeks pulling them out. Especially when water is low, cattails swiftly encroach. It's always best to keep pond banks reasonably clear.

Unfortunately, aquatic weed growth, especially in warm-water ponds, is an ever-present problem. A design for deep basin edges helps inhibit the weeds. Fertilizing a pond also helps. Commercial fertilizers for the purpose are readily available. Various pamphlets from SCS and USDA give full instructions. With fertilization, resultant plankton growth shuts out light penetration needed by rooted aquatics. The water looks cloudy and the plants die. Fertilization also enhances growth of the food chain. To be successful, fertilization must be a continuing routine. Some weed killers that do not harm fish can also be used.

It's extremely important what and how many fish you plant. You must think of managing them like any crop. Species native to the area are always best. Trout, bass, bluegills, channel cat are the mainstays. Trout never should be tried where summer surface temperature rises above 70°F. Get advice from your state fisheries biologists about the proper numbers and species mix recommended for your size pond.

Some states furnish fish, but many do not. Those that do may have rules about pond size and stipulate that it contain no other fish. Whether or not your state furnishes stock, state biologists can offer expert advice. There are numerous private commercial hatcheries from which stock may be purchased.

Properly managing the annual fish crop is extremely important. A friend of mine became so fond of his fish by the time he had nurtured them to catching size that he just couldn't bear to take any out or allow friends to fish. In two years his pond was ruined, vastly overstocked with stunted fish. Another friend caught exactly eleven warmouth bass from a slow creek, only one of them identifiable as a male, and put them into a small, new pond in the fall. What happened the first spring was all but unbelievable. The water suddenly swarmed with tiny warmouths. By summer's end thousands were in evidence, all an inch or 2 long. Nothing else was in the pond to help keep a balance. The only options were to drain the pond or make a total chemical kill and start over.

The fish population balance in any small pond is indeed delicate, both to achieve and to maintain. Once fish are grown, hard fishing is mandatory, and the catch should be at least

After: My son Terry catches a bass in the finished pond.

roughly tallied, with an attempt to keep the bass-bluegill ratio, for example, at a continuing level. One friend regularly seines out scads of small bluegills. Trout, in habitats where they'll live, are in some ways easier. They are automatically controlled by lack of pond spawning of any consequence. Fingerlings can simply be added in proper ratio to fish caught.

Numerous pond owners are now stocking unique hybrid sunfish crosses between two different sunfish species. They grow large; the females deposit only a moderate number of eggs, few of which hatch; and the hatch produces about four times as many males as females. This built-in low production rate practically assures stable population, eliminating the problem so common with the overpopulous, stunted bluegills.

Pond management, even with its problems of weed control and fish-population balance, is an immensely fascinating hobby. For example, we have a rule that no one ever releases a small fish; otherwise, only the big predators would be eliminated. You'd be surprised what small fish we sometimes eat. All in all, owning and working with your own pond is a wonderful experience in broad learning as well as in fishing sport and other recreation, and putting protein in the pan.

It's not a matter of trying to take out enough fish to pay for the pond and its upkeep. Fishing for the pan is only one aspect, unless you decide to raise fish on a commercial basis, which certainly is a growing business and will become ever more important. Some pond owners choose to operate a small fee-fishing business to help with expenses. A pond of your own, however, is fundamentally a hobby. The fish help justify it.

If you want to feel good about the money side of it, though, even without commercial use, consider these facts. Let's say you take out for table use $500 worth of fish annually, and the pond expense for management costs the same. You've made $500: you didn't have to buy fish to eat. The presence of the pond on your property raises the property value double what the pond cost, and this continues to accrue. How can you go fishing whenever you want to and make money any easier?

Following are suggestions for choosing a pond site and a listing of SCS services.

Selecting a Pond Site

Look for	Avoid
Ample spillway room, to spread flood water thinly.	Low, always wet area that may create access problems.
Some type of clay soil; it compacts and holds water efficiently.	Site beneath noisy nuisance, possibly dangerous power lines.
Numerous successful ponds in area, if you must buy tract. Sign of proper soil, adequate water.	Easement through another's land, if you must buy tract.
Dam site where valley narrows, requiring only short dam to back up maximum water.	Soil of sand or gravel; shale; rock outcrops, loose rocks, rock ledges.
Eroded gully; it means ample runoff and is usually cheap, if you must buy tract.	Large streams with heavy flow and flooding.
Grassy, forested or tree-studded watershed, if water source is runoff.	If runoff water supply, tilled land or land without plant cover.

Typical SCS Services Available

Advice about water source and quality.

Selecting best dam site as related to land contour.

Computing watershed size in relation to water supply and flooding.

Establishing size of pond most advisable.

Determining height of dam required, and width of crown and base necessary.

Designing dam contour.

Computing precisely the area over which water will back up.

Determining width of spillway necessary and its location.

Positioning and overseeing installation of normal overflow ("dribble") pipe.

Positioning and overseeing installation of metal flanges ("seep collars") to stop seepage around pipe.

Positioning and overseeing installation of emergency drainage pipe or gate valve.

Advice on machinery and materials needed for actual construction, and where available.

Estimating materials and construction costs.

Determining soil type and quality, and, if questionable, advice on sealing pond basin with trucked-in clay or a commercial sealant.

Booklets (also available from USDA) detailing pond care and management.

Advice and bulletins on fish stocking related to pond size and locale.

Setting up a fertilization program.

Advice on chemical weed control.

20

Handling Fish Properly From Hook to Pan

An astonishing amount of fish is treated abominably between the catching and the eating. Some winds up hardly fit for consumption. Because the flesh of cold-blooded fish is more fragile than that of warm-blooded game, it requires more attention, more delicate handling. Many fishing boats on both fresh and salt water nowadays have built-in live wells, with the water coming in from outside and circulating as the boat moves. Fish placed in a live well as caught stay in good condition, alive, unless injured during catching and unhooking, until they get to the dock.

CREELS

Centuries ago the wicker creel came into vogue as a "fish basket" that was carried by sport fishers on the streams of England and the Continent. The fundamental design of the wicker creel—recognized by ancient originals—was a container that allowed fish to have room enough not to be packed in and squeezed, and to have air circulating around them. It took into account the comparative fragility of fish flesh. The trout fisherman using a wicker creel invariably placed fresh grass or leaves, wet in the stream, into the creel and laid the fish upon them.

This is one of the traditions of classical trout fishing. Without a wicker creel slung on one side, the properly tailored purist trouter even today would hardly be dressed for the stream. While I have no quarrel with this tradition, I see fewer and fewer wicker creels these days. They are awkward, clumsy to tote, and really do very little to ensure and enhance the quality of the contents that cannot be accomplished in a less awkward fashion.

Years ago, and in fact for years, I carried a cheap little canvas fish bag. At that time it cost possibly ninety-nine cents. It had a shoulder strap of doubled canvas, and the flap was secured by a small buckle and leather fittings. The bottom of the bag had small grommets with drain holes. How many hundreds of trout, and other fish, went into and came out of that bag and its replacements would be interesting even for me to know.

The advantages of such bags are easily explained. When I waded a stream on a warm day, I always wet the bag long before the first trout went in. After that first one, I wet it again, letting stream water drizzle down the side of my waders as I moved along. Every few minutes I dunked the bag in the stream. The soaked bag breathed well and continuous evaporation cooled the interior. I don't know if many readers are acquainted with the old-fashioned canvas water bags that were extremely popular in desert areas some years ago. A couple still hang in our cluttered garage. You filled one with water, corked it, and slung it from a bumper guard on your vehicle, or secured it elsewhere outside the car, where the wind blew on it as you drove. The heavy canvas oozed just enough so that evaporation was continuous.

The same principle was involved in the canvas fish bag. The

warmer the day, the more often I dunked the bag. Never did
I find a trout softened or harmed in the least from being
carried this way. When the fish were removed, I turned the
bag wrong side out and washed it thoroughly. Commonly I
cleaned trout at dusk, sloshed the bag clean, put the gutted
trout back in, wet the bag again, and laid it in the car trunk
until I got home. Obviously, after a few sloshings in water
only to clean it, the bag began to take on an olfactory personality that needed taming. I'd fill a bucket with cold water,
slosh in a husky dollop of bleach, soak the bag an hour or so,
then rinse it. Fresh as an ironed bedsheet. Admittedly, the
wicker creel breathes, but it is difficult to clean thoroughly.

There are fish creels or bags of numerous makes available
today that are of one fabric or another. But beware! Almost
all are fitted with a heavy plastic lining—to keep blood and
fish slime off the fabric. Although these contrivances are sold
by the thousands, they are the worst inventions ever concocted. No air gets to fish placed in one. You can't wet the
material that encloses the fish (the plastic liner), and many a
trout and other fish has been utterly ruined after a few hours
of being carried in one of these.

It amuses me to remember the expression on the face of
the clerk in a sporting-goods store where I bought one of
these, when I asked to borrow his jackknife. This bag was
heavy, porous canvas—exactly what I wanted—but it had a
heavy plastic liner. The clerk had pointed out it also had
separate small zipper compartment, plastic-lined as well, in
which to stow small tackle items, which kept creeled fish away
from tackle and fabric. I slashed the plastic liner out with his
knife. The zipper compartment had to go too, of course, but
the "redesigned" item made a dandy canvas fish bag that I'm
still using. Wet it, keep dunking it periodically, and it's a fine
means of carrying fish on a stream or when fishing from shore
on lake or pond. When it's dirty, I give it the bleach treatment.

When I was a young fellow, sugar always came in close-

woven cotton bags. My mother made several fish sacks for me
from these for use in the old flat-bottomed wooden rowboats
that could in those times be rented at most lakes for a quarter
a day. She fitted the top with a long, stout drawstring. You
looped the string over an oarlock and let the bag drift in the
water. As bluegills or other fish were caught, the bag top was
pulled up out of the water, opened, the fish popped in, and
the drawstring pulled tight. Fish stayed alive in such bags.
Old-fashioned as this sounds, the idea is still as useful today—
if you can locate a proper kind of cloth sack. I know a few old-
timey canepole Texans who use what they call a "tow sack,"
which translates outside Texas and the South to a burlap bag.

Woven wire live nets also are a good way to keep fish,
especially the smaller ones, if you are in a boat, or even fishing
from shore. The whole idea, whether you keep caught fish
alive or dead, is to keep them wet and cool, always out of
direct heat. One way I've done it for some years now when
fishing in hot summer weather is to carry in a boat an ice
chest with a thick layer of crushed or cubed ice on the bottom.
As I catch fish, I pop them into the chest. This keeps them
perfectly fresh and cold until I'm ready to clean them.

An amazing number of saltwater fish are poorly handled on
piers and on boats. Some pier fishermen carry burlap bags
which they let down into the water and wet, then keep fish
in them, even on the pier planking. That's all right. Most
well-equipped charter and party boats now have large ice bins
into which fish are put as fast as caught. I recall one excursion,
however, when I was after kingfish out in the Gulf of Mexico,
and the skipper had aboard a couple of big metal garbage cans
for fish. As a king was caught, the billy stick or "priest" was
applied with a whack to its head, then it was placed headfirst
into one of the metal cans. After an hour numerous tails stuck
up out of the can. The vicious sun on the open water boiled
down until the can would almost cook the fish. They actually
were not fit to eat by the time we got back to dock, skin

wrinkled leathery dry, flesh soft. Without fail, fish under such conditions should be kept on ice.

A great many anglers string their catch. The small-diameter rope with metal "needle" attached for stringing fish through the gills and out the mouth may be handy, but it quickly kills fish and if they are to be kept lying in water for very long this is a poor idea. The temperature at the surface of many lakes rises into the 70s and 80s in summer. A bunch of dead fish lying in water that warm quickly begins to soften. Safety-pin type stringers of metal or plastic keep fish alive for long periods. They should be strung through both lips if you hope to keep the fish alive, and never dragged when the boat is moved.

Fish kept alive, or at least kept *cold* (iced) between catching and cleaning taste far better, and they keep much longer if you intend to freeze them. During fish runs, for example, when a lot may be caught, it is all but mandatory to go prepared to ice the catch as caught. I've watched fishermen clean fish out in the sun, with perhaps fifty or more to be cared for. If they're just tossed down on a dock, or piled on a cleaning table, by the time the last one is done it is soft and has lost much of its original flavor. By that time, too, if the cleaned ones are also left out in the sun, they're in the same shape. Keeping fish iced between catching and cleaning, and while cleaning, as well, is the best plan. Put some fresh ice in another, perhaps smaller, chest, and as you clean and wash each one, drop it in on the ice.

CLEANING AND FILLETING

If you fillet your fish, for best eating results you should have all the necessary paraphernalia ready before you begin. Fillets can be piled in a big stack, if you're under shady cover or it is cool, or they, too, can be tossed into a chest with fresh, clean ice. You should make every attempt to keep dirt, fish slime, and scales off the fillets. Wash them in cold, preferably running, water, after you've finished filleting and have cleaned up the mess of scales, carcasses, and slime. Dry the washed fillets on paper towels, and don't spare the towels. Fillets can then go into plastic bags, the Zip-loc kind or with a twist fastener, for the trip home.

Fish that are not filleted need three special processes to ensure the best eating, fresh or frozen. (1) Be very certain every bit of the entrails are cleaned out and the vent removed. (2) Be positive all blood has been removed from inside along the backbone. On all fish of moderate size running your thumb

Basic method of cleaning a fish. (1) Slit belly from anal vent to gills. (2) Push knife tip under pointed tip of gill coverings and cut V-tip of coverings from the jawbone. (3) Pull gills downward, stripping out innards. (4) Run thumbnail along cavity to clean out dark matter.

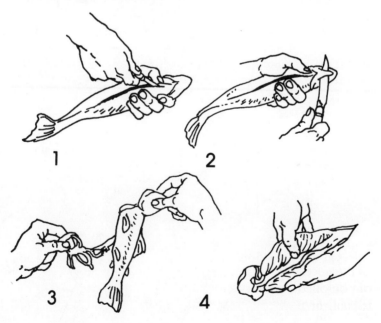

HOW TO FILLET A FISH

1. With a sharp fillet knife cut behind the bony gill covers on a slanting line from *A* to *B*.

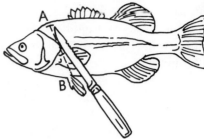

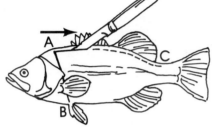

2. Insert knife point at *A* and slice closely along the dorsal fins, down to the backbone, from *A* to *C*.

3. Push the knife blade from *C* through the fish to the vent and then cut toward the tail until the flesh is severed.

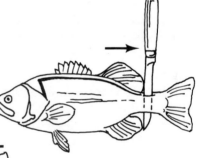

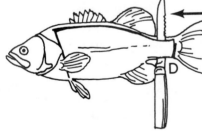

4. Grasping the end of the fillet at *D*, lift it away from the fin bones and slice along the ribs until the fillet is freed.

5. Lay the fillet on a flat board, skin side down, and slice some of the tail skin away from the flesh. Place thumb on skin and, holding knife flat, cut with a sawing motion until meat comes free of skin.

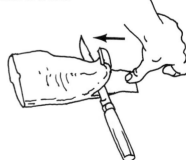

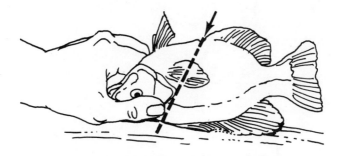

How to clean a panfish. First scale the fish. Then turn the fish belly-side up on cleaning board and, if right-handed, grip it as shown. Start knife just behind the vent and cut forward and down on a slant (dotted line), through the backbone. This removes head, entrails, ventral and pectoral fins. The fish is now ready for cooking.

along the backbone will loosen it; then it can be flushed out. On larger fish use a knife point. Blood left in deteriorates quickly and imparts a poor flavor. Extremely important is the third operation, in cases where heads are left on, which is for some reason traditional with certain varieties, such as trout, salmon, and red snappers, which have edible "cheeks," and often fish to be broiled, such as snappers, flounders, redfish, and sea trout of moderate size. Be sure every bit of the gills is removed. I have even bought (inadvertently) fish in a market that had the gills—presumably to add more weight and make a few more cents for the seller. Gills left in a fish spoil swiftly and can taint or ruin the whole fish.

There is a point to be made about how quickly to cook a fish after catching it for best results. Oddly, few anglers are aware of it. You always read about the delights of yanking the fish out of the cool, clear water and having it in the skillet three minutes later. Certainly fish taste fine that way. And

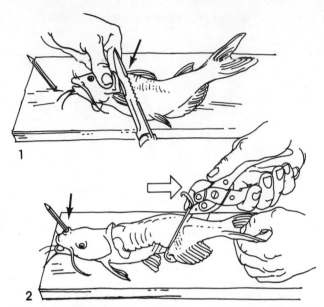

Skinning a catfish. (1) Lay the fish on a board through which you have driven a nail at an angle. Cut through the skin at one side of the fish, just behind the head, and continue across the top to the other side. (2) Impale the head on the nail. Grasp loose skin at the cut with a pair of pliers and pull toward tail. The skin will usually come off in one piece. If it separates along the dorsal surface, two pulls may be necessary.

when camping or about to famish from prolonged fishing, anyone can be forgiven for following that swift routine. However, a fish cooked immediately *never* cooks as perfectly. Small fish in particular, especially trout, which have a limber skeleton, curl up the moment they hit the pan. The skin sticks quite often and peels off, and the meat comes apart.

Fish that have been iced as caught don't do this. For best taste and appearance all fish should be iced or placed in the refrigerator overnight, or at least for several hours, before cooking. This firms the flesh so they neither curl nor come apart in skillet or broiler.

Keeping fish iced from the catching to the kitchen and, if

possible, getting them to the refrigerator or ready for the freezer the same day they're caught is the ideal way, but it can't always be done. However, cleaning fish as quickly as possible, drying off excess water after washing, and getting them iced right away with no exposure to heat still puts them into kitchen or freezer in good shape.

Often we have made trips from our Texas home up into the Rockies for trout fishing. I like to bring home as many as legally possible, and I have a system that works just fine for keeping them several days. I believe it's worth passing along. Because dry ice is not always available en route when needed, I never freeze fish or try to bring them home frozen. I clean the trout, Ellen washes them thoroughly, but also thoroughly dries them on paper towels. We then put them into plastic bags, not more than half a dozen 10-inch (or average) trout per bag. The bags are buried in ice or laid on block ice.

Last summer we traveled four days coming home. Each day we got out the bags of trout, opened them, and wiped each trout with a paper towel. Trout drain and seep liquids slightly, and we never let them lie in this juice in a bag. After wiping, they go into fresh bags and back onto the ice again. I always drain the chest or container they're in, and keep plenty of fresh ice. If you baby them this way, you can keep fish five or six days. We've even wiped, rewrapped, then frozen them after a four-day trip and still found them just fine. But you have to be willing to work at it.

FREEZING FISH

Here are a few suggestions for preparing fish for the freezer. Always measure out whatever you believe you'll want for one meal and wrap no more than that per package. You can open several packages, but if you thaw out too many fish, you have to cook and eat them, whereas large cuts of game can be cooked and refrozen with good results.

It's best to remove the dorsal fins of all spiny-rayed fish that will be wrapped in multiples. A good-size snapper with dorsal spines folded down, and the wrapping carefully done, probably won't puncture the freezer paper. But numerous bluegills in a plastic bag may do so. Trout are no problem, of course, because their fins are soft-rayed. We wrap broiling-size flounders, snappers, and comparable varieties whole in freezer paper. Bass, walleyes, and often saltwater trout and reds we usually fillet. Large fish, such as king mackerel, cobia, and salmon, we like to cut into steaks. Again, only the number of steaks the family can eat at one sitting should be packaged together.

One of the best ways to package and freeze small fish— bluegills, crappies, smelt, yellow perch, and many others— is to freeze enough for a meal or two in water. We use half-gallon milk cartons, thoroughly washed. Just drop in the cleaned fish, cover them with water, and freeze the whole carton. The fish are encased in ice. In place of milk cartons, you can use all sizes and shapes of plastic freezer cartons. Some years ago, when most ice trays in refrigerators were of metal and had removable cube makers, a friend of mine annually filled the trays, cube-maker sections removed, with smelt, covered them with water, and quick-froze them. These blocks were then loosened by running cold water briefly on the bottom of the tray, and the ice blocks with smelt in them were wrapped and put back into the freezer. Six or eight months later, they tasted like smelt just out of the stream.

This same method of freezing small fish in water, in milk cartons or plastic freezer cartons, also works beautifully with small game and birds. Rabbits and squirrels, cut up and frozen this way, are guaranteed airtight. We habitually place doves and quail in cartons and freeze them in water. There's no trouble with punctures from small bones or fin spines, nor any chance for air to get to the meat.

Watching hundreds of fishermen over many years mistreat their catches, even if unwittingly, I long ago came to the conclusion that one reason many people, anglers and others, claim they don't like fish is that the fishermen, fisherwomen, and their fisherkids never bring home fish that taste as they should. As I've said, you have to pamper fish, no matter where and under what conditions they're caught, to enjoy the delicious taste the creatures were born with. The fussing isn't all that much work or bother, however, and if you're going to catch 'em and keep 'em, the least you can do is give them a chance to show off in the pan as well as on the hook.

21

Using the Remnants

One of the lessons of my boyhood, hammered home to me not by a lot of talk but by deed, was that nothing edible was ever wasted. Part of it, I'm sure, was that we were quite poor. My father taught country school for a few dollars a month, and we lived on a little farm, which provided all our food except the staples such as flour, salt, and sugar. In today's society, waste has become virtually a way of life. Whoever heard of saving a leftover fried egg and somehow using it? Who would eat cold pancakes left from breakfast?

Well, my family did. Everything was used. And nobody considered it unusual—that was the point. Nor did all the odds and ends necessarily taste bad. Mothers and grandmothers of that day knew how to use every scrap and fix it up so it tasted just fine. Probably the most interesting examples of this type of frugality concerned meat of any kind. It is a joke of sorts today to say that packing houses putting up pork use everything but the squeal. That wasn't a joke when I was a kid. When we butchered a hog you'd have to fine-comb the place a few days later to find anything discarded.

Much of the use-everything attitude came to America with

settlers from Europe and the British Isles. I remember one time seeing a scrawled sign in a poor-looking farmyard near Petoskey, Michigan, where about thirty years ago we used to do our grocery shopping. It said "Geese." My wife and I decided to stop and buy a goose for roasting. It's not common, hasn't been for years, to find tame geese for sale for cooking. An old German immigrant lady met us, and we struck a bargain for a goose, which she said she would kill and dress for us right then.

During this process she asked, "You vant der blut?" Did we want the blood? Her method of killing the goose entailed bleeding it. I wasn't sure what she thought we might want it for, and she explained, "Blut sup." Blood soup. I assured her we didn't want it, and she asked if we objected to her keeping it. Of course not. We didn't even want to think about goose-blood soup. But later the thought crossed by mind, "How do we know it isn't delicious?"

I've thought of that incident many times, with amusement, remembering some of the game and fish remnants we'd used that would no doubt put unbelieving expressions on the faces of many persons to whom we related such incidents. In an earlier chapter I mentioned some of the offtrail wild meats we've eaten, and some of the remnants we've not wasted. Fish come under a quite different category, and it is surprising how much many modern cooks waste, or overlook.

Some of these, however, would bring no surprised or shuddering looks to the faces of many oldtimers, or, in fact, to many a coast of Maine, or Boston, seafood cook. For instance, when small, local fish markets were common along the East Coast, especially in New England, it was routine for a housewife—not just a poor one, either—to admonish the market owner from whom she bought the fresh cod to be sure to save the head, fins, and backbone for her. These were boiled as a rule, often in a muslin bag, to make soup or chowder stock.

And, after the stock was boiled out, the remnants were often picked over to retrieve whatever bits of meat might still cling to them. This isn't really a startling approach. The French, the British, practically all Old World peoples have since historic times used fish remnants for stock, and the stock was— is—a most important part of many fish dishes.

There is no reason for fishermen of both fresh and salt water to throw away usable parts of a fish. To be sure, remnants of some species are better than others for use in soup or chowder making. You find out which by trying them. It's surprising what delicious dishes can be concocted from some of the least believable fish-remnant ingredients.

One spring I was fishing in the Ozarks and was invited to eat a noon meal with an old couple who lived near a river in the hills. Something smelled awfully good as I was getting washed up at the pump outside the kitchen door. The lady served a one-dish meal in a big, steaming bowl. The aroma was obviously of fish, mingled with onion and various condiments. There was milk in it, lots of homemade butter, and big chunks of potatoes apparently boiled in whatever was the base for it. It was superb stick-to-the-ribs food.

I didn't want to ask right out what it was made of. But when I leaned back full and content, the old lady asked if I needed any more. I assured her I was full and that her meal was delicious. She thanked me and said, "Pa speared some big suckers a night or two back, and when I cleaned them, I saved the heads and fins to boil up and flavor a batch of potato-and-onion soup."

I'm not certain everyone would choose to save sucker heads for that purpose, but I couldn't quarrel with the lady's results. It well illustrates what can be accomplished in good, healthful meals by using fish remnants.

One item we have used for years that might come under the fish-remnant heading, and that's what most fishermen would call too-small panfish such as bluegills and the other sunfishes. In many states there are no limits on these species, and in hundreds of lakes they are overpopulous. Years ago I began keeping even very small ones, those no more than 4 inches long. I've been laughed at by dozens of fishermen for doing this, but I faithfully clean every one, and my wife has cooked hundreds of them.

If you cut off the head after scaling but leave the dorsal and anal fins intact, then flour and fry these small fish, you'll be surprised how tasty they are. Just pick each up, pull out the dorsal, pull out the anal, and slip a table knife along each side of the backbone, tilting it sidewise each time to lay the boneless flaky tidbits away from the backbone. Each small sunfish has two to four bites on it, and not a bone in the way if you follow this routine.

One time a fisherman I had met and fished with kept trying for bass all afternoon, and I kept popping small bluegills into an ice chest. He made fun of me the whole time. He wound up with a single bass that weighed about 1½ pounds; meanwhile, I had fifty or so miniature sunfish. Just for fun I invited him to eat with us that evening. My wife served a heaping platter of the diminutive sunfish he had scorned. He approached the meal with misgivings, but after putting away eighteen fish he wore a happy look and apologized for making such a pig of himself.

One of the most enjoyable fishing outings I've ever had was with our two boys when they were in their early teens. They were good fishermen by then and had been around me enough to know that I'd try eating almost anything that didn't bite back. They had become the same way. We had seined a big batch of minnows that they intended to use for crappies and bass. But we wound up having as close to a fishless day as was possible; all we had to show for it was a bucketful of 3-inch minnows. The boys had gathered them, and like kids they had laid in a supply that would have lasted a week.

We had a cooking-fire built, and out of the corner of my

eye I watched Mike getting spring water into an iron kettle we carried. He put it on the fire and casually remarked that maybe he and Terry would fix up an experimental stew, or chowder, in lieu of the bass fillets we had intended to eat. Next thing I knew they were dipping the minnows out of the bucket, tying the whole batch up in a big clean bandana, and putting it into the pot to boil. They came up with watercress from a nearby creek, some chunks of hearts from green cattails, whacked up an onion, peeled some potatoes.

After the basic minnow stock had been made, they lifted out the bulging bandana with a forked green stick, set it on a rock, and dumped in their other gleanings. While the vegetables bubbled away, they laboriously picked apart the cooked minnows, pitching the tidbits of meat into the pot. When the spuds and onion were done enough, they added butter, salt, and pepper, cooled down the brew, and poured in some milk from our ice chest. I'm not sure whether this could be called a recipe or just a kid conglomeration. I reflected that, after all, I had eaten canned sardines scores of times knowing the fish were put up entrails and all, so why should I balk at this? Fact is, the concoction was just great. I'm not certain it's legal everywhere to seine minnows for camp cooking, but the experience does illustrate that all sorts of fish remnants are edible, and delicious.

Some tidbits have become famed over the years that actually are remnants from fish. Among these—and many marine fishermen are not aware of them even though they sell at fancy figures in markets when at all available—are red snapper cheeks. On each cheek of a snapper is a meat-filled hollow that is delicate and delicious. The larger the snappers, the larger the cheeks. If you are a trout fisherman, chances are you leave the head on when you cook trout. But most people eat only up to the head and stop there. Many even cut off the heads and discard them. Thick meat reaches forward from about where you'd ordinarily cut a trout head off clear forward to the top of the head. These fine, small remnants of fish should not be wasted.

One of the most interesting uses of fish remnants was shown to me by a Texas friend who is an avid black-bass fisherman. But it doesn't apply just to black bass. Any good-size fish that you fillet is a candidate for this use of otherwise discarded good eating. The first time I fished with this gentleman we came in with ten bass each, a total of twenty. All were in the 2- to 3-pound class, beautiful fish. We filleted them. Like most fishermen who fillet bass, we made a cut behind the head, sliced the whole side off down to the tail, then slipped off the skin. This leaves, as readers know, the head, backbone, tail with two big flaps of skin—all of which ordinarily goes into the garbage.

While I began washing the pile of fillets and putting them into plastic bags, I noticed he was busy cutting off heads, and tails with skin attached, and piling up the long sections of backbone. He explained what should have been obvious: no matter how expertly you fillet a bass, or other large fish, a fair amount of meat is certain to be left on the backbone.

"My wife broils the backbones," he told me, "and we pick the meat off with a fork. You should try it. Delicious, and more than you think." He added that sometimes she also used the backbones to start a chowder, boiling them, lifting them out and shaking the meat off into the liquid, then adding the rest of the ingredients. Some expert of the sort who figures how many people it would take, joining hands, to stretch across the continent, might figure out that from the hundreds of thousands of black bass annually caught in the United States and filleted, if just 1 ounce of meat per backbone is wasted or saved . . .

Everyone knows that when a good-size fish is broiled and served whole, with portions removed by each person at the table, what remains on the plate is mostly skeleton, head, and skin. But invariably a large broiled fish is not all cleaned up.

Where do the meager leavings on the platter go? Almost always into the garbage. But not at our house. We've found that around the fins, maybe along the ribs, near the tail, behind the head, and along the backbone there are small tidbits that can be salvaged. These boneless scraps of fish we wrap in plastic wrap and put into the refrigerator. The "leavings" from a 2- to 3-pound fish broiled whole are usually enough to make, with tartar, red sauce, or whatever condiment you wish, a delicious seafood cocktail for the next meal, or to use in a seafood salad. This is a fine way to use scraps and stretch the value of the catch.

THE ROE

Of all common fish remnants, however, undoubtedly the item most commonly wasted, and most delectable, is the roe. Whether or not one has ever eaten it, everyone knows that shad roe, and caviar, are expensive items. Thousands of us fish during spawning seasons, and I have devoted much space in this book to the gleaning of large catches for the freezer, of the more abundant species, during spawning runs. Yet how many fishermen do you know who ever save, and eat, eggs from the common game fish?

When our boys were very small, we were living where I had opportunity each spring to go after abundant, large bluegills during spawning. The females were always fat with twin sacs of eggs. Saving these egg sacs as I cleaned the fish was routine. The kids, seeing us eat fish, always wanted some, but at that age we worried about bones. So, Ellen cooked the eggs for them. Floured and gently fried, they looked like miniature sausages. The kids licked them up.

Frankly, I envied them. Almost all fish roe is edible, and a delicacy. Roe of gars, as I mentioned earlier, is toxic, but the egg sacs of yellow perch, walleyes, and saugers are excellent. So are those of all the sunfish, the crappies, and the freshwater basses. All of these eggs, prior to full ripeness, are contained in membranes that keep them together. Eggs of trout—browns, rainbows, brook trout—do not stay together quite as well when they begin to mature. Nonetheless, they are fine eating. Ordinarily nowadays one releases a known female trout, but if you happen to clean one that is filled with roe, by all means save the eggs and cook them.

Saltwater fish of many kinds also furnish delicious roe. For several years we had a fish man coming every week to our door. He went down to the Gulf coast every week and brought back a pickup load of iced saltwater fish of several varieties. The little tricks used by commercial fishermen and sellers of commercially caught fish to get money for every possible bit of weight are well known. It always amused me when, during the time when trout (speckled weakfish) were spawning, I'd buy two or three and find big twin sacs of roe inside when I trimmed them and cleaned them up. Most people would throw the roe away and mutter about getting gypped for a few ounces. I never felt gypped. This was a special delicacy.

Thus, if you happen to be catching weakfish, or any of the common saltwater gamesters, during the time when females are full of eggs, by all means save the eggs and use them. I mentioned in an earlier chapter catching small spadefish during spawning. Their eggs are fine, too. I also urged readers who have never done so to try saltwater mullet. The roe of mullet, incidentally, is considered to be first class, and though it may seem curious, so are the sacs or pods of milt of the male, actually the testes. To those who are acquainted with it, this is known as "white roe."

To get the most value from the fish you catch, it is important to use the remnants. All you have to do is put away prejudices and let your taste buds make the final decisions.

22

Bonus Delicacies

The fisherman who is ever alert and also aware of what is available where he fishes can garner many a delectable and unusual meal as a sideline to his angling endeavors. These are water-oriented items that offer gourmet opportunities. Some of them are seldom used, and some are high-priced commodities when you buy them in a market or in a restaurant.

FROGS

Probably the most obvious around lakes and streams are frogs. Now almost everywhere frog hunting or taking is regulated. There are numerous restrictions—season dates, license requirements, limits, in some instances only certain species legal, and of a specified size. In a few states taking of frogs is less severely regulated, or not at all.

The frogs most commonly considered edible are the big bullfrogs. Depending again on the laws in effect, they are gigged, shot with air rifles, and even caught with a fly dangled from a monofil leader, the frog catcher using a fly rod or cane pole. Extra-large bullfrogs—some stretch out 18 inches or so—will strike astonishingly large prey. In my photo files I have a picture of a big fellow that banged a top-water bass lure in broad daylight and got hooked.

Needless to say, frogs legs are delicious; the meat, in case you've never eaten it, white as chicken breast, with a delicate flavor. We often prepare frogs legs floured and with a dash of garlic salt, gently sauteed. Although the large bullfrogs are the focus of most frog hunting, large specimens of meadow frogs are just as good, perhaps even better. But, again, you must check laws carefully. Meadow frogs may not be legal in your area.

Years back, as a kid, I used to hunt them diligently. The legs of a large spotted frog prepared for the pan are about 4 inches long and extremely meaty. My brother and I had a very basic way of hunting them that was not lacking in challenge. We prowled a creek that crossed the farm where we grew up, stalking them in the daytime, carrying sticks we'd whittled that were only about 2 feet long with a handhold and the far end flattened. In order to bop a frog, you first had to get your eye on it distantly, then make a sneak. Usually the frogs chirped and jumped before we got close enough, but by diligence we managed to bring in enough every now and then for a meal. In Mexico today kids still hunt meadow frogs and sell them to restaurants and markets. Most frogs legs served in tourist-city restaurants along the border are the small varieties.

Frog hunting on a commercial basis, as it is done in Florida, for example, is a sporty proposition. Most is done at night from airboats. The frogs are spotlighted, the shine of the eye picked up. Then the light is kept on the frog as the boat moves in, a tricky maneuver indeed, and a gig is used to fetch the quarry into the boat. Similar tactics are used by experienced frog hunters in other areas.

Now and then you may discover a lake or pond that is

Some bullfrogs have legs as big as those of chickens. Be sure to check state regulations for frog hunting.

simply alive with big bullfrogs. My family and I were fishing and camping near such a place a few years ago. Every little while, between fishing forays, the boys and I would try to gather a frog or two. When we left for home, we had an ice chest loaded with redear sunfish and bass, and two dozen pairs of frogs legs almost as big as chicken drumsticks. Retail value on those frogs legs would have been at least $30, perhaps more. It wouldn't have made much difference: at those prices we wouldn't have had them anyway unless we had caught our own.

TURTLES

Another group of delicacies fishermen come across fairly regularly are turtles. During one winter we spent in Florida some years ago, Lake Panasoffkee in the central part of the state was a favorite fishing ground. It was not much built up then, except for a few rickety fishing camps. The son of the owner of the camp where we stayed for some weeks made a substantial living hunting what he called "cooters."

The cooter turtle is one of the freshwater terrapins native to the southeastern United States. The so-called "slider" turtles (they slide into the water when disturbed) are also terrapins. Most terrapins make excellent eating. In fact, most of the best eating turtles are in the terrapin group. Sliders for many years were abundant in markets in the Southeast and South. The once-renowned terrapins of brackish waters along the Atlantic, which sold for tremendous prices in the markets, were too heavily hunted and are no longer on the list of common desirable species for eating.

Before taking any turtles, you should check state laws to make sure what may or may not be legal "game." For example, the large sea turtles that come ashore to lay their eggs have received strict protection over past years. Unfortunately, many are killed annually by poachers, and several are endangered species.

Especially across the southern United States fishermen might be alert for soft-shelled turtles. These creatures have leathery, soft shells, a narrow snout that can inflict vicious— and with large specimens, dangerous—bites. The southern soft-shelled turtle is the largest of the varieties, and may weigh up to 40 pounds, although that is unusual. Other soft-shell species are present westward into Texas and the Rio Grande River. Others appear in the North. Sometimes turtles are caught on a baited hook meant for a fish. The soft-shells, because they are almost entirely water creatures, are often caught this way.

Among southern blacks many years ago the soft-shelled turtle was greatly prized. It is worth noting the curious way in which they were often prepared. When one of pan size was procured, it was slit part way on the underside through the soft, leathery covering, and the entrails removed. Then the entire turtle was rolled in corn meal and placed in a skillet for frying. I confess I've never tried this, but it might be a worthwhile experiment.

The turtles one hears most about among fishermen are the big, ill-tempered snapping turtles. They range very widely, and I doubt there are any restrictive regulations pertaining to them. They are carnivorous critters, killing wild ducklings and eating fish and anything they can seize. Anglers who've never handled a snapper should be warned that it should be approached and dealt with carefully. The jaws of a big snapper can cut off a finger with ease.

Snappers come in sizes from several pounds to 20 or 30 or more. The largest variety, the alligator snapper of the South, grows to 100. Those giants, incidentally, are fine eating and furnish a tremendous amount of food. As with all turtles, there are several shades of meat—from dark to white—in the various parts.

Ten years ago I was the writer-producer-director for a TV fishing film which was shot at Toledo Bend Reservoir on the Louisiana-Texas border. This huge lake is full of drowned timber and harbors a wide variety of animal life. During a run with three boats from one filming location to another, the lead boat struck its motor prop on some submerged object with such a jolt that it almost threw the occupants into the water.

A 45-pound alligator snapping turtle. These large turtles are
excellent table fare, furnish a tremendous amount of meat.

We hauled up to survey damage, if any, and discovered we
had struck a huge alligator snapper. The turtle was killed, but
floated long enough to be grabbed by the tail. We finally got
it aboard and took it to dock, cleaned it, and the cook in the
restaurant where our crew all ate agreed to fix us a turtle
dinner, starting with turtle soup and going on from there.
That alligator snapper, just an average one, weighed 44
pounds. It was excellent fare.

The common snappers range over a large area of the United
States, north to south, throughout the plains, as well as eastward. Some fishermen who've found out what good eating
they are catch them in turtle traps. Others use baits of meat
or fish; some, a small-caliber weapon. Wherever legal, the

snappers, terrapins, sliders all make fine food, offering a worthwhile bonus to the catch of fish.

Turtles are no special problem to clean. Usually the head is cut off and the animal allowed to bleed well. Then it is either cut from the shell, or the plastron (bottom of the shell) is removed and the cleaning proceeds from there. Nor should there by any great puzzlement over how to cook turtle. Practically all fish and game cookbooks, and quite a few standard ones, contain turtle recipes. One I checked lists turtle steaks, soup, stew, pie, goulash, and fried turtle.

CRUSTACEANS

The various crustaceans are of course among the most highly prized of all seafood. These are the lobsters, crabs, and saltwater crayfish (often called spiny lobster, rock lobster, or clawless lobster), but the freshwater crayfish also should not be overlooked. Some years ago many people along the Florida and Pacific coasts used to dive for saltwater crayfish. But crayfish are no longer that common close to shore. Only rarely can one succeed at this.

However, catching marine crabs along the coasts is both fun and a means of gathering superb eating that is presently so high priced it is not on the average home menu. Several varieties of crabs are easily catchable. The blue crab is the most abundant and common. Currently marine crabs are regulated almost everywhere, and for the most part may not be taken during spawning. Anyone fishing the shores, however, can easily catch big crabs during those times when they are legal. They are taken in simple crab traps (available in coastal sporting-goods stores), baited with fish or meat, or on similar baits dangled on a string. When a crab takes hold, it is slowly lifted to near surface, and a dip net slipped under it.

Picking the meat from your catch of blue crabs is something

of an effort, but worth the trouble. When I've watched professionals do it at a processing plant, it looks so fast and simple. It has always been an ordeal for me, yet I can't resist. Any good cookbook will explain, if you don't already know, how to clean and cook crabs.

When my wife and I were first married we lived where we could gather blue crabs easily. I remember evenings of patiently boiling and cleaning the catch, then picking out crab meat most of the next day. Our fingers would be cut from the shells, but were we ever proud of perhaps the pound or so of white crab meat that we had gleaned. Truly an accomplishment. Ellen would bake potatoes the next evening, with the tops slit, then scoop out the interior. The potatoes were mashed and mixed with abundant crab meat and seasonings she decided might taste "just right," and put back into their skins. With ample butter spread on, and paprika sprinkled over them the stuffed potatoes were slipped for a few minutes under the broiler, until their tops were browned. Surely eating anything that delectable must breach the commandments!

Stone crabs are not as abundant nor as easily taken. They are the big fellows with enormous claws. I've seen stone crab claws that weighed a pound each. We used to collect stone crabs in the bays of the western Florida coast, instructed by a native. He used a steel rod with a short right-angle bend at the bottom end, as a kind of hook. On low tide he went out in shallows in the bay and could spot small depressions in sand where a crab had burrowed down. He pushed the crook down into the soft sand and pulled the crab out. I remember that even then there was a law that limited a stone-crab hunter to one claw only from each crab. That was so the creature was left with protection. The claw taken for its meat would eventually regenerate.

In some places along the Gulf there are even sport-fishing seasons for shrimp. Obviously you must have a proper boat, and also a shrimp trawl. I've known quite a few Texans who've made a point during open seasons of gathering shrimp for their freezers. This of course is a specialized business, but worth looking into.

Collecting freshwater crayfish, conversely, is anybody's game. Headquarters for crayfish in the United States is southern Louisiana. Here they are not only gathered commercially, particularly in the Atchafalaya basin, but are now being cultured commercially in ponds. The general public across the South catches them in traps, or in baited, small, flat nets let down into a ditch or bayou, or even fishes for them. This is great fun for kids. It can be done anywhere across the nation where crayfish are found, using bait dangled from a line on a pole and dropped among rocks or beside submerged logs. One man holds the pole, one a small dip net. When the crawdad takes hold, it is lifted slowly, but not out of the water because it will probably let go. The net is slipped under, and up it comes.

Baited traps catch crayfish faster. I have even waded rock-rubble shallows in small lakes where crayfish were abundant and grabbed them up by hand. It takes a lot of crayfish to make a meal, but once you try them, you're hooked. This is one of the prime bonus delicacies of freshwater. We've even gathered crawdads for bait, then decided the heck with fishing, we'd just eat the bait. Crayfish pie, gumbo, *etoufee*, crayfish boiled whole in water variously seasoned—these homely little "mud bugs" are the aristocrats of bonus delicacies for anglers.

MOLLUSKS

The various mollusks also should be considered. In some areas along our coasts, you may gather oysters during specified seasons, in specified places. Clams of numerous varieties also are available. Make sure of regulations concerning them.

Some of the most delightful experiences of bonus-gathering I've ever had occurred along the Pacific coast, gathering clams. I hunted pismo clams, with size and numbers limited, in California, and how delicious they were! In Oregon there were razor clams and soft-shelled clams. Wherever marine clams are abundant, you can get so involved in gathering legal limits that you sometimes forget fishing. Clam chowder, clam stew, clam patties made with egg and cracker crumbs but so full of clams they're like big, fat hamburgers—these are gourmet memories not soon forgotten.

Mussels of several kinds are easily collected along both Atlantic and Pacific coasts. A caution, though: at times they

Digging marine clams on a Florida beach. Many varieties of clams are found the length of both coasts.

These clams, from an Oregon inlet and beach, are of two delicious marine varieties: upper four, soft-shelled clams; lower three, razor clams.

may be toxic. California has long regulated the taking of mussels to certain periods for that reason. In fact, all mollusks when in polluted water may be inedible. The way in which both univalve and bivalve mollusks feed, pouring water through their digestive tracts and filtering out plankton, allows them to become saturated, under certain circumstances, with dangerous chemicals or bacteria. Thus you should never gather marine mollusks except where taking them is certified safe by authorities.

One mussel almost entirely overlooked by fishermen is the freshwater kind, often called a freshwater clam. As a matter of fact, there are numerous varieties. They range almost throughout the country, in lakes, ponds, and streams. Ancient Indians indicated how good mussels are by leaving countless huge mounds of freshwater mussel shells along river courses and beside lakes. In the Midwest, mussel shells are used for making buttons and several other items. There is still some commercial mussel dredging in the large rivers of the interior of the country, in Iowa, Missouri, and Arkansas. The last time I saw a mussel dredge in operation was on the Cache River in Arkansas.

Some southern fishermen use mussel meat as the prime bait for big yellowbreast and other sunfishes. Not many anglers eat them, yet they are indeed tasty, although inclined to be tough. I recall fishing a small lake one time, for bluegills, and noticing that in several feet of water the bottom was littered with live mussels lying in the soft mud. Out of curiosity I began scooping them up in a dip net. I took a big batch of them home and put them in a tub of clean water to purge them. Leaving them overnight or for a day or two allows a lot of water to go in and out of their suction devices and wash out elements that may cause a muddy flavor.

These were big ones, and I was certain they'd be tough. So we opened the shells, scooped out the meat, and ran it through a food grinder. We used the ground meat to make a mussel chowder. It was great. We have also made patties from ground mussels, as well as soup (made much like oyster soup).

Among my mollusk-eating experiments, I cannot resist relating what is probably the most unusual. Back in the mid-'40s I camped for a few days in a small trailer at the south end of Bahia Honda Key in the Florida Keys. There was nothing there then, just sand and coral, moonflower vines, flocks of shorebirds, and not even any great amount of traffic on the highway. The only people I saw were a couple from New Jersey, who came in and pitched a tent.

I wandered the shallow flats, fishing and fiddling. The area of shallow water was littered with conch shells, live ones. I got wondering what conch might taste like. I knew that old-timers who'd spent a lifetime on the Keys eking out a living fishing or in similar pursuits were sometimes called "conkers," named from their poor-folks habit of eating "conk" in stew, chowder, soup, and even fried.

I brought in a few big conches. Bear in mind that in those years they were tremendously plentiful. The conch, as most readers will know, is a univalve. The animal lives wound round and round the several whorls of the interior of its shell. The large foot muscle is the edible part, just as the adductor muscle that opens and closes the shell is the edible part of the bivalve scallop.

Of course, the conch creatures withdrew snugly inside their shells when taken from water. How was I to get them out? I decided to boil them first, then pull them out and remove the edible foot muscle. This done, I cut up one strip of muscle into squares, and fried it. The result? You couldn't have shot a hole in the resultant juice. About then the people from the tent came over, wondering what I was doing. They remarked that whatever I was cooking smelled good. I told them my problem. This couple, Fred and Maude Forrest, were the sort who were curious about everything. Why not, Mrs. Forrest suggested, put the conch meat in a pressure cooker, with vegetables, and make a conch stew? They just happened to have a pressure cooker with them.

Out it came along with their Coleman stove. She furnished the other ingredients, and I furnished the conch meat—what must have seemed like an overample amount. In the cool, quiet Key sunset we sat wolfing down conch stew as though we'd never get any again. It was superb. The truth is, I've never had any since, and I don't suppose the Forrests have, either. A pleasant punch line to the story is that since our mid-forties introduction over a bowl of "conk" stew almost forty years ago, the Forrests and I have kept in contact to this day.

There is one other marine mollusk that must be mentioned—this is the coquina. Perhaps many readers already know what a coquina is. For those who do not, it is a tiny bivalve, like a miniature clam; adult specimens range one-half to three-quarters of an inch long. The shells appear in a wide variety of colors, from gray to brown, white, pink, and always with starbursts or stripes in one pattern or another. Coquinas are found at surf line along the warmer beaches of the southern United States. Where present, they are usually in awesome abundance—literally hundreds of thousands of them.

They are especially abundant around Florida and across the Gulf to Texas. To illustrate how abundant they can be, coquina rock, a mixture of coquina shells and concrete, was a common building material years ago in Florida. Also years ago, several people who knew how delicious the flavor of the coquina was tried to commercialize canned coquina broth. Their endeavors met with varying degrees of success, the main hurdle the difficulties of gathering the tiny creatures economically in commercial quantities.

We learned about making coquina soup and broth thirty-odd years ago in Florida, and have often done so along the Texas coast. (I've never seen anyone else on that coast utilize these tiny mollusks, however.) You hunt along a stretch of sandy beach until you find a colony. As each wave rolls in, many are uncovered. They promptly dig back down into the sand. By the time the wave recedes, the swarms of coquinas have disappeared.

The usual way to gather them, aside from laboriously picking up one or two at a time until you have a quart or a gallon, is to make a topless box with a quarter-inch-mesh hardware-cloth bottom. When you locate a big coquina colony, you shovel sand into the box, wade out, and slosh it in the water. The sand goes through, the coquinas, and probably odds and ends of seashells, stay in. Each gather is placed in a bucket with seawater in it, to make sure the coquinas live.

After a couple of quarts have been collected, you have enough to make a fair batch of broth. Place the coquinas in a big pot of water and boil them. Strain the resultant liquid through a couple of thicknesses of muslin to remove all the shells and the sand. The tiny meats, though delicious, are mighty gritty. We've tried making patties of them—good, but just too much sand that can't be removed.

The less water you use for boiling, the thicker and stronger the broth. Coquina broth can be cooled and refrigerated. It makes a delightful cold cocktail, far more delicate and tasty than clam juice. It can also be used, with diced celery, butter, milk, and seasonings, as a soup. Or, by adding diced potatoes, celery and seasonings, you can create a marvelous and delicate chowder.

There are other bonus delicacies fishermen can gather. The ones suggested here should set you on the right track. Whether you are looking for these, or fishing, or hunting, the whole purpose of this book—which I hope has been evident from the beginning—is to show that these outdoor participant sports fundamentally have three parts. Undoubtedly, the most important is the mere fact of being outdoors, of imbibing the beauties of one's surroundings, using the fishing and hunting as means and excuses to be there. Next comes the heady action, the sport of bagging game and catching fish. But after the action has subsided, the third part of the equation is at hand: using the game bagged and the fish caught—the feast. In this new philosophy of hunting for the pot and fishing for the pan, this portion of the sequence shares equally with the other two in importance and enjoyment.

Index